WOMEN AND THE DIVINE

WOMEN AND THE DIVINE
TOUCHING TRANSCENDENCE

Edited by Gillian Howie and J'annine Jobling

First published in 2009 by PALGRAVE MACMILLAN® in the
United States—a division of St. Martin's Press LLC, 175 Fifth
Avenue, New York, NY 10010.

Where this book is distributed in the UK, Europe and the rest of
the world, this is by Palgrave Macmillan, a division of Macmillan
Publishers Limited, registered in England, company number 785998,
of Houndmills, Basingstoke, Hampshire RG21 6XS.

Palgrave Macmillan is the global academic imprint of the above
companies and has companies and representatives throughout the
world.

Palgrave® and Macmillan® are registered trademarks in the United
States, the United Kingdom, Europe and other countries.

ISBN-13: 978-1-4039-8413-5
ISBN-10: 1-4039-8413-1

Library of Congress Cataloging-in-Publication Data

Women and the divine : touching transcendence / Gillian Howie and
    J'annine Jobling, (eds.).
      p. cm.
    ISBN 1-4039-8413-1 (alk. paper)
    1. Women and religion. 2. Women—Religious life. 3. Transcendence
of God. I. Howie, Gillian. II. Jobling, J'annine.

BL458.W5756 2008
200.82—dc22   2008019901

A catalogue record of the book is available from the British Library.

Design by Scribe Inc.

First edition: January 2009

10 9 8 7 6 5 4 3 2 1

Printed in the United States of America.

Contents

ACKNOWLEDGMENTS

A number of chapters in this volume were first aired at the conference on "Women and the Divine," organized by Gillian Howie, J'annine Jobling, and Patrice Haynes; this took place in Liverpool, United Kingdom, during June 2005. We are particularly grateful, therefore, to those who sponsored that project: Liverpool Hope University, Liverpool University, the British Academy, the Subject Centre for Philosophical and Religious Studies, and Liverpool's Capital of Culture fund.

BIOGRAPHICAL NOTES

Pamela Sue Anderson is a reader in philosophy of religion at the University of Oxford and a tutorial fellow in philosophy at Regent's Park College, Oxford. Anderson published *Ricoeur and Kant: Philosophy of the Will* (Scholars Press, 1993) and *A Feminist Philosophy of Religion: the Rationality and Myths of Religious Belief* (Blackwell, 1998) and co-edited, with Beverley Clack, *Feminist Philosophy of Religion: Critical Readings* (Routledge, 2004). She has also published various articles on feminist philosophy, philosophy of religion, and ethics. She is currently completing *A Philosophy of Love: The Heart Has Its Reasons* (Oneworld Press) and is working on a collection of her own essays, *Goodness, God and Gender: Enlightenment Secularism and Protestant Feminism*.

Hannah Bacon lectures in the Department of Theology and Religious Studies at the University of Chester. Her research interests include the Christian doctrine of the Trinity, feminist methodology, postmodern methodology, and feminist issues surrounding Christian orthodoxy. Her current interests pivot around a driving concern to interrogate the relationship between feminism and understandings of Christian orthodoxy within contemporary, postmodern contexts. At present she is working on the book *What's Right with the Trinity?*

Claire Colebrook is a professor in the Department of English Literature at the University of Edinburgh. She has written books and articles on the philosophy of Gilles Deleuze, irony, literary theory, and gender. Her most recent book is *Milton, Evil and Literary History* (Continuum, 2008).

Daphne Hampson is a a professor emerita of divinity at the University of St. Andrews, where she held a chair in Post-Christian thought. She is the author of *Theology and Feminism* (Blackwell, 1990), *After Christianity* (SCM, 1996; 2nd ed., 2002), and *Christian Contradictions: The Structures of Lutheran and Catholic Thought* (Cambridge

University Press, 2001). Hampson teaches and researches at Oxford and is also a life member of Clare Hall, Cambridge. Her forthcoming work includes an exposition and critique of Kierkegaard and writing in theology and Continental philosophy.

Patrice Haynes is a postdoctoral teaching fellow at Liverpool Hope University. She is currently working on a book titled *Transcendence Matters: Rethinking Transcendence and Materialism in Deleuze, Irigaray and Adorno*, which explores contemporary philosophical attempts to rethink the divine in this-worldly, materialist terms.

Gillian Howie is a senior lecturer in philosophy at the University of Liverpool. She is the author of *Deleuze and Spinoza: Aura of Expressionism* (Palgrave, 2002), editor of *Critical Quarterly's* special issue on higher education (2005), and co-editor of *Gender, Teaching and Research* (Ashgate, 2003), *Third Wave Feminism* (Palgrave, 2004), and *Menstruation* (Palgrave, 2005). She is currently writing *Fugitive Ethics: Feminism and Dialectical Materialism*.

Luce Irigaray is director of research in philosophy at the Centre National de la recherche scientifique in Paris. A doctor of philosophy, Luce Irigaray is also trained in linguistics, philology, psychology, and psychoanalysis. Now acknowledged as a key influential thinker of our times, her work focuses on the culture of the two subjects, masculine and feminine—particularly through the liberation and construction of a feminine subjectivity—something she explores in a range of literary forms: the philosophical (from *Speculum of the Other Woman* [1974; 1985] to *The Way of Love* [2002] and *Sharing the World* [2008]), the scientific (*To Speak is Never Neutral* [1985; 2002]), the political (*Democracy Begins Between Two* [2000]), and also the poetic (*Elemental Passions* [1982; 1992] and *Everyday Prayers* [2004].

Haifaa Jawad is a senior lecturer in Islamic and Middle Eastern studies in the Department of Theology and Religion at the University of Birmingham. She previously taught at al-Mustansiriyah University, Baghdad; Exeter University; New England College, Arundel; and Lancaster University. In 2004 she was a visiting professor in contemporary Islam at the University of Alabama in the United States. She has specialized in a range of areas, including Islamic Thought, Islam and the West, Islamic spirituality, and women's issues in Islam. Among her publications are *The Middle East in the New World Order* (editor and contributor; Macmillan, 1997) and *The Rights of Women in Islam: An Authentic Approach* (Macmillan, 1998). Currently, she is working on *The Contribution of European Converts to Islam: Britain as a Case Study* for Continuum International.

J'annine Jobling is an associate professor of theology and philosophy at Liverpool Hope University. She works in the crossover between philosophical, theological, and literary texts. She is author of *Feminist Biblical Interpretation in Theological Context* (Ashgate, 2002); she has co-edited *Theological Liberalism* (SPCK, 2000) and *Theology and the Body* (Gracewing, 1999) and has recently written about novelists such as Kazuo Ishiguro, Iris Murdoch, and Anthony Burgess. Her current projects include a book on spirituality and fantasy fiction for young adults.

Morny Joy is a university professor in the Department of Religious Studies at the University of Calgary. She has an MA from the University of Ottawa (1973) and a PhD from McGill University (1981). Morny's principal areas of research are philosophy and religion, especially continental philosophy. She has edited a number of books and has written many articles in the area of women, philosophy, and religion. Her most recent book is *Divine Love: Luce Irigaray, Women, Gender and Religion* (University of Manchester Press, 2006).

Mike King has four degrees from British universities spanning the disciplines of art, science, and religion. He regards each as complementary inquiries into the deep structure of human experience, and he has published more than forty papers on the intersection of these fields. Mike has exhibited his digital artworks nationally and internationally. He is a Visiting Research Fellow at London Metropolitan University. He is the author of *Secularism: The Hidden Origins of Disbelief* (2007) and *Postsecularism: The Hidden Challenge to Extreme Religion* (forthcoming), both published by James Clarke and Co. Other books in preparation include one on American cinema and one on religion and film.

Beverly Metcalfe is a professor of international management and development at Liverpool Hope University; she taught previously at Manchester, Hull, Staffordshire, and Keele universities. Beverly has undertaken consultancy and advisory roles on women's development and empowerment and human resources issues in the Middle East for the Bahrain and Islamic Republic of Iran's education ministries. Her research focuses on the following areas: human resource development and management learning; gender, development, and organization analysis; and feminist theory and leadership.

Melissa Raphael is professor of Jewish theology at the University of Gloucestershire. She is the author of a number of books, including *The Female Face of God in Auschwitz: A Jewish Feminist Theology of the Holocaust* (Routledge, 2003) and the forthcoming *Judaism and the Visual Image: A Theology of Jewish Art* (Continuum, 2008).

Introduction

Gillian Howie and J'annine Jobling

In a silence
Without any appearing
A wonderful touch
A kind of river that flows.
Intimacy exists beyond nearness,
Bodily memory of the contact
Engendering a running liquid
Cool and continuous.
Strange mystery of the living.

—Luce Irigaray, *Prières quotidiennes*

There is an essential link between theology and ethics, metaphysics and spirituality. Throughout all religions, the practice of knowing or loving God is considered to have a direct bearing on self-transformation: an orientation to the divine evinces a reorientation to our neighbors. The divine-human relationship is though more than a means to an end but is an end in itself. But if this divine were considered completely mysterious, an epistemic problem would arise, for how might we say anything about something that is wholly other? Merold Westphal describes the Wholly Other as that which enters my experience on its own terms and not mine, as that which permanently exceeds the forms and categories of my transcendental ego and permanently surprises my horizons of expectations (Westphal 3). "Touching transcendence" takes this as the way to begin a conversation about the relationship between transcendence and immanence or transcendence and embodiment.

Within recent, especially poststructuralist or postmodernist, theory, the transcendence-immanence doublet is often taken to be a problem and one characteristic of modernism. Immanence has two features: one formal and the other ontological. Formally, a philosophy or theory that can be called immanent is one that does not appeal to anything outside the terms and relations accounted for by the theory (Kerslake 10). Ontologically, a theory is described as immanent when it considers thought to fully express being: where there is no moment of transcendence of being to thought. For Negri and Hardt, immanence is the primary event of modernity (leading us into postmodernity): the moment when Spinoza released powers of affirmation from the "otherworldly" principles of rationality. This otherworldliness is captured by the opposing term "transcendence."

Transcendence is an idea that can suggest going beyond the present and going beyond that which can be known or represented. According to Jean-Paul Sartre, it is the process whereby consciousness goes beyond the given in a further project. Transcendence is to be distinguished from the transcendent, which means—for Kant at least—a regulative idea of reason, such as God, the Soul, and freedom, which has no corresponding sensory intuition. For Westphal, a transcendent God is one found "beyond" or "outside" the world (as well as within it) and self-transcendence is the moment that draws us away from our natural preoccupation with ourselves (2). Often conflated, transcendence and transcendent have come to stand for the principles of thought or symbols of authority that organize the way we think about and experience the present as well as the way we project ourselves into the future. A further term can be added to form a triumvirate, "transgression," suggesting that there is always something that remains uncaptured, possibly produced, by the system and that this uncaptured element or excess can disrupt the system.

The "divine," as a form of transcendence, is emerging from feminist theology as a central category of critical thought. Regina Schwartz draws a distinction between vertical and horizontal transcendence. The former signifies a relationship to another world or a negation of immanence. The latter refers us to the experience of an incomplete present invigorated by the ceaseless movement of consciousness projecting toward an incomplete future. Within feminist theory, "the divine" shifts uneasily between the vertical and horizontal. It reopens

questions of love, truth, grace, and the spiritual within the quotid-
ian but risks recovering a closed and hierarchical relationship between
sexed human subjects and a transcendent Subject. It reopens questions of premodern, decentered subjectivity but risks sacrificing modern autonomy central to the emancipatory project of feminism.

The relationship of transcendence to feminism then is awkward.
This awkwardness is only exacerbated by the influence of psychoanalytic theory on feminist theory. Within psychoanalytic theory, the feminine either signifies the "unsayable" or the excess within the system.
In this psychodynamic model, the "feminine" actually is a moment of
transcendence or transgression. According to Luce Irigaray, because
this psychodynamic model is tenaciously masculine, a metaphor, or an
image, will always take place within the context of a phallogocentric
system of representation. Any attempt to figure the feminine then
is perilous because it risks provoking "common sense," which will
either associate the feminine with nature as beneficent, supportive,
and nurturing or as destructive, wild, and abandoning. Yet, without
such images, women are "a blank space," a refusal of representation.
So Irigaray considers a third way to imagine women: "by resolutely
focusing on the blank spaces of masculine representation, and revealing their disruptive power" (Berg, quoted in Whitford 71). Ideas of
transcendence, which can be glimpsed "flickering ambiguously amidst
the images which have cast us in their net," can be refigured in such a
way as to disrupt orthodox systems of representation (Kosky 13). By
taking this risk within the masculine symbolic, there is then an opportunity to convert a form of subordination into affirmation, a moment
of silence into an image of "emancipation." But the reconfiguration
must occur; otherwise, "the feminine" will remain only that which
marks a boundary. By bringing together feminism and transcendence,
we hope to show how "the sensible" and "transcendental" are con-
stituent elements of a synthetic unity.[1]

The risks are worth taking. Without rethinking transcendence in
this way, we are left with theory—philosophy, theology, and cultural
theory—which conceives transcendence and immanence, as well
as the finite and infinite, as opposing terms. Such theory tends to
empty the infinite of content and to make a virtue of the radical
inaccessibility of transcendence. The future then recedes into a pattern of (affirmative) repetition. Prioritizing one term in the doublet, the apparently "radical" move is to consider all elements within
the system to be of the same order. For instance, Gilles Deleuze, by
gathering together the ethical and the empirical, the ontological and
epistemological, the finite and infinite, and by finding a place even

for excess within the same system, draws all elements together into "an immanent plane of consistency" (271; see also Žižek, 242).

Slavoj Žižek argues that this postmodernist "radical immanence" can lead to an ontology without ethics; it can lead us straight back to the very modern and thoroughly disenchanted world (242). An enchanted world is one animated by spirits, gods, and magical forces. In a disenchanted world, a scientific way of thinking lauds the formal over the conceptual, rule and probability over motive and cause.[2] Because of this privilege, reason is driven into incoherence. With Kantian philosophy, for example, the problem is to find a way to ground the metaphysics of morals given an epistemological skepticism about moral realism framed in terms of "the good" or "god." The God of faith must always remain abstract and dead and is set "apart from the living world of faith and knowledge" (Kosky 17). The apparently vacuous system of regulated maxims forces the individual into defending moral action by stealth. When moral judgment is described as "nonsense on stilts," it is not just moral philosophy that suffers. Enlightenment results, in the end, with values that are unable to orient, regulate, and give meaning to practical life.

Modernism does not entirely abandon the idea of transcendence but depicts it either as absolute presence (the aesthetics of the sublime) or absolute absence (meaninglessness embodied in kitsch). But religious and mythical thought share a rational kernel, and there is a religious strand running through modern rationality. According to Gillian Rose, secular modernism is actually founded on an unrevealed religion. It is a religion that devotes us to our own individual inner-worldly authority "but with the loss of the inner as well as the outer mediator" (Rose 127). The protesting cry against the third term turns into an ethic without ethics and a religion without salvation. At this point, transgression becomes fetishized as a moment of freedom within an overly administered world. The truly "radical" move is not to flatten all elements onto a plane of consistency but to reveal and engage with the theological strains that resonate throughout secular modernity; perhaps to rethink the modernist-postmodernist doublet itself.

Philosophical theology, for Georg Wilhelm Hegel, reinterprets the death of God as a fundamentally Christian truth in which God, brought to earth, can be known by human subjects. Kosky argues that unfortunately rather than opening a way to bring together the infinite and finite, God and subject, philosophical theology actually prepared the way to make Man origin, means, and end. Friedrich Nietzsche's Zarathustra teaches the "death of God" to release subjects from the spell of transcendent powers but leaves us with scientific forces and earthly powers. This thorough and pure immanence is the horizon within which Western contemporary philosophy and philosophical theology moves. This is one of the reasons that Patrick Sherry gives for turning to literature, art, and history to provide a fresh understanding of ideas that have grown stale in the hands of the preachers and theologians (2). A heart and imagination stirred by images of atonement, redemption, and salvation may detect within the mundane astonishing acts of love and kindness and hear the call to bear witness to the wounds of terror. The feminine divine, a reconsideration of transcendence and embodiment, may hold the key with which to read anew the present in light of a past thrown toward a future.

This volume brings together reflections on women and the divine—or put otherwise, women in the contexts of transcendence and immanence. The majority are developed in dialogue with the work of Luce Irigaray, as a paramount contemporary thinker in this field and who has contributed the opening chapter of the book. There follow three chapters specifically analyzing the concept of transcendence from philosophical perspectives—by Pamela Sue Anderson, Patrice Haynes and Claire Colebrook. The three subsequent chapters explore ways in which women's "divinity" and integrity can be developed: Morny Joy, in close dialogue with Irigaray's work, looks at the sacrificial economy as exploitative of women; Beverly Metcalfe suggests that contemporary leadership theorizing may be enhanced by "returning to the Goddess" and looking at alternative interpretations of the story of Deborah and Jael in the Book of Judges in the Hebrew Bible; Mike King argues that the traditional monotheist modality of spirituality needs "cutting down to size" in favor of a fivefold schema. Daphne Hampson then addresses the question of how best to conceptualize the dimension of reality traditionally named "God," with a focus on "Abrahamic" religions. The three chapters thereafter look at women and the divine in specific religious and spiritual traditions: Haifaa Jawad, Melissa Raphael, and Hannah Bacon reevaluate theologies and spiritualities within Islam, Judaism, and Christianity, respectively.

Luce Irigaray opens our collection with a reflection on the question of how women may find, define, and practice a spiritual doctrine, and what kind of divine may assist the becoming of women? She reiterates both her belief in two separate subjectivities and her insistence that this does not equate to positing subjectivity upon a biological destiny. Man and woman have a relational identity, held between nature and culture and based on certain bodily givens; sexuate belonging is a matter, however, not only of the body but also the psyche. The two irreducible subjects require a different manner of becoming divine; women need to be able to transcend history as it already exists in order to affirm a culture as women. She posits the "two lips" as privileged place of self-affection for the feminine; this is not, however, simply autoeroticism, but the capacity to stay positively in one's self. The task for a woman is keeping a transcendental dimension between herself and the other that cannot be overcome, resulting in a carnal transcendental. Becoming divine is not only a concern for the mind but requires a transmuting of our material dependency into a spiritual autonomy; this is not achieved through relinquishing sensory perceptions but through modifying the manner of perception. We need to stay at the crossroads between a vertical transcendence (relating with an Other who corresponds to Same) and a horizontal transcendence (relating with the other in respect of their differences). This meeting with the other requires entry into an other culture—a culture of intimacy that is a matter of touch. This touching, this intimacy, concerns not only the touch of a hand but also listening, opening to, meeting with a breath, or heart, or soul; it is the passage from self-affection to affection for the other; it leads us, says Irigaray, to a possible Other in the path of becoming divine.

Pamela Sue Anderson offers an analysis of "transcendence" from a feminist philosophical perspective, in critical dialogue with Irigaray's work on a feminine divine. She raises the question whether Irigaray and her followers can avoid the forms of transcendence-in-immanence that lead to ethical debilitation, as pointed out by Simone de Beauvoir in her consideration of the immanence of the female narcissist, lover, and mystic. A key point is whether the "sensible transcendental" actually subverts the degradation of the female body and oppressive patterns of love relations. Anderson takes as an example the apotheosis of man and woman in the relations of God the Father and the Virgin Mother, critiquing Irigaray's reconfiguration of Mariology. Ultimately, Anderson argues that serious issues arise in Irigaray's account by her preference for the strictly psycholinguist over against the sociological and the historical. Anderson returns to de Beauvoir's contribution, which, she argues, allows for the possibilities and subordination in the context of a Western woman in love and elucidates the relational exchanges between women and men. For Anderson, it is through the historical and social that the damaging imagery of both traditional ideas of transcendence and of the female body can be transformed. Transcendence for Anderson is not to be sought in the immanence of bodily self-love or in a god in one's own image. Rather, transcendence can be situated in the reality of goodness—the concrete relations of self-transcending subjects mutually seeking truth and justice between one another.

Patrice Haynes also provides a philosophical consideration of the nature of transcendence, suggesting that transcendence should be rethought and reclaimed in the construction of a theological materialism. She starts from the premise that transcendence is frequently regarded with suspicion by feminist theorists. This is grounded in the typical position of Western thought: the body and the material are what is to be transcended; given femaleness is normally associated with just these things and relegated to an (inferior) position of materiality and immanence, it is not surprising that feminism has sought to deconstruct concepts of transcendence and immanence that are perceived to be patriarchally constructed and inherently both dualistic and hierarchical. It is further argued by some feminists that a focus on transcendence detracts from giving due attention to the lived materialities of existence. This has led to a thinking of the divine in terms of immanence and a relocation of the transcendent to within the world. Haynes sets out to reclaim the traditional theistic idea of divine transcendence as one that can actually affirm both materiality and embodiment. She builds on the nontheistic work of Theodor Adorno in order to construct a model of transcendence as divine mind that actually secures the inherent meaningfulness and particularity of the sensuous.

Claire Colebrook takes a further look at the philosophical concepts of transcendence and immanence to argue, counter prevailing trends, for transcendence as the possibility of ethics. Like Haynes, she begins with an examination of arguments that urge us to jettison "transcendence," in this case through reprising the arguments of Deleuze and Guattari and Foucault. For the former, transcendence is the primary illusion enslaving thought to false notions of foundation and presence rather than becoming. Their creation of the concept of "becoming-woman" in a move toward liberation indicates also that the problem of transcendence is itself sexed. Similarly, Foucault sees the institutionalization of philosophy's notion of transcendent truth to be tied to a process of normalization; transcendence then figures thought's tendency to be emasculated by its own productions. Yet, the question can be raised: if we do not have transcendent criteria, how do we appeal to a mode of life other than the present? If thought is entirely self-enclosed, are we left with a heightened subjectivism that cannot recognize the other? Such a subject, Colebroke argues, is highly masculinist. She then considers the issues of beauty, religion, and pornography to elucidate how the transcendent can move us beyond a preoccupation with the self. This is to move toward a transcendence in relation, rather than as an alien imposition on the self; it opens us to risk, contingency, and difference. Colebrook closes by showing the intersections between Irigaray's philosophy of sexual difference and becoming divine and transcendence as the possibility of the ethical.

Morny Joy examines the phenomenon of sacrifice as a paradigmatic example of the economy of exploitation in operation on women; for instance, women provide the resources to fuel the economy but are denied any say in their allocation. Women, she argues, have been denied not only symbolic status but also what she names "ontological integrity"—the capacity to determine and affirm their own self-worth. She identifies a male-controlled sacrificial economy, undergirded and empowered by the concept of a masculinized, omnipotent, and transcendent deity. In this economy, women are objects of exchange. Joy dialogues closely with Irigaray's work in order to reflect on the question of what would happen if women undermined the present symbolic system. For both Irigaray and Joy, the religious dimensions to this should not be ignored because of the religious roots of most symbolic systems. Different forms of symbolic expression are required to promote women's agency and ontological integrity—for women, in fact, to "become divine." This also requires a rethinking of the concept of transcendence, one that incorporates a recognition of both responsibility and limitation. Joy expresses the indebtedness of feminist thinking to Irigaray's insights but also sounds a number of notes of caution—for example, with respect to Irigaray's focus on heterosexuality as the fundamental form of relation. She nevertheless commends her reframing of the encounter between man and woman in ways that point toward female divinity and integrity and which challenge the classical body/spirit dualism. This breaches certain of the barriers denying women symbolic status. Joy also notes, however, that the adequacy of such a strategy for addressing actual social and political abuses has been questioned. Joy calls for the value of Irigaray's work to be recognized but suggests that some may prefer also to explore other models of equitable relation and acquisition of symbolic status.

Beverly Metcalfe intertwines a consideration of female leadership with a consideration of the feminine divine. She draws on the work of Irigaray and other feminist scholars to demonstrate how a rereading of conceptions of feminine wisdom and leadership can help us move toward a situation of transcendence, in which human beings may take their place as embodied living subjects in their own right. To do this, she examines the tale of Deborah in the Hebrew Bible in the Book of Judges, with a view to casting light on contemporary leadership theorizing through the inscription of a feminine logic. Men, masculinity, and leadership are typically associated with one another. This chapter, as an act of destabilization, reimagines leadership as intrinsically feminine: returning to the Goddess. This is achieved through looking at two alternative readings of leadership based on Deborah and her female supporter Jael. On the one hand, Deborah is portrayed as a "lesser" leader despite her achievements; Jael's triumphs are accounted to her success as seductress. On the other hand, the feminine leader has achieved a closeness to God, embodies a female sacral power, and can represent a transcendent position.

Mike King argues that monotheism offers us only an attenuated language in which to understand the spiritual life. He takes the term "transcendence" as in itself illustrative of this, since in Christian traditions it tends to posit a binary opposition to immanence that is not apposite for nonmonotheistic traditions. "God," as a masculinized construct of Abrahamic and text-centered monotheism, needs cutting down to size: This will allow space for other religious frameworks and for women's spirituality. King suggests that four other significant spiritualities should be able to take their place at the table alongside the "God" traditions, leading to five in total: shamanism, goddess polytheism, warrior polytheism, monotheism, and the unitive (transcendent). These five modalities of spiritualities represent historical epochs. They also, however, represent five personal spiritual impulses. The boundaries between are understood to be fluid. King offers an analysis of each of these five modalities, concluding that a fivefold schematic of this kind allows us to see monotheism in a global and epochal perspective. As such, it retains significance but not oppressive dominance at the expense of other modalities—in particular, in its denial of the feminine. King ends with a consideration of how Irigaray's call for a culture of two subjects might intersect with his own fivefold model.

Daphne Hampson examines ways to reinterpret and reconceptualize concepts of "God" or the "divine"; she argues that only by effecting a shift in our conceptual understanding and in our language can freedom be hoped for. She acknowledges that the so-called historical religions may have acted as a vehicle for human awareness of "God"; however, these paradigms have also skewed our understanding and new language, imagery, and concepts need developing. She puts forward "experience" as a starting point—what is it about their experience that makes any concept of "God" credible to people? In reconceptualizing, epistemological and ethical considerations are then held to be key criteria. Reconceptualizing "God" also goes hand in hand with reconceptualizing common Western concepts of the self—as both "centered" and "open." She suggests that the traditional Abrahamic religions are untenable both ethically and epistemologically and calls for a wholly new paradigm.

Haifaa Jawad provides us with a reevaluation of the feminine dimension in Islamic spirituality. She notes the popular perception, especially in the West, that Muslim women are oppressed, subordinated, and denied active religious participation. Jawad accepts that this can be discerned in certain parts of the Muslim world but seeks to demonstrate that these are not related to Islam as such—rather, they constitute the actual disfiguration of Islam. She suggests that an emphasis on the spiritual dimension of Islam offers a corrective to such ideological distortions. She highlights the openness of the spiritual life within Islam for both men and women, showing the Quranic roots of such a philosophy. Further than this, Jawad also seeks to show that, historically, it is possible to identify a type of spirituality within the Islamic tradition that has distinctly feminine attributes. She looks especially at the Sufi tradition in order to demonstrate this, arguing that the feminine dimension of the Divine Reality is enshrined at the very heart of authentic Islam tradition. Taken seriously, such an affirmation of the female in spiritual terms leads to women being treated with reverence rather than contempt.

Melissa Raphael looks at Jewish women's experiences during the Holocaust. She uses recent research into gender and the Holocaust and, more specifically, the oral histories of mothers and daughters who survived. She seeks to demonstrate how the suffering of mothers can point to a reconfigured understanding of the covenantal relationship between God and Israel. Centrally, her argument is that female love, power, and providence can in fact be seen to resist evil; the power of motherhood is not simply a sentimentalized ideal but tells us something deeply important about the nature of both divine and female love. This includes its resistance to oppressive powers and regimes. Read in this way, the suffering of mothers and children offers us insight into the nature of God and provides resources for the construction of a maternalist theology. The face of *Shekhinah*, she suggests, is dimly perceptible in the smoke clouds of Auschwitz—a face expressive of divine maternal wrath and yearning for what was being lost but also offering the redemptive kiss at dying. Raphael moves from this into a Jewish feminist, post-Holocaust engagement with Irigaray's work, in particular the spirituality of self-affection or the closed lips; she questions whether such an approach is able to offer consolation to the suffering other, and prefers the opened divine lips of the *Shekhinah*.

Hannah Bacon reassesses the doctrine of Incarnation within Christianity, with a view to establishing the sacramentality of female embodiment. The Incarnation, in its affirmation of the value of fleshed existence, has been held by a number of feminist theologians to subvert patriarchal conceptions of materiality, including the denigration thereby of female existence as "immanent." However, the maleness of Christ remains problematic: The gendered particularity of the Incarnation has traditionally justified a gendered differential of male and female embodiment with relation to the divine. This has led to a feminist tendency to focus on the cosmic, rather than particular, significance of Christ. In this chapter, Bacon argues that the very particularity of the Incarnation in fact promotes feminist desire to affirm the body, both female and male; more, the Incarnation can destabilize phallocentric economy itself. Bacon deploys concepts drawn from Irigaray's work to construct a theology of the Incarnation that, she argues, secures and affirms bodily goodness; "body" is understood as "situation" rather than essentialist given. Taking the particularity of Jesus's body seriously undermines attempts to focus on any singular aspect of that particularity as theologically more significant; all bodies, in their own particularities, differ from that of Jesus. The theological importance of the Incarnation is that the Word becomes flesh in history and that others in history—both men and women—can Incarnate God, becoming co-redeemers. The body of Christ may thus be deemed "extendable." As such, the particular body of Christ is opened out to irreducible plurality; it therefore subverts phallocentric logics of the same.

The essays that follow, then, are plural in nature, espousing different methodologies, aims, and perspectives. We hope, however, that they all, each in their own way, offer us illumination in our consideration of those two terms variously considered so far apart, and yet so close together: women and the divine.

NOTES

1.   "Transcendental" here is intended to invoke Irigaray's "sensible transcendental," rather than Kant's method as laid out in the *Critique of Pure Reason*, trans. N. K. Smith (London and Basingstoke: Macmillan, 1983).

2. For an account of this, see Theodor W. Adorno and Max Horkheimer, *Dialectic of Enlightenment*, trans. John Cumming (London: Verso, 1997).

BIBLIOGRAPHY

Adorno, Theodor W., and Max Horkheimer. *Dialectic of Enlightenment*. Translated by John Cumming. London: Verso, 1997.

Deleuze, Gilles, and Félix Guattari. *A Thousand Plateaus: Capitalism and Schizophrenia*. Minneapolis: University of Minnesota Press, 1987.

Hardt, Michael and Antonio Negri. *Empire*. London: Harvard University Press, 2000.

———. *Multitude*. New York: Penguin Books, 2004.

Irigaray, Luce. *Prières Quotidiennes* [Everyday Prayers]. Translated by Luce Irigaray with Timothy Mathews. Paris: Maisonneuve et Larose, and Nottingham: University of Nottingham, 2004.

Kant, Immanuel. *Critique of Pure Reason*. Translated by Norman Kemp Smith. London and Basingstoke: Macmillan, 1983.

Kerslake, Christian. "The Vertigo of Philosophy: Deleuze and the Problem of Immanence." *Radical Philosophy* 113 (May /June 2002), http://www.radicalphilosophy.com.

Kosky, Jeffrey. "The Birth of the Modern Philosophy of Religion and the Death of Transcendence." *Transcendence: Philosophy, Literature and Theology Approach the Beyond*. Edited by Regina Schwartz. London: Routledge, 2004.

Rose, Gillian. *Love's Work*. London: Chatto and Windus, 1995.

Schwartz, Regina. *Transcendence: Philosophy, Literature and Theology Approach the Beyond*. London: Routledge, 2004.

Sherry, Patrick. *Images of Redemption: Art, Literature and Salvation*. London: Continuum, 2003.

Westphal, Merold. *Transcendence and Self-Transcendence: On God and the Soul*. Bloomington: Indiana University Press, 2004.

Whitford, Margaret. *Luce Irigaray. Philosophy in the Feminine*. Routledge: London, 1991.

Žižek, Slavoj. "The Descent of Transcendence into Immanence or, Deleuze as a Hegelian." In *Transcendence: Philosophy, Literature and Theology Approach the Beyond*, edited by Regina Schwartz, 235–48. London: Routledge, 2004.

Chapter 1

Toward a Divine in the Feminine

Luce Irigaray[*]

How can we find, define, and practice a spiritual doctrine appropriate to women? How can we return to ourselves in a way that allows us autonomy and freedom enough to discover what sort of divine is suitable for us? A divine, that is to say, that can assist our becoming as women, including the becoming divine of the women that we are by birth. From birth I am a woman, not only through my body. I am not only a female but a woman because I belong to a subjective world, a subjective identity, different from those of a man. Such a subjectivity can be analyzed as a specific way of relating with myself, with the other or others, with the world. For various reasons, this manner of relating is different in the case of a girl and a boy. As I have already said many times, to affirm that man and woman are really two different subjects does not amount to sending them back to a biological destiny, to a simple natural belonging. Man and woman are culturally different: This corresponds to a different construction of their subjectivity. The subjectivity of man and that of woman are structured, starting from a relational identity specific to each one, a relational identity that is held

---

[*] The English version is by Luce Irigaray, with a rereading by Mary Green.

between nature and culture, and which assures a bridge from which it is possible to pass from one to the other while respecting them both.

This specific relational identity is based on different irreducible givens: A woman is born of a woman, of someone of her gender, whereas a man is born of someone of another gender than himself; a woman can engender in herself like her mother, whereas a man engenders outside of himself; a woman can nourish with her body, whereas a man nourishes only thanks to his work; a woman can engender in herself the masculine and the feminine, whereas a man, in fact, intervenes as man above all by engendering the masculine.

The first relational situation is thus very different for the girl and the boy. And they build their relation to the other in a very different way. The girl immediately finds herself in a relation between subjects of the same gender that helps her to structure a relation to the other, which is more difficult for the boy to develop. On the other hand, the girl, a woman, is made fragile by the intervention of the other in her: in love, in motherhood. From the very beginning, sexuate belonging concerns not only the body but also the soul.

Sexuate belonging has to be cultivated in a different way, not only as a sexual dimension of subjectivity but also as an entire and comprehensive determination of subjectivity, hence my use of "sexuate" and not "sexual" in order to indicate this total reference.

Becoming Divine in the Feminine

Thus, the matter for a woman is not of becoming a man and joining a becoming divine in the masculine. This could remove us from the fulfillment of our subjectivity. Of course, it is not a question of agreeing to be secondary with respect to man. The historical perspective that maintains that only one subject exists—presumed neuter and universal, but elaborated starting from the necessities of man—has to be overcome to reach a culture of two subjects: one masculine and one feminine. These two subjects are irreducible, the one to the other. They cannot be substituted the one for the other, nor subjected to a hierarchical assessment. They really are two, two who are qualitatively and not quantitatively different. There is not a first subject followed by a second subject less perfect than the first. Two subjects exist who correspond to different values, different beings and Beings, and who need different subjective accomplishments or fulfillments. Each subject requires a different manner of becoming divine. To take the place of the other subject amounts to a lapse, a fault, toward the other and toward oneself. And one could say the same when only one subject is recognized as existing or as valid, or when the relation between the two subjects is not considered.

I would like to stress the following: I am not talking here about sexual relations strictly speaking, but about sexuate identity or subjectivity. I believe that a lack of respect for the identity or subjectivity of each one is the most important fault since this amounts to a kind of murder: a spiritual murder, the most serious murder and also the most serious suicide. How to escape this kind of murder or suicide? It is not always obvious. But perhaps this is the first question to which we should pay attention on the path of becoming divine.

It is even less obvious that we live in a time in which sociology lays down the law. Now sociology talks only about what already exists, in the past or at best in the present (which becomes the past when referred to by sociology). Furthermore, sociology talks about that which exists at the level of a social belonging, which itself already exists. From such a viewpoint, becoming divine could only make sense as a process in a past sociological context. As far as sociology is concerned, my own becoming, as a process that is strange to the history and society in which I am situated, amounts to a mere dream or a utopian view: in fact, a sort of madness or psychosis. In a way, sociology locks us up for a second time in a patriarchal tradition. It claims that only that which already exists—or better, existed—can be, or is, true. Thus, for sociology, a culture of two subjects, which does not yet exist, cannot be and cannot correspond to the truth. I, as a woman, we, as women, can only then be second with respect to man, to men, as was the case in our past patriarchal or phallocratic tradition. Becoming what or who we are makes no sense. More generally, becoming makes no sense, apart from being subjected to what already exists: for example, rules, norms, and stereotypes.

In fact, Simone de Beauvoir understood a feminine becoming only in this sense: to passively submit oneself to that which already exists in the form of social norms, rules, and stereotypes. Thus, becoming a woman could not have a positive meaning for her. In my opinion, we can do better today. Firstly, by considering that sociology is more limited than we ourselves are, that is to say, that sociology approaches only an aspect of human beings, not the whole. It is true that our epoch would like to reduce human beings to sociological beings. But is it then a question of humanity? It is certainly not a question of the fulfillment of our humanity because it is up to humanity to go beyond that which already exists, including what we consider as humanity itself. It is in this aspiration that our subjective concern regarding divinity has its origin, but, more generally, our concern regarding transcendence as such.

The problem for a woman today is how to overcome history as it already exists, rather than submitting to and entering it. The problem is: how to escape the feminine status of our past tradition in order to affirm and promote a culture of our own as women, a culture appropriate not only to our body but above all to the relational world that is ours from birth? Therefore, the first task is how to return to ourselves in spite of our belonging to a culture that is not built by us but that we have in some way supported?

THE TWO LIPS: THRESHOLD OF THE FEMININE SELF

We can have recourse at least to our experience and tradition for this return. I could give the example of the two lips, which I have already suggested many times to be a privileged place of self-affection in the feminine. Self-affection here does not refer to a mere autoeroticism or narcissism. Rather, self-affection refers to the capability of staying in oneself with a positive feeling. The lips can represent the threshold of the feminine self, which allows a woman to remain within herself when her lips touch each other, and open to the outside when her lips relinquish this position of self-affection. I discovered the importance of the lips through personal experience. But I verified the relevance of this experience thanks to some cultural traits of our tradition, to which I have already alluded in *Marine Lover* and in a more recent text, "The Return."

For example, in the archaeological gallery of Syracuse in Sicily, there are many statues of the goddess Kore. The most interesting aspect of these statues of Kore is that their lips change according to the century in which they were sculpted. The most ancient of them have their lips closed, touching one another, and they could be an illustration of self-affection in the feminine. In later statues, the mouth is open and the lips no longer touch each other. And, finally, the mouth remaining open, the lips are also deformed.

Such an evolution can be explained by the story of Kore, taken from her mother, the great Goddess Demeter, by the God of the underworld. He raped her and kept her in the underworld—even changing her name—until her mother provoked a great famine on earth so that her daughter would be restored to her. You could understand, in this way, that the evolution of Kore's lips is linked to a change in self-affection, which leads her to become dependent on an external instrument, or an other as instrument, for self-affecting, as is a boy or a man. You could also perceive here what I intend to mean when I talk about the virginity of woman as a condition for autonomy. I allude to an ability to affect oneself through the lips, touching one another without any external intervention or tool. It suffices that woman cares about gathering with herself and remains concentrated on the affect that results from this touching. It is interesting to experience what then happens, is felt, notably with respect to the two in a relationship. Such a gesture allows woman to come back to the self, within the self, and to respect the other, preserving a free space between the two.

How could we save this privileged place of self-affection in order to be able to return within ourselves, to be faithful to our self, and to cultivate our own becoming—a necessary condition for entering into a dual relation with the other, that does not amount to a repetition of the first link with the mother? How can we reach a relation in two that does not reduce itself to a "dyad" or to a pair of opposites? This requires another culture to be elaborated.

Also, in the case of feminine subjectivity, a process of cultivation of sensible immediacy is necessary but in a different way from that which is needed by masculine subjectivity. The feminine world is, by birth, more relational than the world of the boy, notably because of a privileged situation of the girl with respect to the mother, a same as the girl. Which permits a duality of people from the very beginning, in particular through a relation to engendering different from that of a boy, of a man. The girl knows what it means to beget; it is a familiar experience for her, notably through intuition or feeling. Turning back to birth, or beyond, does not seem a dangerous abyss to cover, to veil, even with a God, as is the case for a masculine subject. The problem for feminine subjectivity is how to escape from a solely natural state, both at the level of herself as a living being and in relations with the other(s)—be they the mother, the lover, or the child, for example. What woman has to do is maintain an irreducible difference between the other and herself, while preserving her natural origin, her natural roots or existence. This can happen by placing and keeping a transcendental dimension between the other and herself, particularly the other who belongs to a different origin, beginning with the masculine other. The task, for a woman, is one of interposing, between the other and herself, a negative that cannot be overcome. Thus, the transcendental would not be immediately, but abstractly, deferred to the absolute "you" of a God—who, in fact, then substitutes himself for the mother, the first other. The transcendental must unceasingly intervene between the other and myself—the "you" and the "I"—turning the sensible immediacy of the relation into a cultivation of affect. This can save the irreducibility between the other and myself, the insuperable difference between the two: the "you" and the "I." This will end in a transcendental feeling that remains carnal, sensible, and which does not relate only to the mind.

SELF-AFFECTION AS RELIGIOUS DIMENSION

Thus, experiencing the two lips touching one another can represent a crucial place of self-affection for a woman. And we can try to return to such an experience in our own lives as a concrete everyday means of recovering our own self. We can also observe that the positive, indeed the religious, sense of the two lips touching each other has not totally disappeared from our tradition or other traditions, but we are often unable to recognize its value, that is, our own value, as woman.

For example, most women interpret only in a negative way the silence of the figure of Mary. But perhaps it indicates a means of keeping self-affection as woman, and not losing herself in a discourse that is not fitting for her. We could at least wonder about this, instead of rejecting all that which represents a possible feminine divine value, in a sort of spiritual masochism. Freud did not think of this feminine masochism because it could throw into question his own cultural belonging, in particular his interpretation of the desire that Dora felt to keep her lips touching one another rather than agreeing to be kissed by her therapist. In my opinion, it was wise on her part, and not pathological as Freud claimed, to act in this way, above all when looking at a procession, that is, in a religious context. In fact, Freud, as the god Hades did with Kore, wanted to rape Dora, to take Dora from herself, from her self-affection. Freud was then causing hysteria rather than curing it. But such a cure required him to interrogate his own desire, to question his own self-affection and the need he felt to take Dora from her self-affection in order to affect himself.

The silence that accompanies her lips touching one another is thus not necessarily negative but can represent a privileged place of self-affection for a woman. Through this gesture, we could cure by ourselves the hysteria that a phallocratic culture has aroused in us by taking us away from ourselves. Joining our lips, just as joining our hands, is a way of gathering with ourselves, of reuniting the two parts of ourselves for self-affecting.

Experiencing, and always turning back to, this self-affection through the two parts of ourselves touching each other is necessary so that we can feel self-affection in the relation with an other different from us, without losing ourselves. In these cases—the two lips, the two hands, the two sexes—the word *eteros* was used in earliest Greek language. In these cases, it is a question of two, and it is essential to start and to return to the union of the two that we are, before being able to reach being two with an other in difference. Without this, we always run the risk of confusing the other with a part of ourselves, of mistaking the other for a part of ourselves.

In a phallocratic historical time such as ours, we often forget the value of the feminine lips touching each other and of the silence that accompanies such a gesture. But it is not the case in all traditions. For example, although in the Western tradition words are favored in relation to silence, this is not the case in certain Eastern traditions. For Hegel, the end of our journey ought to be a gathering of all possible discourses. In contrast, for the Buddha it ought to be becoming able to reach silence. Of course, silence does not then amount to a lack of words but to the safeguarding of that which has not yet been manifested, of that which has not yet appeared, of that which does not yet exist.

And we again find such a teaching about keeping silent when closing our lips with the universal sacred syllable: *aum*. In this syllable, the enunciation of the last letter, *m*, which requires one to close one's lips, is presumed to safeguard the not yet manifested, and would correspond to the color black. I could add that the linguist Jakobson has stated that the letter *m* is used by the baby to designate the mother in many languages. But the *m* is then followed, at least in French, by an *a*, the clearest of all vowels, and, contrary to *aum*, we go here from darkness to clarity: the mother being the representation of the darkness of our origin.[1]

We could thus consider in another way the silence of Mary, and more generally the silence of a woman. Mary is the one who keeps that which is not yet manifested, not only at the level of a natural birth but also at the level of a spiritual or divine coming into the world. To enter into a new era of our tradition, the time of incarnation, God has needed the existence of Mary and her consent.

"Yes" is one of the sole words pronounced by Mary according to the Bible. But this "yes," for which Mary opens her lips, is nothing less than the threshold that makes it possible for us to enter into another era of divine becoming. Such an interpretation is possible, and it gives to woman a decisive part in the figuration of divinity. Many women are today unable to recognize this privileged role in the manifestation of divinity. They make their own the most disparaging discourse about Mary, relinquishing in this way their founding part in the divine becoming of humanity.

But, also in other traditions, there are figures rather similar to Mary. The Indian god Shiva, who corresponds to our era, can lead the world to its destruction or to its salvation, depending on the woman who is his lover. And the woman who can help our salvation, and thus avoid our damnation-destruction, is closely related to the figure of Mary. For example, she is said to be the woman of the mountain; that is, she represents the fresh or pure aspect of Shiva. Mary also frequently appears on a mountain or a hill, and she also represents freshness or purity with respect to the Lord. We are here approaching some universal paradigms of the divine dimension.

THE PATH TOWARD INTERNALIZATION

Other words attributed to Mary in the Bible are words of praise for the marvels that the Lord made for her: the *Magnificat*, for example. People often interpret such words today as a testimony of servitude. But it would also be valid to hear them as Mary's capability of feeling divine bliss or beatitude and of expressing it through singing, as the birds do when they enjoy the return of spring. In fact, consenting to receiving divine bliss is not so remote from enjoying a ray of sun—as is shown by iconographies of the Annunciation. No doubt it is then a more internalized experience, and it requires a path toward internalization that cannot amount to submitting to a truth external to oneself but to transforming oneself.

After succeeding in turning back to our own self, we have to make our way toward an internalization appropriate to ourselves: an undertaking that requires us to intertwine, at every moment, a doing and letting do, a being and letting be. Such a wedding between an active and a passive gesture already exists when our lips touch one another. The two dimensions take part in self-affection. And we must care about their permanent interlacing in order to be faithful to a becoming of our own. But the more we advance along the path of internalization, the more subtle this interlacing becomes. How to avoid being mistaken?

Some criteria could be of help. For example, if I am out of breath, that is, if I am losing the rhythm of my breathing, something goes wrong in my self-affecting. It is rather easy to verify this by ourselves.

We have to remain capable of inhaling and exhaling for the same length of time, and of holding our breath inside ourselves or staying without breathing—that is, without inhaling or exhaling—during a short time, between breathing in and breathing out.

Another criterion could be of help. If I am worrying too much about something or someone, this means that I have lost harmony in self-affecting and have probably taken too mental a path. To turn back to my self-affection, I could try to stay peacefully in a quiet place, keeping my lips touching one another, until I find the capability of being well and remaining silent. Walking alone in nature is also a means of turning back to oneself.

Furthermore, and contrary to the religious teachings of our tradition, I also think we have to cultivate our senses, not as a way of appropriation or seizure, as has too often been the case in Western culture, but as a way of passing from solely a physical level to a spiritual level without despising or leaving our body. For example, gazing at a flower can lead to the blossoming of concentration and contemplation. Gazing at an other can help us to pass from a visible to an invisible dimension—as I have tried to explain in some of my texts, for example in *I Love to You*, *To Be Two*, and some poems in *Everyday Prayers*.

In our times, the cultivation of listening—to music, to the song of the birds, or to the words of an other—is a manner of restoring our self with respect to a culture that privileges images and representations. Cultivating our senses can contribute to the conversion of our vital energy into a spiritual energy, and it is a better way of becoming divine than submitting ourselves to abstract laws that we do not understand with our whole being.

Becoming divine cannot amount only to a concern of the mind. The question is how to turn our original material and dependent existence into an autonomous and spiritual existence through a change of our energy. And the problem here is not of relinquishing our sensory perceptions but of modifying our manner of perceiving.

Such a transformation is necessary in relating with ourselves, with nature, or with the world, and also to and with the other(s). If we do not keep our sensory perceptions, we cannot meet with the other in a global way. We then subject the one and the other to norms and truths that are already defined and which do not allow us to enter into presence. Now this aspect of our humanity is really crucial. Neglecting it and its cultivation is the cause of many crimes, including religious crimes, against humanity or its surroundings.

FROM BEING TWO IN ONESELF TO
BEING TWO WITH THE OTHER

We lack a culture of relating with the other. Not only a profane culture, not only a moral culture but also an ethical culture, ethics being
understood here as respect for the place and the dwelling of the other,
for their difference and for the space between us. We lack a culture
of the divine in our relations with the other. We have too quickly
subjected the other, present to us here and now, to the Other. It
could be suitable, also with respect to this Other, to cultivate relations with the other(s), present here and now to us, with us, without
too simply projecting all that we are onto a presumed God, who is
then made according to our image and not the reverse.

In fact, our everyday cross, our internal and invisible everyday cross,
consists in staying, every moment, at the crossroads between two transcendences: a vertical transcendence and a horizontal transcendence.
The first transcendence exists in relating with an Other who corresponds to the absolute perfection of ourselves; that is, the absolute
Same. The second transcendence exists in relating with the other here
and now in respect for their difference(s), for our difference(s), that is,
for our concrete and irreducible singularities. This requires a cultivation of our entire way of being, of our total Being. And this cannot be
reduced merely to a concern of the mind as is too often the case with
morality itself.

Meeting the other, meeting with the other, requires us to enter
another culture than that which has been provided by our Western
tradition, at least until now. The relations to and with the other cannot simply be subjected to the relation to God: they have to be and
to remain both earthly and divine. Thus, they cannot only be submitted to the logos, to words already pronounced. They need a wording
appropriate to our present and unique encounter.

The meeting with the other cannot be merely ecstatic with respect
to real surroundings or our bodies, nor can it become reduced to a
sensible immediacy. In the words that the one tries to speak to the
other, the bodies and the earthly dwellings in which they live have
to be heard. Each time the words must reach, for each one and in
each one, their belonging to earth and to heaven, to humanity and
to divinity. We have to hear something of this belonging from one
another. If each one takes care of their own part of earth and of sky, of
the human and of the divine, then approaching one another becomes
possible. But when these polarities are distributed between the one

and the other—between man and woman, for example—coming closer remains impossible.

Another important difference with respect to our tradition which privileges seeing and the visible: the approach to the other requires opening a path that is not primarily inspired by showing something or making something appear. To make one's way toward closeness does not demand here passing from the darkness of the night to the light of day, but rather finding a manner of speaking that could go with a nocturnal luminosity. To turn one's eyes toward the heart of the intimate risks undoing intimacy's touch—by dividing, distinguishing, cutting off and thus isolating. Our eyes are not capable of contemplating intimacy, at least not directly. They can only imagine something about intimacy through the light, the gestures, the words that it radiates. Intimacy as such will remain invisible, irreducible to appropriation, thus foreign to Western discourse. Intimacy allows itself neither to be seen nor to be seized. Nevertheless, it is probably the core of our Being. And any attempt to appropriate it risks annihilating Being itself. However, it is not a question here of magic, of irrationality or of madness. It is, rather, a question of touch.

But touching does not only correspond to touching or grasping a body. Touching, or being touched, can concern an intimacy that cannot be approached with the hand. It is rather a question of listening to, of opening to, of accepting to feel a breath, a heart, a soul. To go toward the other does not end just in meeting with a body. We are also meeting with a breath, a heart, a soul. Often the call that compels us to move toward the other is confused with a mere physical attraction. And thus we elude the question that implies meeting with an other, reducing them to a simple body. Or, we lapse into the contrary: considering the other only as a cultural vehicle. Whereas the other is always both a body and a soul, belonging to nature as well as to culture—be they a lover, a child, or a foreigner. In any case, the matter is how to find, and keep finding, the crossroads where we could meet and share. In fact, we always meet the other at a crossroads if we try to escape fusion, reducing the one to the other, subjecting the one to the other—that is to say, if we remain two.

TO CONCLUDE: TOUCH AS GUIDE TO APPROACH DIVINITY

We are thus again, and once more, situated at a crossroads. It is not the same crossroads as that between the other and the Other, but neither is it absolutely strange to it. What then could guide us on the good path, the path of our becoming? Certainly, not only a mental care, especially one that is determined by laws defined outside ourselves. Our way could be touch itself, not only an external touching through our senses but also an internal touching.

It is touch that can help us to pass from self-affection to affection for the other and with the other, and also lead us toward a possible Other. Touch can be our guide, our star, one could say, along the path of becoming divine. But this touch has to be cultivated while remaining capable of immediacy and sensibility.

If you read, or read again, the text "The Mysterique" in *Speculum*, you will remember that the guide on the path of the mystics is touch: an immediate touch that is still lacking in mediations and is thus often hurting, cutting, striking, or dazzling. The closure of the Western tradition within metaphysics probably made such a violence necessary in order to reach an intimate touching in a culture dominated by the light of the logos, by a logic ruled above all by a mental economy. Furthermore, the exile of woman from herself can explain why she was only passive in meeting with divine grace.

Perhaps we could today prepare or pave the way for grace in a continuous manner, a manner that includes both passivity and activity, a manner in which passivity will be actively cultivated to open ourselves to receive grace, all sorts of graces, coming from different sources, with different intensities and impacts on our life.

I have indicated some stages for the journey toward our becoming divine: faithfulness to self-affection; sharing with the other in respect for their/our difference(s); crossroads between horizontal and vertical transcendences. In fact, it is difficult to express all these suggestions in a few words; furthermore, through a discourse that has to remain logical and rational, and is addressed to a wide audience. You could, with more time, quietly read some more poetic texts in *Everyday Prayers*, *The Way of Love*, and also *Key Writings*. In some traditions—even at the beginning of our own—prayer, thought, and art were not separated one from the other. This seems wise in order to express and talk (to) our whole beings. And I am sure that you will be touched in a more intimate way by certain of my poetic texts than by this more argued speech. Nevertheless, I hope that you have already received today some lights for your own path, your own journey.

NOTE

1. See Roman Jakobson,"Pourquoi 'Papa' et 'Maman'?," in *Langage Enfan-
    tin et Aphasie*, translated by J. P. Boons and R. Zygouris, 120–30. 1960.
    Paris: Les Editions de Minuit, 1969.

BIBLIOGRAPHY

Irigaray, Luce. *I Love to You*. Translated by A. Martin. 1992. New York: Rout-
ledge, 1996.
———. *Key Writings*. London and New York: Continuum, 2004.
———. *Marine Lover of Friedrich Nietzsche*. Translated by G. C. Gill. New
York: Columbia University Press, 1991.
———. *Prières Quotidiennes* [Everyday Prayers]. Translated by Luce Irigaray
with Timothy Mathews. Paris: Maisonneuve et Larose, and Nottingham:
University of Nottingham, 2004.
———. *Speculum of the Other Woman*. Translated by G. C. Gill. 1974. Ithaca,
NY: Cornell University Press, 1985.
———. *The Way of Love*. Translated by Heidi Bostic and Stephen Pluháček.
London-New York: Continuum, 2002. From the French *La Voie de
l'amour* (not yet published in France).
———. *To Be Two*. Translated by M. M. Rhodes and M. F. Cocito-Monoc.
1994. New York: Routledge, 2001.
Jakobson, Roman. "Pourquoi 'Papa' et 'Maman'?," in *Langage Enfantin et
Aphasie*, translated by J. P. Boons and R. Zygouris, 120–30. Paris: Les
Editions de Minuit, 1969.

Chapter 2

Transcendence and Feminist Philosophy

On Avoiding Apotheosis

Pamela Sue Anderson

> She gives up her transcendence,
> subordinating it to that of the essential other,
> to whom she makes herself vassal and slave.
> *It was to find herself*, to save herself,
> that *she lost* herself *in him* in the first place.
>
> —Simone de Beauvoir, *The Second Sex* (emphasis added)

This chapter intends to treat the title *Women and the Divine: Touching Transcendence* as a philosophical topic, offering one response to Luce Irigaray's "Toward a Divine in the Feminine" (Chapter 1 in this volume), while also drawing from her "Divine Women" and "I Love to You." I would like to raise a critical question for my readers: Can Irigaray, or those who follow her, avoid the ethically debilitating forms of transcendence-in-immanence that Simone de Beauvoir successfully uncovers in the immanence of the female narcissist, lover, and mystic?

Beauvoir confronted a philosophical conception of transcendence (*pour-soi*) as moving beyond or outside the immanence of the body (*en-soi*). She also demonstrated how the female body has been represented symbolically as a prison in the texts of Western philosophy. Today we confront an alternative conception to this dominant Western symbolism in Irigaray's "sensible transcendental." But can this sensible transcendental subvert the degradation of a woman's body as immanent and the oppressive patterns of a woman's love relations? From the outset, I suggest that even if Irigaray herself avoids degrading forms of female immanence, it is not immediately clear how she guides philosophical thinking about women and the divine. But let us take a closer look.

Various feminists have attempted to follow Irigaray's call "to become divine women." In fact, the position to be defended here has some affinity with Irigaray's "a divine in the feminine" when it comes to ensuring the integrity of and fidelity to the self; but I also turn to Beauvoir's philosophical assessment of transcendence, female immanence, and love. To see how Beauvoir's conception of transcendence can significantly develop Irigaray's notion of the sensible transcendental, it is necessary to unearth Irigaray's conception of divinity as a form of transcendence. The challenge for contemporary women who seek the divine in love (relations) remains to transcend the oppression that persists in relation to a woman and herself, a woman and a deified man, and a woman and a divine reality. Disagreeing with Irigaray, I intend to argue that women must be more cognizant of their place in history and society. To subvert their degradation, women can recognize themselves as subjects in everyday relations within a transformable history and transformative society and so transcend what have been ethically debilitating forms of love.

Irigaray and I might agree that transcendence should become the critical focus for both feminist philosophers and theologians. Yet, I will distinguish Irigaray-influenced theologians from feminist philosophers by the theologian's conception of divine women who function in a theological picture of creation and redemption (Beattie, "Redeeming Mary" 107–22). The feminist philosopher resists the internally and ethically contradictory conception of transcendence, which, in particular, emerges in the Mariology of orthodox theology. Despite that which is philosophically problematic, the contradiction inherent in the gendered accounts of the Christian God as Father and the Virgin as the Mother of the Son of God is embraced by "post-secular philosophers" who have also called themselves "radically orthodox theologians" (Blond 1–66; Ward, "Bodies: The Displaced

Body of Jesus Christ" 175–81, and *Christ and Culture* 129–58). My contention is that this contemporary reappropriation of Mariology shapes those postmodern Irigarayan theologians who are, consciously or unconsciously, guided by the implicit ideals of divinity for men and women. In brief, not unlike Irigaray herself, the radical orthodox theologian in particular relies on a pre-Enlightenment portrait of the Virgin Mother and God the Father; this reliance goes with a post-Enlightenment rejection of secularism.

Against this particular theological exclusion of Enlightenment philosophy, and so the virtual rejection of philosophy of religion as a modern project, I propose that a contemporary perspective in philosophy can enable a critical openness to self-transcendence insofar as there is a serious, reflexive engagement with both secular and religious thinking. In avoiding apotheosis (i.e., in not deifying men and women), self-transcendence could restore Enlightenment values of critical reflective openness and of active dialogue between different religious and secular philosophies (Anderson, "An Epistemological Approach to Philosophy of Religion" 87–94). Self-transcending relations to others and to the world would not rely upon apotheosis. Instead of seeking to become divine, these acts of self-transcendence would adhere to newly enlightened views of humanity, of mutual attention, and of concrete manifestations of truth.

TRANSCENDENCE AND THE
CONSTRUCTION OF A GENDER TYPE

Generally, in Western philosophy and myth, transcendence has not been associated with female bodily life. Instead, transcendence has been attributed to male subjects who seek the divine by devaluing and/or thinking beyond the body. Yet narrative configurations that gender the personhood of the gods and goddesses continue to enter Western philosophical discourse about transcendence from Christian theology and classical mythology. Western theology in particular idealizes Christ as the Son of God whose incarnation in a male body can be given an ambiguous gendering by, or in, a female form. Christ's mother is also frequently treated as a divine in the feminine. These configurations of divinity generate philosophical questions about the nature of that which is beyond human form. Why, in trying to comprehend the divine, is God given a gender? When God is conceived to be two persons, does this imply uniting two gendered forms? What makes a godlike transcendent reality both terrifying and fascinating

for human persons? Should the apparently unknowable reality of transcendence be associated with goodness and truth without a body?

Iris Murdoch, who was a British contemporary of Beauvoir, dis-
tinguishes bad, or false, from true transcendence. Murdoch turns to
Plato in her moral philosophy to demonstrate how true transcendence
is intrinsically bound up with goodness and how what is intrinsically
valuable is still perfectible (Murdoch 55, 57–70). This does not mean
that Plato himself—nor Murdoch herself—avoids treating the female
body as that which must be transcended to reach goodness. Just the
opposite is true: in Plato's dialogues, we find the mythology about
the human condition conceived symbolically as a womblike cavern
and imagined as a bodily prison out of which the philosopher must
struggle to achieve goodness, beauty, and truth. In Murdoch's novels,
we find women who are often trapped in the most demeaning stereotypes. Nevertheless, feminist philosophers can borrow from Plato
himself and from Murdoch's Platonic conceptions of intrinsic worth
and transcendence in goodness, while disagreeing with other aspects
of Platonic philosophy.

I borrow from Plato and Murdoch to conceive forms of self-transcendence in concrete acts of recognition and practices of goodness
that have a universal significance. Again Irigaray might agree with me
that it is not enough for women simply to reject or to reconfigure
the philosophical imagery of the Platonic cavern, home, or womblike
"dwelling"[1] from which the divine emerges: No reversal of the hierarchy of gendered imagery from masculine to feminine would achieve
mutual recognition as the ground for goodness in our discursive and
bodily practices. A feminist reversal of the hierarchical ordering of theological concepts according to their gender[2] would also fail to discover
how women and men can cultivate practical reasoning in mutually
constructive, social, and material relations. Furthermore, a (feminist)
theologian who rejects or opposes Western philosophy because it has
been gendered masculine not only reinforces the diremption of masculine philosophy from feminine spirituality but finds herself in the
mystifying space of her own apotheosis.

Irigaray herself tries to avoid this mystification by playing in a different way with the morphology of a divine in the feminine. Yet, there
are difficulties in her cultivation of belonging as "sexuate": this not
only means belonging to "the body" but also to "the psyche" as a
total "determination" of the place of a woman's subjectivity (Irigaray,
Chapter 1 in this volume, 14). This twofold sexuate belonging is identified as the "privileged place of self-affection" in the woman's two sets
of lips (cf. Irigaray, *This Sex Which Is Not One* 132–33). A significant

difficulty is whether this imagery of sexuate belonging can provide the basis for either true transcendence or the intrinsic good. Can truth and goodness be recognized both in concrete forms of sexually differentiated bodies and in their universal significance? Although Irigaray seeks transcendence in the sensible dimension of a female body—that is, in her "morphology"—those philosophical readers who attempt to make sense of this female body language may find it to be narcissist, if not incoherent.

I wonder whether it makes sense to accept Irigaray's construction of a gender type in terms of a "comprehensive determination of subjectivity" (Chapter 1 in this volume, 14). Yet she insists on "relating with an Other who corresponds to the absolute perfection of ourselves; that is, the absolute Same" as a "a vertical transcendence"—while still maintaining our differences in relation to "the irreducible singularities" of "a horizontal transcendence" (Chapter 1). Presumably, when the vertical transcendence is added to the horizontal transcendence, Irigaray's conception supports her claims about becoming divine women; that is, the twofold nature of transcendence creates the conditions for a divine in a woman's own gender (Irigaray, "Divine Women" 69–72). Horizontal transcendence seeks to establish "a transcendental dimension between the other and herself": the other belongs to a "different origin, beginning with the masculine other" (Irigaray, Chapter 1 in this volume, 17). In this way, a gap remains between the sexually differentiated forms of self and the other. Together the vertical and horizontal transcendences not only imply a female apotheosis but also an ontological difference: the two transcendences ground a woman's distinct gender type and her distance from another gender type. To translate my reading of this construction of a distinct gender type into Irigaray's shorthand: "sexual difference" is both the natural and transcendental condition for becoming subjects.[3]

Yet it remains unclear how exactly Irigaray's apotheosis of the female, in establishing sexual difference, can be a concrete solution to the problem of transcendence in philosophy. Positing an irreducible difference between masculine-male and feminine-female bodily origins, alongside the absolute Same (above), does not necessarily give a less abstract or more positive picture of a woman's body; her formative bodily practices and her relations to other bodies and to the world remain unclear. A major obstacle for feminist philosophy in overcoming the asymmetry of bodily difference is not removed if the philosophical imaginary that shapes our gendered practices continues to devalue and disinherit women precisely because the feminine-female subject as sexually different is not imagined to have ideas of her own—"having ideas" has distinguished the masculine-male subject only (Le Doeuff, *The Philosophical Imaginary* 108–28). This imaginary exclusion and real subordination of the very possibility of women having ideas cannot be undone by the apotheosis of women's subjectivity, especially if this means a sexually different language in the shape of female psychosexual bodies. Instead, I would urge that this psychosexual imaginary be changed. Otherwise, real concrete and positive changes in thinking and acting across sexual barriers remain inhibited by both the deification of a woman's bodily nature and the self-deification of a female psyche.[4]

To see the problem with Irigaray's psychosexual language, consider her account of virginity. Irigaray claims that "the [two] lips can represent the threshold of the feminine self, which allows a woman to remain with herself when the lips touch each other, and open to the outside when her lips relinquish this position of self-affection" (Irigaray, Chapter 1 in this volume, 16). This opening and closing of a woman's sex is "the threshold" to a feminine self; this self is violated when the two lips are broken open and no longer touch each other. In this way, female morphology renders the feminine self always deeply and vitally vulnerable to the other sex. This psycholinguistic analysis places the source of female degradation, of a woman's bodily imma-nence and psychological subordination to men, in the loss of virginity that implies a violent and damaging sexual encounter. For Irigaray, preserving female virginity symbolically, if not literally, enables a simple apotheosis that ensures a fidelity to self. Yet I suggest that this excessive preoccupation with the female threshold would prevent one from seeing what is there outside one. Irigaray's work on love might attempt to see the other. Yet insofar as one becomes preoccu-pied with one's own female (or male) virginity in love, the concrete issues making up the everyday reality of self-transcendence for most women, especially in their relations to men and to the world in gen-eral, are obscured.

For a philosophical example of the above problem, Irigaray's mim-ing of female self-affection confronts the paradox of the Kantian self who is both active and passive in bringing intuitions under concepts. The decisive difference between Irigaray's mime of self-affection and Kant's empirical and transcendental subjects remains the twofold movement of deification: preserving virginity by keeping the two lips together renders the female subject both sensible and transcen-dental. Yet ironically, this sensible transcendental remains both too disembodied—deified as transcendent virginity—and too narcissis-tic—focused exclusively on the sensibility of an individual (female) virgin. So Irigaray's "solution" to the paradox of self-affection cannot achieve a sensible and transcendental horizon; and it fails to establish a constructively relational and concrete gender type. I propose that we replace Irigaray's impossible sexuate ideal by recognizing self-transcendence in practical actions: Self-transcending acts already connect each of us with one another in concrete forms of goodness.

POSTSECULAR METAPHYSICS AND ENLIGHTENED SECULARISM: MARIOLOGY OR MORALITY

As already suggested, apotheosis is a common occurrence in classical and contemporary myths. The transformation of women and men into goddesses and gods in mythical terms has often demonstrated the close relations of human and divine. Yet this occurrence in myth also betrays a common illusion, that is, idolatrous perfection in patriarchal constructions of erotic relations between men and women.[5] What makes Enlightenment philosophy "secular" for some thinkers at least is its decisive challenge to this illusion of idolatry—of which the myths of apotheosis are examples. It is in this spirit of secularism that Beauvoir, Murdoch, and, currently, Michèle Le Doeuff as women philosophers reject any form of apotheosis. In direct opposition, postsecular philosophers (i.e., theologians) reject any form of secularism, while reconfiguring the divine God-man and the Virgin Mary in line with radical Christian orthodoxy. Irigaray's imperative that we become divine tends to fit nicely with what would seem to be premodern theology. To illustrate the contrast of postsecular metaphysics and enlightened secularism, let us turn to Le Doeuff.

Le Doeuff is adamant that women should avoid apotheosis for the sake of themselves and the welfare of humanity more generally. This sense of welfare connects goodness to transcendence: Here it is not a matter of going beyond the human but going beyond badness and inhumanity. Le Doeuff's spirit of enlightened secularism addresses both women and men. Her imperative is twofold: (1) to allow no one to think in one's place, so as to use one's reason and (2) to disallow the idolization of the woman whose sacrifice is blindly passive due to her fundamental lack of choice (i.e., in the face of being divinized by a male god). True transcendence would reject bad transcendence as a form of alienation: apotheosis alienates one's practical reasoning from oneself, undermining one's autonomous relations to others, goodness, and collective historical experiences.[6]

Le Doeuff builds on Beauvoir's account of transcendence by turning to lived experiences and to the concrete situations of real life in an explicitly feminist political project. In *Hipparchia's Choice*, Le Doeuff retrieves Beauvoir as "a philosopher" in her own right ("Third Notebook" 135–209); she also turns feminists to a crucial, dialectical tension: to make something of what the world makes of us. Le Doeuff insists that what young girls and the rest of us need is precisely *not* to become divine. The implication is that, in the spirit of Beauvoir's *The Second Sex*, she directly challenges Irigaray's claim: "The only task, the only obligation laid upon us is: to become *divine* men and women, to become *perfectly*, to refuse to allow parts of ourselves to shrivel and die that have the potential for growth and fulfillment" ("Divine Women" 68–69; emphasis added).[7] Furthermore, Le Doeuff's "Spirit of Secularism" provides an attractive alternative to Irigaray's "Divine Women" and to the French Roman Catholic imagery of a glorified (m)other and a maternal sacrifice, of a suffering and silent body.[8] Unlike Irigaray, Le Doeuff outlines a secular philosophy that directly challenges the theologically orthodox story of women becoming divine like (as) the Virgin Mary. Irigaray has a closer affinity to those contemporary theologians who advocate a postsecular philosophy in the spirit of a radical orthodoxy that, I insist, revives premodern problems for women today.[9]

There is a real danger that the theology underlying Irigarayan "feminism" may be uncritically influenced by the premodern orthodoxy about becoming divine.[10] Philosophical scrutiny of the gender norms (or, "paternal law") presupposed by the story about the Virgin Mother remains essential for feminists who seek to avoid the danger of allowing theology to mask what exactly is going on when the followers of Irigaray talk about women, sexual difference, and a divine in the feminine. In consenting to the man-God, Irigaray's Mary subordinates a woman's practical reasoning about goodness, herself, and other selves; that is, submission to her divine role as Mary, to a perpetual virginity, Annunciation and Assumption (i.e., to Mariology), means that her decision is actually determined in a strong sense. Yet I suggest that the apotheosis of a female body creates a mystifying attraction (or false comfort) in the divinely determined consent of a virgin—a woman who, some say, also had an immaculate conception—to become the mother of God (Beattie, "Redeeming Mary" 113–22).

Despite Irigaray's reconfiguration of virginity as a fidelity to self, giving self-worth to both genders, an implicit Mariology assumes the passive sacrifice of a virgin to become a mother by the act of an all-powerful God the Father. This paradigmatic story mystifies not only submissive women but arguably Christlike men in deifying gender ideals (Ward, *Christ and Culture* 129–58). Because I am not an orthodox theologian, I cannot see how the relations of women to men are helped by justifying self-sacrifice on the self-deceptive grounds of both a virgin birth and sacrificial death of the virgin born son. The norms of this story of virginity and divinity support an acceptance of patriarchal oppression, that is, of blind submission to the will of the Father. So, even with Irigaray's best intentions in reconfiguring Mary in the form of a woman's "consent" to suffering, as a distinctive female form of maternal suffering, this gender ideal (type) of an innocent mother with a divine son whose love remains submissive to the point of violence and death renders passive those women who emulate it, not just as individuals, but as a collectivity.

In philosophical terms, the incompatibilist reading of Mary's freedom is that she claims to consent, but does not actually consent, since the incarnation of God the Son is already determined by the will of God the Father. The "consent" of Mary, then, subordinates a woman's gender formation to that of an all-powerful God-man. As a collectivity, women form a group in which each woman requires all other women to resist the justification—as well as the particular cases—of sexually specific suffering for themselves and for other women globally, across past, present, and future history. Oppressive standards of gender as a social kind, in this case, as the innocent suffering of the Western mother/lover, can only be finally overturned when individual tokens of real, dissenting women begin to work together to change the imposition of a concept of gender that serves to justify the sexual subordination of women generally. The relevance of the present critique of female apotheosis in the form of a Mariology—but, also potentially, in other forms of mythology which deify a certain kind of woman—becomes clear once we recognize the serious role of gender in either constraining or liberating the reality of women's social and material relations.

Even if a theological hierarchy of gender types as social kinds rather than natural kinds is granted, the power of one gender type to determine the other gender needs to be carefully monitored. For this reason, feminist philosophers who take up Irigaray's mimetic proposals should become aware of the concepts and imagery of both French psycholinguistics and Mariology. Making explicit the process of gendering should disallow the exploitation of symbolic meanings: creating a sharp opposition of feminine fluidity to masculine rigidity illustrates what can happen to particular tokens of the general type (Canters and Jantzen 8–32, 124–27). The critical step of elucidating the instantiation of a gender type in particular tokens takes seriously our epistemic practices (Fricker 27–29, 37–41, 147ff.).

It can be very helpful to construct an ethical argument against an idealized type of the female lover that devalues or, worse, subordinates women on the grounds of their reproductive or sexually specific potential. To illustrate this, we can take up tokens of the ideal type: take the token of a feminized Christ. The idealized gender type found in a feminized Christ serves as a general standard, or social norm, justifying the sexually specific suffering of women by way of gender-specific forms of self-sacrificial behavior. This is notable in the token of a Christlike *kenosis* in a woman's act of self-abnegation.[11] Another token of this type is the apotheosis of the female body as Mary's consenting, silent body: this example poses the same urgent problem, indicating a general norm for a woman's social and material subordination. Whether performing a kenotic act, following the exemplar of the divine son (Christ) or the Virgin Mother (Mary), female bodily practices are deified and justified by way of a specific gendering of the Christian story.

To be fair, Irigaray acknowledges the serious implications of subordinating women to religious imagery, which exploits the female body in the reproduction of a man-God. To avoid these, she provocatively reconfigures Mary's virginity in terms of female self-affection (as already mentioned): she seeks fidelity to the sexuate unity of body-psyche and effectively "morphs" the imagery of two sets of lips from her earlier writings. Yet the nagging question is whether her attempt to disruptively mime the female sex of Mary for contemporary women can avoid the negative implications of the material that she mimes. Does this move us decisively beyond both the misogyny and the narcissism, which can be silently—and are all too easily—imitated in each woman's reconfiguration of Mary's story?

Even if secular and Protestant feminist philosophers are not easily persuaded by arguments concerning the Virgin Mary as the female type for the metaphysics of transcendence in philosophical theology, we should notice the serious metaphysical weight in the haunting attraction of Irigaray's imagery of virginity. A crucial element of this mythology wrongly assumes human knowledge of certain sorts of reality: We actually cannot know anything about a virgin mother and a divine father. That said, Christian mythology is treated as representing a known reality insofar as the myth is given real social significance in the lives of Western religious women and men. The paradox rests in the story of Mary giving birth as a virgin to a divine son: even when "known" to be an incomprehensible story of male and female bodies, its symbolism is taken to represent real cognitive, conative, and affective capabilities for women in sexually specific ways.

Once deified and treated as a God-given fact about the nature of woman, this gender is fixed and so its significance rendered beyond change. The apotheosis of Mary can justify ignoring, or not knowing, whether the implications of her gendering include pernicious human practices toward virgin women. Irigaray reads female virginity as the symbolic feature, which preserves a woman's integrity. Yet, in this light, how can anything positive be said about the integrity of real women who lose their virginity in sexual practices to give birth? A further difficulty is that what is said to be known by God and to be a divine in the feminine is associated with God's sexual intervention as a gift of excessive love; and as such, this love is beyond critical scrutiny. Ultimately, this association of God's love with Mary's virgin birth only increases the anxiety of a feminist philosopher who recognizes the potential for mystification and illusion at play in the slippage from an unknowable reality, which is treated as "known" and excessive "love" that requires innocent suffering. Who can be certain that any individual woman will not be persuaded to believe that a horrendously evil act is "known" to be a divine form of excessive love and so accept her own exploitative suffering? This being the case women would be better off practically and ethically without such divine love.[12]

IRIGARAY, BEAUVOIR, AND *THE SECOND SEX*

Beauvoir's feminist task is to achieve relational autonomy and material equality. But Irigaray dismisses Beauvoir's feminist argument against passive submission, as well as Beauvoir's assertion of active resistance. Irigaray is categorical: "Simone de Beauvoir understood a feminine becoming only in this sense: to passively submit oneself to that which already exists in the form of social norms, rules, and stereotypes. Thus, becoming a woman could not have a positive meaning for her. We can do better today" (Chapter 1 in this volume, 15). Is this fair? I suggest that Irigaray fails to distinguish between Beauvoir's historical description of a woman's immanence in submitting passively to social norms and her phenomenological account of a woman's "original" situation of solicitude. Irigaray not only misreads Beauvoir but fails to benefit from the historical account of the situation of women in love, a situation that can be changed. Beauvoir describes a threefold set of unsatisfactory, historical alternatives in which women in European societies attempt to survive under patriarchy as man's other: these are the narcissist, the lover, or the mystic who under Western patriarchy have each lost the possibility of transcendence.

Irigaray herself mimes the role of the female mystic, lover, and narcissist.[13] However, while Beauvoir argues on philosophical grounds that the socially constructed situation of these three sorts of female figures in love needs to be transcended, Irigaray reads this as the natural situation that should become the transcendental condition for a woman's sensible ecstasy.[14] Her account slides from an existential act of self-transcendence to an abstract metaphysical conception of transcendence; that is, she confuses the natural situation, which for her includes the transcendental condition, with the contingent situation making up the social-material conditions of a woman's subordination. In doing so, "divine women" become naturally and transcendentally grounded, yet appear very much like the women in love who are the object of Beauvoir's 1949 critique. The sensible transcendental obscures changeable situations and confuses philosophical categories.

Irigaray is unable to locate her account of women's social subordination historically and so to recognize this historical situation as contingent: a recognition that could make all the difference for transforming the lives of women. Moreover, Beauvoir assumes that the original condition is one of solicitude and solidarity between women and men. She returns women to this positive, even if thought-to-be neutral condition.[15] Again Irigaray dismisses sociology and history, while Beauvoir tackles the subordination of women by social-material and historical relations.[16] The result, then, is that Irigaray disallows the possibility that women's liberation should come through both historical and social reality.

In contrast to a psychosexual discourse, Beauvoir's "Justification," in book 2 of *The Second Sex*, develops concrete descriptions of lived experiences; that is, her "existential phenomenology" of our collective experiences uncovers the fundamental condition of our *Mitsein*, that is, being with.[17] *Mitsein* appears to establish the solicitude in which women and men find themselves primordially. This solicitude is prior to any historical divisions between subject and object, body and psyche, or gendered agent and objective world. On the assumption of a relational world of fully embodied and conscious subjects, Beauvoir uncovers the primordially incarnate and relational nature of our lived experiences. What Irigaray later sees as strictly negative in Beauvoir is not what should or has to be. Instead, Beauvoir's threefold account of the oppressive situation of a woman in love represents a degradation of the female into immanence.

If women and men are born into a relational world that becomes conflictual, then the original condition provides human subjects with some capacity for reciprocal relations of solidarity (Beauvoir 172–73,

740–41). Hope springs forth here. Conflict and lack of solidarity represent a situation requiring transformation back into its original condition. Given a capability for relationality prior to the bad and false situation of oppression, women and men can return to the natural state of being a human couple, with both solicitude and solidarity. Beauvoir's distinctive appropriation of Heidegger's *Mitsein* counteracts the difficulties of the Hegelian position of relentless struggle between woman and man, which haunts so much of contemporary French feminism. In fact, the problematic Hegelian struggle between subjects haunts some of my own readings of Irigaray's disruptive engagement with the texts of philosophers. The question remains whether Irigaray and her followers avoid the trap that Beauvoir elucidates as a moral fault, that is, the falling into self-deception that after Jean-Paul Sartre is *la mauvaise foi*. For Beauvoir, there is a specifically female form of self-deception, that is, a woman's "bad faith."[18]

A Sensible Transcendental: Or, Falling Back into Bad Faith

Irigaray's conception of divinity for woman as a form of transcendence appears in several essays. In *The Forgetting of Air in Martin Heidegger* Irigaray's rereading of transcendence could bring her close to Beauvoir. Yet instead of turning to her text on Heidegger, let us remain with the three ways in which Irigaray seeks a sensible transcendental in women's love-relations.[19] Each of these ways of loving has an affinity to Beauvoir's account of a woman's relation to a divine reality, a divine subject, and a divine body.

First, Irigaray's disruptive miming of the Platonic ascent of *eros*, which exploits the female intervention in the voice of Diotima, seeks a divine reality in the go-between. In this manner, Irigaray opens up a space between a sensible reality and its transcendental ground for a becoming, a space that would avoid any opposition between transcendence and immanence. A sensible transcendental is a horizon: like a beatific vision of beauty in love, or like a god whose advent is always ahead of each man and of each woman. To cite from Irigaray's account of Diotima's Speech in Plato's *Symposium*: "This person would have then attained . . . a *sensible transcendental*, the material texture of beauty . . . He would have contemplated the 'nature' of the divine?

"At the beginning of her remarks . . . she held love to be the mediator of a state of becoming with no objective other than becoming . . . what she proposes to contemplate, beauty itself, is seen as that which confounds the opposition between immanence and transcendence. As an always already sensible horizon on the basis of which everything would appear" (Irigaray, "Sorcerer Love" 32–33).[20] What is necessary is a habitation for women, which does not imprison her in sensibility, in the immanence of her degraded and forgotten body. This imprisonment from which the female body must extricate itself comes close to Beauvoir's mystic who is trapped in her own solitude. But Irigaray's horizon for an apotheosis of sensible reality in the form of "becoming beautiful in love" is dangerously ambiguous. Diotima herself indicates the lack of concrete space for the apotheosis of female bodies in the *Symposium*.

Second, Irigaray conceives divine women as seeking transcendence-in-immanence by becoming in exchanges with another subject. But these exchanges cannot be primordial, or originally given. Irigaray's sensible transcendental is both a horizon and a mediating threshold for the divine. It is for women to become divine subjects themselves.[21] Perhaps, this project could be required for Beauvoir's woman in love? Much ink has been spilled concerning Irigaray's provocation in "Divine Women," which asserts that "the only diabolical thing about women is their lack of a God" (Irigaray 64; see also Hollywood 207, 211–35). In what sense, if any, is this true? Is a woman's lack of God, or a personal God in "her own gender," a diabolical thing? In what sense exactly do women—all women presumably—lack a God? Unanswerable questions about the provocation to become divine persist. Seriously large and significant questions remain unanswered concerning the sexually specific nature of female morphology, anthropology, and subjectivity. My question is whether in becoming divine women and men share any common ground. Each subject could simply move to its own gendered horizon blocking any vision of the other in love.

Third, in her latest writings, Irigaray seeks to realize a sensible transcendental in the practice and ideal of breathing and breath ("A Breath That Touches in Words," 121–28). This ideal of breath comes into her account of Mary, as well as in the more general account of breathing to access the divine. Sensible reality together with a transcendental condition constitutes a habitation or in-dwelling; breathing opens up a horizon for a woman's own bodily life. For Irigaray, air is both a primary element of nature and something apparently required a priori like a transcendental condition of the possibility of life itself. This imagery of air also takes female readers back to their primary stage of narcissism in self-affection. To see this, let us read Irigaray's words on self-affection in breathing:

We have to make our way toward an internalization appropriate to ourselves . . . a wedding between an active and a passive gesture already
exists when our lips touch one another. The two dimensions take part
in self-affection . . .

For example, if I am out of breath, that is, if I am losing the rhythm
of my breathing, something goes wrong in my self-affecting. It is rather
easy to verify this by ourselves. We have to be capable of inhaling and
exhaling for the same length of time, and of holding our breath inside
ourselves or staying without breathing—that is, without inhaling or
exhaling—during a short time, between breathing in and breathing
out. (Chapter 1 in this volume, 20–21)

At first glance, this extraordinary account of breathing sounds great
for a spiritual meditation on the divinity and the sexuate belonging
of a female body. It enables recognition of the uniqueness of the
female sex in self-affection. However, the psychosexual context of this
account excludes all questions of social and historical relations making
up the real oppression of a woman's situation. And to be blunt, how
many women would agree that a woman's bodily subordination to
men and to a masculine divine can be completely sorted out by learning to breathe differently?

Ultimately the critical question for Irigaray's sensible transcendental becomes: Are women still dragged down by their association with
female immanence? Each of the forms of transcendence-in-immanence—of beatification, deification, and self-affection—locates sexual
difference within a sexually specific female incarnation. The pressing issue persists, whether locating a woman's difference in sexuate
belonging avoids the subordination of women individually and collectively. If not, Irigaray's sensible transcendental could trap a woman
in the solitude of her own servitude. Beauvoir had stated the problem
of transcendence-in-immanence cogently: "There have been . . . and
. . . are many women trying to achieve individual salvation by solitary
effort. They are attempting to justify their existence in the midst of
their immanence—that is, to realize *transcendence* in immanence. It is
this ultimate effort—sometimes ridiculous often pathetic—of imprisoned woman to *transform* her prison into a heaven of glory, her servitude into sovereign liberty, that we . . . observe in the narcissist,
in the woman in love, in the mystic" (*The Second Sex* 639, emphasis added). The realization of being incarnate in a female body, as
sexually different from a man, has dangers for a woman, crucially for
her becoming imprisoned within herself. Even supposing Irigaray's
vertical transcendence, where or what is the absolute Same? What is

there to help a woman move beyond the horizon of this self-same gender ideal? If nothing, then it is not only unclear but uncertain that a woman can avoid servitude, imprisoned in her own body and psyche. The idiosyncratic nature of the transcendental dimension for a woman's sensible ecstasy in breathing, or in consenting to the will of a male God, does not instill much hope that a woman will transcend the oppressive situations of patriarchy, especially those that Beauvoir cogently elucidates. A woman who is situated in love could follow Irigaray in projecting her self as autonomous; she could find a horizon for her own becoming in a sensible transcendental; and yet she could lack any reciprocal relations. She, then, has nothing except the image of her own apotheosis.

With this problematic of the sensible transcendental, we easily find ourselves back in the situation exposed by Beauvoir's concrete unveiling of the decisive dangers for the divinized female in love. Irigaray's project for women to become divine may have great psychological benefits, especially for the traditional Roman Catholic woman who lives within the imaginary of the virgin Mary story; but this would only be as long as its positive implications within Catholicism are not undermined by pernicious ramifications. But then, Beauvoir appears to be the more radical feminist insofar as Irigaray reestablishes a conservative picture of sexual difference compatible with orthodox and Roman Catholic theology. With the significant parallels in the positions of Irigaray and of Beauvoir, we recognize the distinctive nature of each of their attempts to transcend the degradation of the female body as the product of a pernicious masculinism. They each confront a body constructed conceptually by the male subjects who have dominated in fixing the gender types for the theology of Western forms of patriarchy. Their distinctive confrontations each generate new, critical knowledge concerning women and the divine.

There is also little doubt that Beauvoir's twentieth-century account of the strategies of the female lover suffers from her own preoccupation with a female sexual fantasy in the form of a narcissistic apotheosis. Uncovering this self-defeating form of apotheosis is important as a critique; that is, Beauvoir offers women a hermeneutics of suspicion for their self-deceptive patterns in love. Yet this critique does not create a completely fair picture of every female mystic and her desire; certainly, her account of maternity has supported a rejection of motherhood.[22] So Irigaray's explorations give a different psychological alternative for some women that, at some level, gives an ideal for women in relation to the divine. However, if we accept Irigaray's conservative picture of virgin women, then the fundamental nature of her contribution to women and the divine is not only to be a more accurate account of the reality of the lives of female subjects.

More strongly stated: Is Irigaray's vision of female apotheosis the very sort of illusion that Beauvoir, Murdoch, and Le Doeuff each aim to uncover and decisively criticize? Whether in the erotics of her mystical experiences or the becoming divine of a consenting virgin subject, the narcissist's obsessive concern with her own self-image haunts and so destabilizes the account of a sensible transcendental.

If narcissism undermines the Irigarayan account of divine women, then Irigarayan feminists fall back into the pernicious patterns of Beauvoir's women in love. This would block the reciprocity of subjects in love, especially the capacity to be mutually self-giving and self-making with another sexuate subject. Solipsism would also block a collective historical awareness of other women who have and do struggle on behalf of all women to transform the conditions of their subordination. Take Beauvoir herself, for example, about whom Irigaray dedicates an essay in memory of a woman, potentially, a mother for the next generation of feminism; but because Irigaray herself, who could have been a sort of daughter, was not taken seriously by the other woman, the upshot of her essay is odd, if not damaging to Beauvoir. Irigaray concludes—and the readers of the latter have tended to agree—that Beauvoir should be dismissed as a first-generation feminist who focuses exclusively on equality for women, and so irrelevant to the second generation who put their focus on the sexual difference of women.[23]

But the failure to come up with any possible agreement on the nature of Irigaray's project is precisely the problem with her fluid and subversive reconfigurations of texts, including Beauvoir's own text.[24] Irigaray offers her poetic subversion of relations within philosophical texts between herself as the reader and the author as another subject. An agreed way forward in philosophy or philosophical theology—let alone in our collective history—will always be lacking. Admittedly, this is a problem for all poststructuralist philosophy. She may be subjectively helpful to individual women, but her proposal that women are represented by fluidity is collectively problematic.

There is novelty in Irigaray's account of a sensible transcendental. This is the sensible for which she reconceives a transcendental condition or dimension to make it possible to redeem and transform a woman's body. But we have also chosen to recall Beauvoir's condemnation of a woman's falsehood as words of caution: "Deified by the master's embrace, she believes she has always been divine and destined for the god—she and nobody else. But male desire is as ephemeral as it is imperious; once allayed, it dies rather quickly . . . She must either suffer or lie to herself. Most often she clutches at the straw of false-hood" (669). At the end of the day, Irigaray creates serious ethical and material problems by disparaging both sociology and history and opting, instead, for a strictly psycholinguistic project in a divine in the feminine. This project runs into the falsehood of self-deception.

CONCLUSION: TRANSCENDENCE IN GOODNESS AS DIVINE

I would like to stress Beauvoir's contribution to "Women and the Divine" as a philosophical topic: She accounts for both the possibili-ties and the subordination in the situation of the Western woman in love. Elucidating the oppression of a woman's situation directs this chapter to an indestructible link between self-transcendence and goodness, which can be transformative in concrete ways. In particular, Beauvoir addresses the moral fault implicit in a relational world that has subordinated women. This, I contend, includes the subordination that is represented by Mary's consent to the powerful God-man. But I also rely upon Beauvoir's awareness that this fault is not a woman's original condition, that is, not natural or a priori.

The Second Sex sets out the problem of transcendence, which has been the focus of this chapter. Under patriarchal oppression, tran-scendence is the prerogative of male subjects only; yet, even this tran-scendence fails as long as a woman lives her immanence as *en-soi*; this Sartrean dichotomy undermines the real possibilities in the reciprocity of embodied subjects, their solicitude, and solidarity, which constitute the original condition.[25] For Beauvoir, true transcendence does not depend on sexual difference. If asked, Irigaray would probably admit a debt to Beauvoir's Heideggerian understanding of transcendence. Yet in giving value back to virginity and the sexually specific body, Iri-garay may well return us to Beauvoir's problem of female immanence (*en-soi*). In Beauvoir's own words:

> Every subject plays his part as such specifically through exploits or proj-ects that serve as a mode of transcendence; he achieves liberty only through a continual reaching out towards other liberties. There is no justification for present existence other than its expansion into an indefinitely open future. Every time transcendence falls back into immanence, stagna-tion, there is a degradation of existence into the—"*en-soi*"—the brutish life of subjection to given conditions—and of liberty into constraint

and contingence. This downfall represents a moral fault[26] if the subject consents to it; if it is inflicted upon him, it spells frustration and oppression. In both cases it is an absolute evil. Every individual concerned to justify his existence feels that his existence involves an undefined need to transcend himself, to engage in freely chosen projects.

. . . what peculiarly signalizes the situation of woman is that she—a free and autonomous being like all human creatures—nevertheless finds herself living in a world where men compel her to assume the status of the Other. They propose to stabilize her as object and to doom her to immanence since her transcendence is to be overshadowed and for ever transcended by another ego (*conscience*) which is essential and sovereign. The drama of woman lies in this conflict between the fundamental aspirations of every subject (*ego*)—who always regards the self as the essential—and the compulsions of a situation in which she is the inessential. (28–29)

These words of caution address a relational situation that continues for some women and men. Our main example has been the apotheosis of man and woman as portrayed in the relations of God the Father and the Virgin Mother; but this is an old drama, in which a woman's salvation rests in the myth of Mary as the second Eve: Mary undoes Eve's downfall in the transformation of her sinful desire. For me, Irigaray's reconfiguration of a freely consenting Mary in the annunciation and assumption of her female body is deeply problematic. The danger in the twofold deification of man as God the Father and woman as the Virgin Mother/Lover is the persistent imprisonment of women in their own bodies and psyches. Beauvoir's grasp on the reality of the lives of men and women remains relevant insofar as the material and social conditions of women have not fundamentally changed in relation to male transcendence.

To conclude, I suggest that the damaging traditional imagery of transcendence and the female body can be transformed in and through both human history and society, despite Irigaray's dismissive comments. This historical transformation is essential for solicitude and for intimate relations between men and women. Social transformation is also required for the sake of women as a collective. We should not forget that socially and historically women rise and fall together. The hope of transcendence lives in goodness, that is, in concrete acts of self-transcending subjects whose relations seek mutual exchanges of truth and justice between one another. The point is not to seek transcendence in the immanence of an always potentially narcissistic love of one's body, of a man who deifies his beloved, or of a god in one's own image, but to recognize true transcendence in the reality of the good. This reality would join each of us equitably to the other, to the livable reality of one and another. If nothing else is, the reality of this good certainly should be divine.

NOTES

1. "Dwelling" is employed by Martin Heidegger and Emmanuel Levinas, who each describe a primordial way of being as a habitation in the intimacy of home. For the early Levinas, this intimacy of dwelling is ensured by the gentleness of the Other as "the feminine," who is missing from Heidegger; see Levinas, *Totality and Infinity: An Essay on Exteriority*, trans. Alphonso Lingis (Pittsburgh, PA: Duquesne University, 1969), 152–74; see Heidegger, *Being and Time*, trans. J. Macquarrie and E. Robinson (New York: Harper & Row, 1962; Oxford: Blackwell, 1990), 80n1, 87–89n2. For this background, I am indebted to Kathryn Bevis, whose DPhil thesis, "Refiguring the Self: Levinas, Transcendence, and Metaphor," offers illuminating insights on the changes in Levinas's conceptions of dwelling from the "dwelling-as-home" in his *Totality and Infinity* to a fundamental "in-dwelling" within the human body in his *Otherwise than Being*, trans. Alphonso Lingis (The Hague: Martinus Nijhoff, 1981). For Irigaray's reconfiguring of Heidegger's dwelling (*die Wohnung; la demeure*), see Irigaray, *The Forgetting of Air in Martin Heidegger*, trans. M. B. Mader (London: Athlone Press, 1999), 63–71; see Ellen Armour, "Divining Differences: Irigaray and Religion," in *Religion in French Feminist Thought: Critical Perspectives*, ed. M. Joy, K. O'Grady, and J. L. Poxon (London: Routledge, 2003), 32–40.

2. "Gender" refers to a general category under which a concept with certain characteristics can be grouped along with other concepts that fall under the same general category; but instead of treating gender as a natural kind, founded on the natural world, I follow a recent definition of gender as a social kind, since its reality is socially founded; see Sally Haslanger, "Gender and Race: (What) Are They? (What) Do We Want Them to Be?" *Nous* 34 1 (2000): 31–55, reprinted in *Feminist Theory: A Philosophical Anthology*, ed. A. E. Cudd and R. O. Andreasen (Oxford: Blackwell, 2005), 154–70; "What Are We Talking About? The Semantics and Politics of Social Kinds," *Hypatia* (Fall 2005): 10–26; "What Good Are Our Intuitions? Philosophical Analysis and Social Kinds," pt. 1, *Proceedings of the Aristotelian Society* (2006): 89–117.

3. For the distinction between natural and social kinds, which is useful in working out whether Irigaray implies that gender as sexual difference is a natural kind, see Haslanger, "Gender and Race."

4. For an exploration of what it would be like to be immortal, in a way deified by timelessness, see Simone de Beauvoir, *All Men Are Mortal*,

trans. E. Cameron, based on the original English translation by Leonard M Friedman, with an introduction by Jacqueline Rose (London: Virago Press, 2003), vii–x; see also A. W. Moore, "Williams, Nietzsche, and the Meaninglessness of Immortality," *Mind* 115 (April 2006): 311–30.

5. Psychoanalysis has traditionally interpreted the psychic and spiritual problems in terms of the Oedipus myth. In contrast, feminist philosophers have turned to the myth of Psyche and Cupid (a male god), including Cupid's goddess-mother, Venus, for an account of beauty that contains an apotheosis of Psyche, rendering her divine like her husband and mother-in-law; see Pamela Sue Anderson, "Beauty," *Encyclopedia of Religion*, ed. Lindsay Jones (Farmington Hills, MI: Thomson Gale, 2005), 2:810–14. For a critical assessment of this Psyche myth in a discussion of love, considering the usefulness of an alternative myth about Dawn (Aurora) who as a female figure does not become divine, but preserves human reason, love, and goodness, see Anderson, "Liberating Love's Capabilities: On the Wisdom of Love," in *Transforming Philosophy and Religion*, eds. N. Wirzba and B. E. Benson (Indianapolis: Indiana University Press, 2008), 201–26.

6. On the collective historical experience of women, or their collectivity of thought, see Michèle Le Doeuff, *Hipparchia's Choice: An Essay Concerning Women, Philosophy, Etc.*, trans. Trista Selous, 2nd ed. (New York: Columbia University Press, 2007), 121–33. For a parallel discussion of collectivity in terms of Heidegger's *Mitsein* ("being with" as a fundamental condition of living) to include interdependence, see Eva Gothlin, "Reading Simone de Beauvoir with Martin Heidegger," in *The Cambridge Companion to Simone de Beauvoir*, ed. Claudia Card (Cambridge: Cambridge University Press, 2003); see also Beauvoir, *The Second Sex*, trans. and ed. H. M. Parshley (London: Random House, Vintage Classic, 1997), 66–69, 84, 88–91, 608–39; *The Ethics of Ambiguity*, trans. Bernard Frechtman (New York: Citadel Press, Kensington Publishing, 1976), 96–114.

7. On the indestructibility of goodness and true transcendence, see Iris Murdoch, *The Sovereignty of Good* (London: Routledge & Kegan Paul, 1970), 59–50. Compare this goodness to such terms as "human dignity," "integrity," and "moral respect" that are employed by feminist philosophers, including Beauvoir herself, who follow, however indirectly, Kant on the topic of the intrinsic moral worth of persons. For a significant rereading of Beauvoir's conception of human dignity, especially in its difference from the strictly formalist Kantian conception, see Catherine Wilson, "Simone de Beauvoir and Human Dignity," in *The Legacy of Simone de Beauvoir*, 90–114.

8. Le Doeuff tells a story that plants the seeds for a new Enlightenment ethic, drawing on the Spanish author Maria Zambrano's symbolic narrative about a girl named Dawn who remains human unlike the goddess

"Dawn" of classical literature. Dawn's heart symbolizes what needs to be protected in the various relations of the young girl to herself and others—whose reason is cultivated as long as no one forces the girl's apotheosis; Dawn teaches those who love her how to be tender and attentive to the vulnerability of a child's ethical and rational development. Le Doeuff leaves us to wonder whether the heart of a young boy is more easily protected from the illusions and oppression of imposed social-sexual stereotypes. For "*la philosophie imaginaire*" rejection of traditional gender stereotypes of divine women, see Maria Zambrano, *De L'Aurore*, trans. Marie Laffranque (Paris: Éditions de L' Éclat, 1989); for "le coeur," see Zambrano, *Les Clairières Du Bois*, trans. Marie Laffranque (Paris: Éditions de L' Éclat, 1989), 65–80. Le Doeuff's new Enlightenment story can be contrasted to Irigaray's "*La Mystérique*" (28–39), "Divine Women" (40–48), and "When the Gods Are Born" (59–67) in *French Feminists on Religion: A Reader*, ed. Morny Joy, K. O'Grady, and J. L. Poxon, with a foreword by Catherine Clément (New York: Routledge, 2002).

9.   For a productive contrast, see Michèle Le Doeuff, "The Spirit of Secularism: On Fables, Gender and Ethics," Weidenfeld Professorial Lectures (lecture 4, University of Oxford, Trinity Term 2006): "Not a Goddess She!"; and John Milbank, "Problematizing the Secular: The Post-Postmodern Agenda," in *Shadow of the Spirit: Postmodernism and Religion*, ed. P. Berry and A. Wernick (London: Routledge, 1992), 30–44; 'Sublimity: The Modern Transcendent,' *Transcendence: Philosophy, Literature and Theology Approach the Beyond*, ed. Regina Schwartz (New York: Routledge, 2004), 211–34.

10.   This is a strong statement that should be seen in relation to an incisive criticism of my failure to recognize the profound significance that the Virgin Mary has had for women in the history of Christianity and could have for feminist philosophy of religion. For a defense of Mary's virginity in particular, and Mariology in general, including Irigaray's contribution to this, see Beattie, "Redeeming Mary" in *Feminist Philosophy of Religion: Critical Readings* (London: Routledge, 2004), 107–22.

11.   Ward unpicks the corporeal ambiguity, which he finds in the Christian accounts of Jesus's body as it is directed toward the ascension from the moment of the annunciation; this body undergoes a series of displacements, whereby Jesus's body continues to reconfigure a masculine symbolics until the particularities of one sex give way to the particularities of bodies that are male and female; Graham Ward, "Bodies: The Displaced Body of Jesus Christ, *Radical Orthodoxy: A New Theology*, ed. John Milbank, C. Pickstock, and Graham Ward (London: Routledge, 1999), 163ff. Also, see Ward, especially chap. 5, "Divinity and Sexual Difference" in *Christ and Culture* (Oxford: Blackwell, 2005), 129–58.

12. Recall Murdoch's argument in "On 'God' and 'Good,'" in *The Sovereignty of Good*, 55–59.

13. For guidance to the relevant texts by Irigaray, see Amy Hollywood, *Sensible Ecstasy: Mysticism, Sexual Difference, and the Demands of History* (Chicago: University of Chicago Press, 2002), 173–241, 329–45.

14. Beauvoir's philosophical conception of a woman's situation includes having a female body and a specific social and cultural perspective (Beauvoir, *The Second Sex*, 66); a situation includes substantial matters that differentiate a woman's lived experiences from a man's. So in feminist theoretical terms, Beauvoir is neither essentialist about a woman's nature nor a formalist about a woman's equality or autonomy. Instead, she takes on board the social and material conditions that shape the sexual differences between men and women; yet, often Beauvoir has been unfairly reduced to a feminism of equality and opposed to Irigaray as a feminist of sexual difference.

15. This "original" condition of concern for other people, or solicitude (*Fürsorge*), is a Heideggerian conception, deriving from a continental tradition of phenomenology with roots back to the original condition ("destination to goodness") that remains even when it goes wrong ("propensity to radical evil"); see Kant, "Religion within the Boundaries of Mere Reason," in *Religion and Rational Theology*, trans. George De Giovanni, ed. A. W. Wood and G. Di Giovanni (Cambridge: Cambridge University Press, 1996), 39–215; Paul Ricoeur, *The Symbolism of Evil*, trans. Emerson Buchanan (New York: Harper & Row, 1967), 156. For an account of Beauvoir's feminist appropriation of Heidegger, see Gothlin, "Reading Simone de Beauvoir," 50–59; cf. Heidegger, *Being and Time*, 237–38.

16. See Irigaray, "Toward a Divine in the Feminine," Chapter 1 in this volume.

17. Here I owe a debt to Ben Morgan for significant conversations on Heidegger and Beauvoir. Also, see Gothlin, "Reading Simone de Beauvoir," 45–65; and Nancy Bauer, *Simone de Beauvoir, Philosophy, and Feminism* (New York: Columbia University Press, 2001), 131–35; cf. Beauvoir, *The Second Sex*, 66–68.

18. Beauvoir's conception of the moral fault, as the way in which we go wrong, derives from a phenomenon, described by Heidegger as, "falling" from a primordial condition of "the at-home of publicness" to the "not-at-home" or uncanny, since still conditioned by the at-home; see Beauvoir, *The Second Sex*, 29, also see 66–69; cf. Gothlin, "Reading Simone de Beauvoir," 59–65; and Heidegger, *Being and Time*, 227–35.

19. On the possible role of the sensible transcendental in her miming of love (*eros*) in Plato, see Luce Irigaray, "Sorcerer Love: A Reading of Plato, *Symposium*, 'Diotima's Speech.'" *An Ethics of Sexual Difference*, trans. C. Burke and G. C. Gill (London: Athlone Press, 1993), 20–33;

see also 32 and 115; cf. Irigaray, *Sexes and Genealogies*, trans. Gillian C. Gill (New York: Columbia University Press, 1993), 57–72. For the possibility of conceiving transcendence and immanence, consider Irigaray on the four elements (air, earth, fire, and water; ibid. 57–58), which make up the fundamental reality of pre-Socratic philosophy; cf. Armour, "Divining Differences," 29–40; and Hanneke Canters and Grace M. Jantzen, *Forever Fluid: A Reading of Luce Irigaray's Elemental Passions* (Manchester: Manchester University Press, 2005).

20.   Irigaray's sensible transcendental brings together the opposing terms (or, worlds) kept apart by Plato, including sensible and intelligible, the world of appearances and the world of reality; that is, the forms of beauty, of goodness and of truth in the divinity of love; cf. Alison Ainley, "Luce Irigaray: Divine Spirit and Feminine Space," in *Post-Secular Philosophy*, ed. Philip Blond (London: Routledge, 1998), 334–45.

21.   Irigaray, "Divine Women"; and *Je, Tu, Nous: Toward A Culture of Difference*, trans. Alison Martin (London: Routledge, 1993).

22.   See Beauvoir, *The Second Sex*, 652, 661, and 689.

23.   See Luce Irigaray, "A Personal Note: Equal or Different?" in *Je, Tu, Nous*, 9–14.

24.   See Pamela Sue Anderson, "Life, Death and (Inter)subjectivity: Realism and Recognition in Continental Feminism," *International Journal of Philosophy of Religion*, Special edition, *Issues in Continental Philosophy of Religion* 60, no. 1–3 (2006): 41–59. DOI 10.1007/s11153-006-0013-6.

25.   Note that what make the possibilities of reciprocity for Beauvoir's "lived body" different from Irigaray's reciprocal relations of sexually specific subjects is that the former's phenomenological description of the lived experience of subjects does not make sexuality dimorphous: subjects experience their desires and feelings in diverse ways that do not neatly correlate with heterosexual norms; it is in this light that we should understand Beauvoir claims that "One is not born, but rather becomes, a woman" (*The Second Sex* 295).

26.   Hampton also describes this moral fault as created by a woman with traditional (self-sacrificing) values: she accepts abuse and so becomes "a roadblock to ending the abuse: . . . [insofar as] it is soul-destroying for them and for the women who will follow them—they must develop forms of thinking and acting that prevent their propensity to care from being the source of their abuse and exploitation"; Jean Hampton, "Feminist Contractarianism," in *A Mind of One's Own: Feminist Essays on Reason and Objectivity*, ed. Louise M. Antony and Charlotte Witt (Boulder, CO: Westview Press, 1993), 245–46; cf. *Feminist Theory*, 294.

BIBLIOGRAPHY

Anderson, Pamela Sue. "An Epistemological-Ethical Approach to Philosophy of Religion: Learning to Listen." In *A Feminist Philosophy of Religion: Critical Readings*, edited by Pamela Sue Anderson and B. Clack, 87–102. London: Routledge, 2004.

———. "Beauty." In *Encyclopedia of Religion*, 2nd ed., edited by Lindsay Jones, 810–14. Farmington Hills, MI: Thomson Gale, 2005.

———. "Liberating Love's Capabilities: On the Wisdom of Love." In *Transforming Philosophy and Religion*, edited by N. Wirzba and B. E. Benson, 201–26. Indianapolis: Indiana University Press, 2008.

———. "Life, Death and (Inter)subjectivity: Realism and Recognition in Continental Feminism." *International Journal of Philosophy of Religion*, Special edition, *Issues in Continental Philosophy of Religion* 60, no. 1–3 (2006): 41–59. DOI 10.1007/s11153-006-0013-6.

———. "Myth and Feminist Philosophy." In *Thinking through Myths: Philosophical Perspectives*, edited by Kevin Schilbrack, 101–22. New York/London: Routledge, 2002.

———. "Postmodern Theology." In *The Routledge Companion to Philosophy of Religion*, edited by C. Meister and P. Copan, chap. 47. London: Routledge, 2007.

Armour, Ellen T. "Divining Differences: Irigaray and Religion." In *Religion in French Feminist Thought: Critical Perspectives*, edited by Morny Joy, K. O'Grady, and J. L. Poxon, 32–40. London: Routledge, 2003.

Bauer, Nancy. *Simone de Beauvoir, Philosophy, & Feminism*. New York: Columbia University Press, 2001.

Beattie, Tina. *God's Mother, Eve's Advocate: A Marian Narrative of Women's Salvation*. New York: Continuum Press, 2002.

———. "Redeeming Mary: The Potential of Marian Symbolism for Feminist Philosophy of Religion." In *Feminist Philosophy of Religion: Critical Readings*. London: Routledge, 2004.

Beauvoir, Simone de. *All Men Are Mortal*. Translated by E. Cameron based on the original English translation by Leonard M. Friedman. With an Introduction by Jacqueline Rose. London: Virago Press, 2003.

———. *The Ethics of Ambiguity*. Translated by Bernard Frechtman. New York: Citadel Press, Kensington Publishing, 1976.

———. *The Second Sex*. Translated and edited by H. M. Parshley. London: Random House, Vintage Classic, 1997.

Blond, Phillip, ed. *Post-Secular Philosophy: Between Philosophy and Theology*. London: Routledge, 1998.

Canters, Hanneke, and Grace M. Jantzen. *Forever Fluid: A Reading of Luce Irigaray's Elemental Passions*. Manchester: Manchester University Press, 2005.

Fricker, Miranda. *Epistemic Injustice: Power and the Ethics of Knowing*. Oxford: Oxford University Press, 2007.

Gothlin, Eva. "Reading Simone de Beauvoir with Martin Heidegger." In *The Cambridge Companion to Simone de Beauvoir*, edited by Claudia Card, 45–65. Cambridge: Cambridge University Press, 2003.

Hampton, Jean. "Feminist Contractarianism." In *A Mind of One's Own: Feminist Essays on Reason and Objectivity*, edited by Louise M. Antony and Charlotte Witt, 234–49. Boulder, CO: Westview Press, 1993; reprinted by permission in *Feminist Theory: A Philosophical Anthology*, edited by A. E. Cudd and R. O. Andreasen, 285–94. Oxford: Blackwell, 2005.

Haslanger, Sally. "Gender and Race: (What) Are They? (What) Do We Want Them to Be?" *Nous* 34, no. 1 (2000): 31–55; reprinted in *Feminist Theory: A Philosophical Anthology*, edited by A. E. Cudd and R. O. Andreasen, 154–70. Oxford: Blackwell, 2005.

———. "What Are We Talking About? The Semantics and Politics of Social Kinds." *Hypatia* (Fall 2005): 10–26.

———. "'What Good Are Our Intuitions?' Philosophical Analysis and Social Kinds." Supplementary volume, *Proceedings of the Aristotelian Society* 80, no. 1 (2006): 89–118.

Heidegger, Martin. *Being and Time*. Translated by J. Macquarrie and E. Robinson. New York: Harper & Row, 1962; Oxford: Blackwell, 1990.

Heinamaa, Sara. *Toward a Phenomenology of Sexual Difference: Husserl, Merleau-Ponty, Beauvoir*. Landam, MD: Rowman & Littlefield, 2003.

Hollywood, Amy. *Sensible Ecstasy: Mysticism, Sexual Difference, and the Demands of History*. Chicago: University of Chicago Press, 2002.

Irigaray, Luce. "A Breath That Touches in Words." In *I Love To You: Sketch of a Possible Felicity in History*, translated by Alison Martin, 121–28. London: Routledge, 1996.

———. "A Personal Note: Equal or Different?" In *Je, Tu, Nous: Toward A Culture of Difference*, translated by Alison Martin, 9–14. London: Routledge, 1993.

———. "Divine Women." In *French Feminists on Religion: A Reader*, edited by M. Joy, K. O'Grady, and J. L. Poxon, with a Foreword by Catherine Clément, 28–39. New York: Routledge, 2002.

———. "Divine Women." In *Sexes and Genealogies*, translated by Gillian C. Gill, 57–72. New York: Columbia University Press, 1993.

———. *The Forgetting of Air in Martin Heidegger*. Translated by M. B. Mader. London: Athlone Press, 1999.

———. "Introducing: Love between Us." In *I Love To You: Sketch of a Possible Felicity in History*, translated by Alison Martin, 19–33. London: Routledge, 1996.

———. "*La Mystérique*." In *French Feminists on Religion: A Reader*, edited by M. Joy, K. O'Grady, and J. L. Poxon, with a foreword by Catherine Clément, 40–48. New York: Routledge, 2002.

———. "Plato's Hystera." *Speculum of the Other Woman*, translated by Gillian C. Gill, 243–364. Ithaca, NY: Cornell University Press, 1985.

————. "Sorcerer Love: A Reading of Plato, *Symposium*, 'Diotima's Speech.'" In *An Ethics of Sexual Difference*, translated by C. Burke and G. C. Gill, 20–33. London: Athlone Press, 1993.

————. "Toward a Divine in the Feminine." In *Women and the Divine: Touching Transcendence*, edited by Gillian Howie and J'annine Jobling. New York: Palgrave Macmillan, 2008.

————. "When Our Lips Speak Together." In *This Sex Which Is Not One*, translated by Catherine Porter, 205–18. Ithaca, NY: Cornell University Press, 1985.

————. "When the Gods Are Born." In *French Feminists on Religion: A Reader*, edited by M. Joy, K. O'Grady, and J. L. Poxon, with a foreword by Catherine Clément, 59–67. New York: Routledge, 2002.

Jantzen, Grace M. "'Barely by a Breath . . .' Irigaray on Rethinking Religion." In *The Religious*, edited by John D. Caputo, 227–40. Oxford: Blackwell, 2002.

————. *Becoming Divine: Towards A Feminist Philosophy of Religion*. Manchester: Manchester University Press, 1998.

Joy, Morny. *Divine Love: Luce Irigaray, Women, Gender, and Religion*. Manchester: Manchester University Press, 2006.

Kant, Immanuel. "Religion within the Boundaries of Mere Reason." In *Religion and Rational Theology*, translated by George De Giovanni, edited by A. W. Wood and G. Di Giovanni, 39–215. Cambridge: Cambridge University Press, 1996.

Le Doeuff, Michèle. *Hipparchia's Choice: An Essay Concerning Women, Philosophy, Etc.* 2nd ed. Translated by Trista Selous. With an Epilogue (2006) by the author. New York: Columbia University Press, 2007.

————. *The Philosophical Imaginary*. Translated by Colin Gordon. London: Athlone Press; Stanford, CA: Stanford University Press, 1989; reprinted New York: Continuum, 2002.

————. *The Sex of Knowing*. Translated by K. Hamer and L. Code. London New York: Routledge, 2003.

————. "Not a Goddess She!" In *The Spirit of Secularism: On Fables, Gender, and Ethics, Weidenfeld Professorial Lectures*. Lecture 4. Rev. ed. University of Oxford: Trinity Term, 2006. [revised text]

Levinas, Emmanuel. *Otherwise Than Being, or Beyond Essence*. Translated by Alphonso Lingis. The Hague: Martinus Nijhoff, 1981.

————. *Totality and Infinity: An Essay on Exteriority*. Translated by Alphonso Lingis. Pittsburgh, PA: Duquesne University, 1969.

Martin, Alison. *Luce Irigaray and the Question of the Divine*. Leeds: Maney Publishing, 2000.

Milbank, John. "Problematizing the Secular: The Post-Postmodern Agenda." In *Shadow of the Spirit: Postmodernism and Religion*, edited by P. Berry and A. Wernick, 30–34. London: Routledge, 1992.

———. "Sublimity: The Modern Transcendent." In *Transcendence: Philosophy, Literature, and Theology Approach the Beyond*, edited by Regina Schwartz, 211–34. New York: Routledge, 2004.

Milbank, John, C. Pickstock, and G. Ward, eds. *Radical Orthodoxy: A New Theology*. London: Routledge, 1999.

Moi, Toril. *What Is a Woman? And Other Essays*. Oxford: Oxford University Press, 1999.

Moore, A. W. "Williams, Nietzsche, and the Meaninglessness of Immortality." *Mind* 115 (April 2006): 311–30.

Murdoch, Iris. *The Sovereignty of Good*. London: Routledge & Kegan Paul, 1970.

Plato. *The Complete Works*. Edited by J. M. Cooper. Indianapolis: Hackett, 1997.

Ricoeur, Paul. *The Symbolism of Evil*. Translated by Emerson Buchanan. New York and London: Harper & Row, 1967.

Russell, Norma. *The Doctrine of Deification in the Greek Patristic Tradition*. Oxford: Oxford University Press, 2004.

Walsh, Lisa. "Introduction: The Swell of the Third Wave." In *Contemporary French Feminism*, 1–11. Oxford: Oxford University Press, 2004.

Ward, Graham. "Bodies: The Displaced Body of Jesus Christ." In *Radical Orthodoxy: A New Theology*, edited by John Milbank, C. Pickstock, and Graham Ward, 163–81. London: Routledge, 1999.

———. *Christ and Culture*. Oxford: Blackwell, 2005.

Warner, Marina. *Alone of All Her Sex: The Myth and Cult of the Virgin Mary*. London: Weidenfeld and Nicolas, 1976.

Whitford, Margaret. *Luce Irigaray: Philosophy in the Feminine*. London: Routledge, 1991.

Wilson, Catherine. "Simone de Beauvoir and Human Dignity." In *The Legacy of Simone de Beauvoir*, edited by Emily R. Grosholz, 90–114. Oxford: Oxford University Press, 2006.

Zambrano, Maria. *De L'Aurore*. Translated from Spanish by Marie Laffranque. Paris: Éditions de L' Éclat, 1989.

———. *Les Clairières Du Bois*. Translated from Spanish by Marie Laffranque. Paris: Éditions de L' Éclat, 1989.

CHAPTER 3

TRANSCENDENCE, MATERIALISM, AND THE REENCHANTMENT OF NATURE

TOWARD A THEOLOGICAL MATERIALISM

Patrice Haynes

The details of our world deserve our respectful and loving attention.

—Iris Murdoch, *The Metaphysics of Morals*

Nothing could be experienced as truly alive if something that transcends life were not promised also.

—Theodor W. Adorno, *Negative Dialectics*

OUT OF THIS WORLD?
THE PROBLEM OF TRANSCENDENCE

Contemporary feminist theorists typically regard the notion of transcendence with suspicion. By "transcendence" is meant "going beyond" or "surpassing" a limit or context. The problem for a number of feminists is that, certainly in Western thought, it is the body, and the material world more generally, that is usually identified as the limit to overcome and so transcend. Given that Western culture traditionally associates bodiliness and materiality with the female sex, "woman" has come to represent the constraints of material imma-nence, and women are thus devalued in the process. In *The Second Sex*, Simone de Beauvoir famously laments the way in which women, defined as the "other" by men, are "doomed" to immanence (29, 726). She urges women to claim transcendence for themselves and, in doing so, to realize their freedom and subjectivity. However, de Beau-voir is often criticized by later feminists for perpetuating patriarchal conceptions of transcendence and immanence.

Indeed, for many feminists, a theoretical commitment to transcen-dence is politically irresponsible because it is held that this ultimately refuses to address the realities of material immanence: the social and historical conditions of women and men's lives. Supposedly, transcen-dence calls for a path out of this world and its material complexities, instead of aiming to effect concrete, social transformation that would promote just relations between human beings and the wider environ-ment. The following remarks by Stella Sanford express the antipathy toward transcendence that dominates much current feminist thinking: "The future of a twenty-first century feminist politics never was going to be found in a metaphysics of transcendence. Such a metaphysics remains *fundamentally incompatible* with a feminist theoretical proj-ect which aims to help transform society through the location of the origin of meanings . . . in the finite structures of the world" (139–40, my emphasis). Philosophical appeals to transcendence are generally seen as "fundamentally incompatible" with the materialist concerns of feminists, which seek to identify and challenge those forms of social organization, structures, and practices that support the subordination of women.

In feminist theology and feminist philosophy of religion, this dis-trust of transcendence is specifically directed at that most archetypal figure of transcendence: divine transcendence. The transcendent God of monotheism presents serious worries to feminists. As radically other—the transcendent source of all goodness and perfections—God stands in complete contradistinction to the world. As such, the argu-ment runs, God's relation to the world serves as the model for the dualistic and hierarchical ordering of reality: God-world, spirit-mat-ter, transcendence-immanence, male-female, human-nature, and so on. The configuration of reality according to hierarchical dualisms is criticized by most feminists for encouraging the denigration of the material realm and, consequently, women, given the latter's symbolic connection with the material. In addition to crowning and bolstering a whole series of hierarchical dualisms, a number of feminists also sus-pect that the transcendent God of monotheism is actually fashioned in the image of man. As Daphne Hampson writes, a "transcendent monotheism" very much reflects the male values of "freedom, power and independence" (152). God's transcendence, then, may turn out to be the grand expression of the male ego, a projection that allows man to assuage his fear of finitude and embodiment.

Given such charges against the divine transcendence of monotheism, it is perhaps not surprising that, for those feminists who do not wish to jettison the category "divine" altogether, many turn toward rethinking the divine in terms of immanence. The transcendence of the divine thus comes to refer to a transcendence within the world, within material immanence: an immanent or materialist transcendence. As one feminist puts it, "If there is any one theme that emerges most clearly [in contemporary women's theologies], it is the assumption of the immanence of the divine. The indwelling of the divine is the foundational assumption on which numerous other concepts rest" (Bednarowski, quoted in Miles 13).[1]

The emphasis on the immanence of the divine in recent feminist discourse is striking. However, conceptions of divine immanence are wide ranging and not always clearly formulated. The influential feminist philosopher and psychoanalytic theorist Luce Irigaray proposes the intriguing idea of a "sensible transcendental" as a way of moving toward "a divine in the feminine" (*An Ethics of Sexual Difference* 30, 70, 74, 109). For Irigaray, the self-affecting female body constitutes a distinct mode of transcendence, a becoming, that is always in and through the sexed body, never a flight from it. Although Irigaray works with a deliberately imprecise notion of the divine, one thing she means by calling for the "becoming divine" of women is the recognition of the divinity that is sexed bodies in their given, irreducible difference (*Sexes and Genealogies* 57–72). For Irigaray, the immanence of female and male sexuate belonging (of body and psyche) *is* divine. Other feminist conceptions of divine immanence are proposed by writers such as Sallie McFague, who revisions the world as "God's body"; Carol P. Christ, who uses process theology to reimagine God as a divine power at one with the ongoing creation of the world; and Sharon Welch, who views divinity as the "relational power" of community.[2]

Whether understood as the sexed body, ethical relations, the cosmos, community, or natural processes, a number of contemporary feminists are keen to develop immanent accounts of the divine and transcendence. My view is that such projects are welcome in that they radicalize concepts of the divine, transcendence, immanence, materiality, and the body, in ways that refuse the hierarchical dualistic thinking characterizing the patriarchal philosophies and theologies enshrined in the Western canon. This recent turn to immanence (also evident outside feminist theorizing) is driven by the worry, outlined earlier, that an emphasis on transcendence must lead, if not to hostile attitudes toward the material, then certainly to a deplorable neglect of embodied life.

Elsewhere I argue that, contrary to expectations, "immanentist" or materialist reconceptions of transcendence or the divine (feminist or otherwise) actually fail to do justice to the material world, particularly to the integrity of embodied subjects (Haynes, *Transcendence Matters*). In this chapter, however, I hope to encourage feminists to reconsider the theistic idea of divine transcendence as one that can actually affirm materiality and embodiment. To this end, I begin with a reflection on the work of Theodor Adorno. Born to a Catholic mother and a Jewish father, Adorno has at best an ambiguous relationship to theology.[3] However, for him the concept of transcendence is crucial and must, if nothing else, refer to a critical standpoint from which oppressive material conditions can be exposed. As such, transcendence can reveal that what is, is not necessarily normative and could exist otherwise given sociopolitical transformation.

In the following section, I outline Adorno and Horkheimer's account of the disenchantment of nature, before going on to highlight the importance of the concept of transcendence for Adorno in the task of reenchanting the world. Thereafter, I aim to show that Adorno's nontheistic vision of transcendence, while compelling, incurs metaphysical consequences that feminists may wish to avoid: namely, the failure to secure the intrinsic meaningfulness of bodies. I hold that these consequences can be overcome by appealing to transcendence understood as divine mind. I propose the idea of a theological materialism that would reclaim divine transcendence in the name of the reenchantment of bodies. Indeed, rather than urging us out of this world, I maintain that divine transcendence inspires us to transform the world in ways that concretely realize love and justice between people and all things.

THE DISENCHANTMENT OF THE WORLD: THE SPELL OF IMMANENCE

In the opening essay of *Dialectic of Enlightenment*, Adorno and Horkheimer cite the domination of nature as the primary motive behind enlightenment. For these two writers, the term "enlightenment" is not limited to a specific point in history but refers to an ongoing process throughout history: the disenchantment of nature, that is, "the dissolution of myths and the ruin of fancy through knowledge" (3, trans. mod.). Enlightenment, then, is the work of demythologization, "the destruction of gods and qualities alike" (8).

It is Adorno and Horkheimer's *dialectical* account of "myth" and "enlightenment" that makes their analysis so distinctive, for they seek to show how the dialectic of enlightenment is at one with the dialectic of myth. Their thesis is famously summarized in the statement "myth is already enlightenment; and enlightenment reverts to mythology" (xvi). But what are we to understand by myth? And, how does enlightenment revert to mythology, thus betraying itself? In what follows, I will briefly review some familiar themes from Adorno and Horkheimer's influential text, including the role of instrumental reason in the disenchantment of the world. However, by linking the dialectic of myth and enlightenment with the idea of the "generation of immanence" (16), I hope to offer a fresh perspective on these issues, as well as provide a basis for the next section where I discuss Adorno's call for transcendence.

Adorno and Horkheimer do not give a comprehensive definition of myth. Nevertheless, it is possible to establish at least two broad ways in which they understand the term. First, myths are what people use to make sense of nature, to represent the world in meaningful ways. Myths provide societies with a public, stable framework through which nature can be understood (Stone 235). In this way, nature need not be encountered in its confusing immediacy, all flux and contingencies. Hence, myth "is already enlightenment" because myths are ways of rationalizing the world so that it becomes more intelligible and less threatening.

However, Adorno and Horkheimer also use the term "myth" to denote animistic views of the world that enchant and mystify. Indeed, broadly conceived as animistic, myths "spiritualised the object" (28), for they assert mysterious givens in the natural world that defy total rationalization. For Adorno and Horkheimer, such givens range from the spirits said to inhabit natural objects in ancient animism to notions of essence and substance in metaphysics. Paradoxically, in explaining nature, myths both enlighten and enchant. They enlighten because they are a form of rationality, and as such, they disenchant nature by subordinating it to the immanence of human thought and practical control. Yet, at the same time, myths enchant because, in their appeal to hidden elements and forces, they acknowledge a moment of nature that transcends human understanding and so cannot be made entirely rational and manipulable. Enlightenment, then, is a moment of myth;

but this means that enlightenment is also ineradicably mythic. We thus begin to grasp how the dialectic of enlightenment and the dialectic of myth are entangled with each other.

According to Adorno and Horkheimer, it is the human desire for self-preservation that drives the pursuit of enlightenment. As Francis Bacon first told us, knowledge is power and this becomes, in Adorno and Horkheimer's words: "what men want to learn from nature is how to use it in order wholly to dominate it and other men" (4). For these writers, the domination of nature is not just that of nonhuman nature, but also the nature *within* man (needs, instincts, desires) as well as the material threat of other men. Nor is it lost on them that enlightenment entails the domination of women by men, given the latter's historical identification of the former with the idea of nature.[4] The authors of *Dialectic of Enlightenment* are keen to emphasize that despite the ever more sophisticated forms of enlightenment that develop over time, archaic domination persists as its logic. However, they are far from presenting an ahistorical account of the domination of nature, for they recognize that with every historical reformulation of enlightenment processes, the expression and extent of domination varies.

For Adorno and Horkheimer, modernity marks the culmination of various stages of enlightenment, with the Enlightenment being a *self-conscious* project of demythologization and human freedom. However, these two thinkers rightly observe that, while instrumental reason emerges as the Enlightenment's unrivaled vehicle of disenchantment, the achievement of modern science and technology, it still remains consonant with mythic rationality. It therefore fulfills the "principle of myth," which is "the principle of immanence, the explanation of every event as repetition" (12). Mythic rationality, both ancient and modern, aims to explicate nature through framing events and things in terms of repetitions and equivalencies, thus establishing patterns, cycles, laws of action and reaction, and so on, believed to constitute the world order. In so doing, it constructs a fixed, closed totality where there can only ever be the eternal return of the same. It is this feature that ensures myth's regressive turn: the institution of fate—an unquestionable, invariable view of the world that restricts human action. Modern rationality strives to dispel mythic fatedness, announcing rather too loudly the arrival of true human autonomy. However, the hegemony of instrumental reason ensures that the Enlightenment merely *refines* mythic fate, accelerating the immanent closure of the world to subjective representation. "Nothing at all may remain outside [immanent representation], because the mere idea of outsideness is the very source of fear" (16).[5]

It is well known that Adorno and Horkheimer charge instrumental reason with the intensification of domination and disenchantment that attends modernity. Instrumental reason—a pragmatic mode of reason that with modernity is elevated to the point of being synonymous with reason *per se*—operates by way of classification, abstraction, simplification, and quantification. It robs objects of their sensuous particularity, subsuming them under universal categories: thus making the incommensurable commensurable. Its aim is the ever more efficient control of nature. When instrumental reason prevails, nature is reduced to a realm of abstract equivalences, a rational totality or *mathesis universalis*, where there is only mythic repetition of the same. However, while mythic animism recognized in nature an otherness that transcends thought, the Enlightenment (modern philosophy, science and capitalism) demands the "extirpation of animism" (5), and, thus, is powerfully disenchanting. In Adorno and Horkheimer's words, "From now on, matter would at last be mastered without any illusion of ruling or inherent powers, of hidden qualities" (6). With the progressive loss of any meaningfulness and value that transcends the immanence of human thought nature is *pari passu* disenchanted. As the modern subject reconstitutes the world in terms of its rational representation, the spell of immanence is cast and recast. Subjective reason renders the world an immanent (almost entirely), closed totality, wherein all phenomena are fully determinate and transparent, thus, comprehensively dominated and directed to meet the ends of self-preservation.

But, as we learn from fairy tales, the danger of casting spells is that they can turn on you. Adorno and Horkheimer seek to show how the spell of immanence reifies the world. The abstract forms of reason take on a thing-like, natural appearance, confronting the subject as an unalterable objectivity that cannot be thought otherwise. A dreadful *re*enchantment of the world haunts modern disenchantment, particularly within the social realm[6] where unjust social relations organized by the capitalist exchange principle, as well as the phallic economy, seem entirely natural, normative and beyond the control of individuals. Adorno and Horkheimer observe: "What appears to be the triumph of subjective rationality . . . is paid for by the obedient subjection of reason to what is directly given" (26). Enlightenment returns to myth. Rather than realizing human freedom, the modern scene merely establishes the "pseudoindividual": (apparently) sovereign yet in reality bound by (apparently) objective laws, and denied their sensuous particularity. A feminist point would also be that the subject of enlightenment is male because the attempt to gain mastery over nature reflects typically male ideals of power and autonomy. Enlightenment cannot register (at least positively) female subjectivity. Indeed, it relies on the negation of all that is female because of the classic association of nature with femaleness.[7] The point I wish to emphasize here, however, is that the rampant disenchantment of the world effected by modern rationality, is also the "immanentization" of the world. Transcendence becomes taboo; but, subsequently, objects are drained of any intrinsic meaningfulness, and their qualitative differences are elided in thought's attempt to create a rationalized totality. Thought, in thrall to the immanence it constitutes, can only think "cycle, fate, and domination of the world reflected as the truth and deprived of hope" (27). Against disenchantment and the mythic fate of modernity, in the next section, I hope to show how Adorno's negative dialectics suggests a way of breaking the spell of immanence. For Adorno, the reenchantment of the world calls for a recovery of transcendence, which he conceives in a way that, I believe, could be used by feminists keen to address the concrete actualities of women's lives.

CRITIQUE, TRANSCENDENCE, AND MATERIALISM: ADORNO AND REENCHANTMENT

Toward the end of *Negative Dialectics*, Adorno considers the possibility of metaphysical experience. It is clear that such an experience would be one of transcendence, and so one that reaches beyond the disenchanting immanence of modernity—the true horror of which having been emphatically exposed in the death camps of Auschwitz. For Adorno, "Transcendence, captured by the immanence of the human spirit is at the same time turned into the totality of the spirit and abolished" (402). Importantly, as will become clear, Adorno does not mean by "transcendence" that which is otherworldly or supernatural. He rejects what he believes is monotheism's false reconciliation of subject and object in a supersensible world, whereupon "our relation to both the world beyond and real existence [becomes] one of impotent longing" (Rose 77). Rather, Adorno's vision of transcendence is thoroughly worldly. Broadly understood, it is more an appeal to material possibilities given the promissory insight at the heart of *Negative Dialectics*, namely, that "what is, is more than it is" (161).

As reason becomes ever more instrumental, it also becomes increasingly absolute. The world must conform to its invariant categories, and whatever does not is irrelevant. A purely instrumental reason mechanically generates the world as a radical immanence, wherein what is, is just what reason determines there to be, and so all that can ever be. Reason thus occludes transcendence such that immanence is strictly limited to fate: the repetition of the same. Adorno's negative dialectics, or nonidentity thinking, names a form of cognition that guards against the becoming total of spirit. In doing so, thought avows its dialectical relationship with transcendence. This has crucial materialist implications that must, I submit, inform the hazardous work that is any emancipatory politics such as feminism. Moreover, as I will contend in the next section, I think that the relation between transcendence and materialism that underpins Adorno's negative dialectics can lead us toward a consideration of theology and materialism in ways that would not necessarily be surprising to Adorno but might surprise and inspire the feminist materialist.

How then does Adorno's negative dialectics aim to resensitize thought to transcendence? In the "Introduction" to *Negative Dialectics*, and the section entitled "Concepts and Categories," Adorno makes it clear that thought becomes trapped in its own immanence when it takes identity as its goal. Indeed, this goal is the very purpose of what Adorno calls "identity thinking." Although he recognizes that "To think is to identify" (5), the real problem occurs when cognition regards the universal category as though it fully expresses the object's nature. Identity thinking simply classifies a particular object by rendering it an instance or token of a general type. However, this enforces an identity on objects that are nonidentical, and, Adorno holds, when cognition stops at identity it serves only to dominate and disenchant nature, ruthlessly negating the sensuous particularity of objects. Moreover, Adorno is clear that the capitalist exchange principle is the social expression of identity thinking. The demands of exchange "imposes on the whole world an obligation to become identical, to become total" (146).

For Adorno, what transcends identity, and what thought must do justice to, is the object in its noninterchangeable, sensuous particularity. This is the aim of negative dialectics, or nonidentity thinking: to orientate cognition away from the universal category toward the unique particularity of material things. To break the spell of immanence, thought must think critically against the appearance of total identity, appreciating that "the concept does not exhaust the thing conceived" (5). Indeed, if nonidentity thinking is to have critical teeth, then the relation between the thinking subject and the object requires refiguring such that the latter is given primacy. To uphold this primacy, thought must check its drive toward totality and unity, thus encouraging the "break-in of what is irreducible" ("The Actuality of Philosophy" 38), namely, the object in its sensuous particularity.

To insist on the primacy of the object is to insist on a *material* transcendence, that is, the specific and mutable materiality of things that eludes full conceptual capture. However, Adorno's thesis of the primacy of the object does not wish to make the object absolute—which would simply be yet another move of the subject. Rather, he wants to emphasize the asymmetry between the subject and object, whereby the subject depends on the object *more* than the object depends on the subject.[8] The subject is not, however, reduced to a mere passive receptacle, for it is through the critical scrutiny of the subject's mediations of the object that the object's primacy emerges.

Negative dialectics is "the consistent sense of non-identity" (*Negative Dialectics*, 5), which is precisely the sense of transcendence against the totalizing immanence of thought. Nonidentity thinking does not seek the comprehensive determination of the object but rather strives "by way of the concept, to transcend the concept" (15) for the sake of the object in its sensuous particularity. The pressing question is, how can the concept escape its own immanence and, with this, the hold of identity? Indeed, for Adorno, this concern is the starting point of metaphysics which must ponder how subjects "embedded in themselves, in their "constitution" . . . are nonetheless able to see beyond themselves" (376). It is Adorno's view that thought transcends itself not by somehow departing the realm of thought, but by thinking against itself, against the appearance of fixed identity.[9] Thought must engage in an ongoing critique of identity if it is not to deny the sensuous particularity of the object.

For Adorno, one key way in which thought can think critically against itself is through constellations. Because no single concept can ever be entirely definitive of any particular object—the universal concept can only grasp a limited range of the object's properties—it becomes necessary to deploy other concepts "around" the object. The limited insights of each concept can, when arranged together, begin to "illuminate" the specificities of the object (162–63, see also Kaufmann 69–70). But it would be a mistake to think that with Adorno such constellations are able to disclose the ultimate or essential truth of the object. Rather than the disclosure of truth about the object, what becomes apparent is the object's historical "experience"; the way in which over time its relations with other objects and concepts have become constitutive of it. Given this, the object revealed through its constellation of concepts is a testament to its ruin and disenchantment by instrumental reason. The light of transcendence, of thought thinking against itself, illuminates the object as a text of its suffering, where its sensuous particularity has been rendered anathema by theoretical and practical processes of rationalization that make the nonidentical identical in the self-preserving drive for unity and totality.

Rather than delivering a consistent and uniform representation of the object, as with identity thinking, thinking in constellations gives the lie to the illusion of full conceptual clarity by exposing the contradictions that attend the determination of the object. Critical thinking draws attention to such contradictions, which are not, for Adorno, simply failures in cognition, but are the conceptual index of "an ontology of the wrong state of things" (11). By this is meant an ontology of a negated state of affairs: The sensuous particularity of the object is (almost completely) negated, not just in thought but in actuality, where the capitalist exchange principle homogenizes people and things for the sake of rendering the world in more calculable, quantifiable terms.[10]

For Adorno, the thought that thinks against itself serves utopia, for it is 'a piece of existence extending—however negatively—to that which is not" (57). And yet might we not complain that, with Adorno, transcendence is too negative, merely the interminable critique of the given that in practice cannot deliver any real transformation of material conditions that engender suffering? I do not think Adorno's nonidentity thinking can be easily charged with this. Although the self-transcendence of thought cannot, for Adorno, show an alternative vision of the world that prescribes how things ought to be, it does reveal that things have possibilities open to them.[11] In Adorno's words: "The means employed in negative dialectics for the penetration of its hardened objects is possibility—the possibility of which their reality has cheated the objects and which is nonetheless visible in each one" (52). By emphasizing the object's mutilation and diminution as the effects of identity thinking, thought functions both critically and redemptively. Thought need not ontologize a negated state of affairs (a problem that I believe haunts Derridean deconstruction) but can discredit the apparent *necessity* of the object's being thus and so (a damaged existent), which nevertheless truthfully attests to its *becoming* thus and so. "What is, is more than it is" (161), and the object is more than a damaged fragment for it has future possibilities: the potential to exist otherwise.

The self-transcending thought enables the hope of what Adorno calls "the transfigured body" (400). This does not refer to some true or authentic way of being that identity thinking has suppressed.

Rather it refers more to a transformed experience, an ethics of thinking whereby thought no longer seeks to totalize itself in all there is, entirely bound by the drive of self-preservation, but desires, instead, affinity (not identity) with the object in its sensuous particularity. A transformed mode of cognition facilitates the realization of peace as "the state of distinctness without domination, with the distinct participating in each other" ("Subject and Object" 140). For Adorno, the emancipated society would be one wherein "people can be different without fear" (*Minima Moralia* 103). And the world properly reenchanted is one where the mysterious, irreducible particularity of people and things stands as a mark of transcendence within the immanence of thought (which never really was, or can be, entirely cut off from transcendence).

Before moving on to discuss the ontological presuppositions of Adorno's negative dialectics, which, I argue, presents problems that an appeal to theistic divine transcendence may be able to address, I would like to summarize two main ways that we can understand the concept of transcendence in Adorno's work. The first is the "transcendence of the object in its sensuous particularity": the object's complex, variable materiality, which cannot be fully determined and reduced to the immanence of thought. The second is the "transcendence of thought thinking against itself": whereby the critique of identity is both critical and redemptive. These two characterizations of transcendence are interrelated. The sensuous particularity of the object is such that while it is determinable it cannot be brought into any final identity with thought without precluding the object's openness to becoming. Given this, and for the sake of the object, thought must guard against its tendency toward self-closure and aim beyond identity.

I contend that the vision of transcendence that can be gleaned from Adorno's work should be of interest to feminists seeking to rethink transcendence in material or worldly terms (an immanent transcendence). Indeed, I think it is important that with Adorno there is no simple call for the divinization and affirmation of materiality, or bodiliness, which we find with, for example, Irigaray and her insistence on the "becoming divine" of women. The problem with such moves (inspiring as they are) is that they risk sidestepping the work of critically analyzing the sociohistorical determinations that have had, and continue to have, such deleterious effects on women's lives. Without such critique the affirmation of the material becomes deeply problematic, for it can only mask social antagonisms, and the experience of contradictory positioning, rather than provide the critical tools with which to identify and practically address these. However, I believe that Adorno's negative dialectics enables feminists to specify the various ways in which a woman's particularity is negated when she is locked within the immanence of masculinist representations.[12] Negative dialectics promises to break the spell of immanence and give hope to the transfigured body.

THE OBJECT AND THE QUESTION OF REALISM

It is the idea of the object in its sensuous particularity that I am keen to examine further because it is the object's irreducibility to thought that ensures its transcendence or otherness. It is clear that Adorno wishes to uphold the primacy of the object against the becoming absolute of thought. However, in his comments on the object, he is unhelpfully ambiguous on what I believe is a crucial point; namely, whether the object has an intrinsic meaningfulness independently of all human mediation. Without an explicitly realist conception of the object—whereby it is understood as existing in determinate, meaningful ways independently of human categories—I think it becomes difficult to support the thesis of the primacy of the object that is central to Adorno's negative dialectics.

The confusion surrounding Adorno's depiction of the object results from his references to the "nonconceptual" or "an objectivity beyond all 'making'" (*Negative Dialectics* 376), and his insistence that the object is not a transcendent Kantian thing-in-itself. By referring to the "nonconceptual," Adorno emphasizes the object's irreducibility to conceptual determination. However, he is keen to avoid presenting the object as a thing with its own inherent truth or reality that thought must somehow fathom or be faithful to. As he writes, "the materialist procedure does all the more justice, the more it distances itself from every "meaning" of its objects and the less it relates itself to an implicit, quasi-religious meaning" ("The Actuality of Philosophy" 32). This suggests that, for Adorno, the object is not some prediscursive given, possessing its own intrinsic meaningfulness. And yet, he also implies that there is something *more* to the object than its subjective determination, and that this "more" is epistemically relevant to thought. Against the constitutive transcendental subject, Adorno maintains that our determinations of the object "will adjust to a moment which they themselves are not" (*Negative Dialectics* 138).[13] For Adorno, thought is not just self-reflexive but is constrained in some way by the nature of the object that it thinks. Nevertheless, if the object has no intrinsic meaningfulness, or determinateness, in what way can it guide our thinking about it? In offering a response to this query, we can begin to establish ontological commitments that, I argue, undermine Adorno's thesis of the primacy of the object.

It is by a somewhat Marxist conception of the object as "sedimented history" that Adorno is able to maintain both that it is something capable of placing constraints on thought, and that it is not a thing-in-itself with its own metaphysical truth. Understood as sedimented history, the object *is* a product of its sociohistorical determinations. In other words, the object (something essentially indeterminate?) is the crystallization of its various determining relations with other objects and subjects, which are constitutive of it over the course of history and within the social totality. It gains its meaningfulness by accruing a mass of human significances over time; the effects of labor, art, and desire are carried within it. The object's sensuous particularity is not by virtue of its pregiven nature but is the objective reflection of the sheer density of its subjective mediations. Because it is collectively produced the object has a determinateness that is independent of, or transcends, any individual subject. In this way then, the object can be without any intrinsic or pregiven meaningfulness, and yet endowed with a meaningful determinateness, acquired over its history, that sets limits to how we can think about it.

This account of the object strikes me as according with what the contemporary philosopher of religion Stephen Clark calls a "social idealism" (*God's World and the Great Awakening* 2). With Adorno, the object is ultimately the product of its social construction rather than constituted by the individual, transcendental subject. As sedimented history, the object is meaningful *only* to the extent that it is subjectively mediated, albeit by human beings collectively. The subject does not need "an impossible noumenal intelligence" (Coole 159) to gain access to the object (which would be the case if it were a transcendent thing-in-itself), because its significance is humanity's own work.

My worry is that by making the meaningfulness of the object completely dependent on (collective) subjectivity, Adorno continues to tie subject and object too closely together. The nonidentity between the two, which grants the object its transcendence, then becomes difficult to articulate. By denying the object any intrinsic determinateness that is epistemically meaningful and grants the object its integrity, Adorno risks presupposing a materiality that is only indeterminate "stuff" to be shaped by the contingents needs and interests of human beings, guided by the dictates of self-preservation alone. To secure the nonidentity between subject and object, and uphold the primacy of the object, I think we should defend a realism about material objects.

More contentiously, it is also my view that such a realism requires divine mind. It is thus in the attempt to advance a materialism that does not reduce matter to an indeterminate base when, I believe, ontology meets theology. And perhaps Adorno, despite his reservations about theology, may not wholly dismiss such a claim for once he wrote, "At its most materialistic, materialism comes to agree with theology. Its great desire would be the resurrection of the flesh, a desire utterly foreign to idealism, the realm of absolute spirit" (*Negative Dialectics* 207).

Toward a Theological Materialism

Central to the project of negative dialectics is the safeguarding of nonidentity. This is particularly important when considering the question of transcendence, because upholding nonidentity between subject and object prevents thought from becoming closed off to the transcendence (or otherness) of objects and so prevents objects from becoming entirely circumscribed by the fixed identities imposed on them by thought. My argument is that realism about material objects is needed if we are to maintain the nonidentity between subject and object. Once again, by realism I mean the metaphysical thesis that objects possess determinations (properties, structures, dynamics) that are independent of the cognitive operations of the human mind. Moreover, such determinations afford the material object an intrinsic meaningfulness. This is because some of them are fundamental in shaping the world in important ways that are not just relative to us, and thus affect how we are able to interact with the world (Haslanger 123).

Adorno's materialism does not explicitly deny that the object exists as something determinate independently of human conceptions. However, by stipulating that it is meaningful only insofar as it bears the marks of its subjective mediation, Adorno inadvertently returns the object to the dictates of (human) mind, thus undermining his thesis of the object's primacy. I must now clarify why realism about material objects is best explained given divine mind. In doing so, I shall espouse views on the role of mind and the transcendence of the divine that are rather at odds with feminist orthodoxy on these matters. While I do not wish to bypass or minimize important feminist criticisms concerning traditional conceptions of the divine in terms of the mind (or spirit) that transcends worldly immanence, I do hope to invite feminists to at least reassess the idea of divine mind as one that could actually support the aims of materialist feminists, rather than inevitably signal a regressive step.

Of course, in the space that remains, I cannot provide a full inquiry into how commonsense material objects are possible independently of the human mind. However, I will highlight one main issue that I believe gives us reason to take the idea of divine mind seriously when thinking the material. According to Clark: "Insofar as we admit . . . of a real world that does not depend on us and what we may say of it, we need to understand how that real world is unified itself. If it can't be unified it remains mere chaos . . . if it comes across as more than that . . . it is as the world of an infinite intellect" (*God, Religion and Reality* 77). Against a picture of the world as chaotic materiality (indeed, if the world were really such we would be incapable of reflecting on it), Clark argues that the unity of the material world depends, if not on us, then on an infinite intellect, which he takes to be divine mind. I think this is correct and therefore agree that it is mind rather than matter that is the principle of unity both for the material world as a whole, and for particular material things.[14] Furthermore, because I wish to avoid founding the material object's determinateness entirely on the human mind, I appeal to divine mind as the intellect affording the determinate independence of material things. If the material object has more than the weak unity of an aggregate of properties then, following the Platonic tradition with Clark, I submit that the object's deeper unity rests in a real form which enables it to be what it is, and that, in turn, this form rests in an eternal intellect—one understood as supremely alive, thinking, and creative.

But is it not question-begging to argue that the unity of the material object must depend on (divine) mind? Might it not be the case that matter is capable of self-organizing into determinate forms? Clark points out that a strictly materialist account of the object's unity faces the ancient problem of an infinite regress: the unity of any material unifier would itself always be brought into question (58–61). This must create difficulties for the materialist who wishes to avoid reducing the material world to simple extension, one space-time locus after the next, at the expense of distinct kinds of things (Clark, *Biology and Christian Ethics* 126–29). However, Manuel DeLanda, inspired by the "new materialism" of Deleuze, would argue that matter possesses its own "immanent and intensive resources for the generation of form from within" (DeLanda 2). His account is complex; yet, it is clear that for DeLanda it is matter's dynamic "processes of becoming" (3) that is significant rather than actual determinate things, which end up having a somewhat epiphenomenal status in his ontology. Although DeLanda may be able to show how matter alone can yield various unities, his strict antiessentialism means that material objects are only temporary, unintentional concretions of occult material forces and thus lack any fundamental meaningfulness in themselves. Such meaningfulness is precisely why I turn to a realist account of the object.

I am aware that feminists in particular may be suspicious of invoking divine mind as the basis of material objects. The concern is that this would reinforce the gendered principles of Aristotelian hylomorphism: The active male *logos* imposes form on passive female matter that is amorphous and undifferentiated. However, I think it is possible to rethink divine mind without such unwelcome implications. In his touching book *God in Fragments*, Jacques Pohier claims that, with respect to creation, "God does not want to be Everything" (261ff). Given this, we could say that divine mind does not seek to totalize itself in its creation. Rather, divine mind is cognition as love. The divine lovingly thinks creation so that each thing may be for its own sake and as such exist as a testament to divine love. Because it is such a testament it is intrinsically meaningful, expressing its own specificity and inherent worth.

The theological materialism I wish to propose is also a theological *idealism* since it holds that divine mind as love is constitutive of the material world. Each thing is, therefore, a concrete manifestation of an idea in divine mind. We should note two points here. First, divine mind is transcendent; it exceeds the material world. However, the theological materialism I advance does not postulate some preexisting matter to be ordered by the transcendent forms of divine mind. Instead, in creation the divine ideas become concrete actualities; they are made incarnate as it were. Material immanence is thus the revelation of divine mind in the realm of finitude: time, limit, and history. This means that the material world is shot through with divine transcendence and thus is marked by an array of distinctions and qualities that God intended. This is in contradistinction to a material world where things are contingent, nonunified arrangements of matter, *pace* DeLanda.

The second point I wish to raise is that divine mind need not be regarded as "overdetermining" the material world, that is, enforcing upon each thing an identity that ineluctably determines every aspect of its existence irrespective of its particular context. While I would maintain that the forms of divine mind do set limits on what a thing can be and do, we can, nevertheless, view such limits in terms of what Serene Jones paradoxically calls a "space of bounded openness" (43). Precisely by being something determinate, that is, a particular kind of thing, the material object can engage in becoming through determining relations with other objects (including human beings), without being entirely reducible to those relations. The object's identity can thus be considered a work in progress.

Although I have only offered some preliminary comments on the idea of a theological materialism, I hope to have encouraged a reconsideration of divine transcendence as that which does not necessarily downgrade the material, but actually lovingly invests it with a determinateness and integrity. Indeed, it is by virtue of the transcendence of divine mind that, I argue, the transcendence of the object in its sensuous particularity cannot be entirely lost to the immanence of the human mind. Given a theological materialism along the lines I am developing, the material object gains its intrinsic meaningfulness as a noninterchangeable embodiment of God's love. Commenting on similar themes, the theologian James Smith writes, "The physical . . . is not a fallen distraction but rather an incarnational index of the [divine] transcendent . . . the physical bears a *positive* relation to the [divine] transcendent" (Smith 107, my italics).

CONCLUSION

In an interview following her work as editor for a special issue of the Italian journal *Inchiesta*, Irigaray laments, "We've generally located transcendence between the 'sky' and 'us' ("A Bridge between Two Irreducible to Each Other" 58). She goes on to say: "We should learn to lay it [transcendence] between us. Each one of us is inaccessible to the other, transcendent to him/her" (58). Here Irigaray expresses a general feminist discontent with the traditional idea of transcendence found in religion and philosophy, where the concept signifies that which is beyond the material world. Like a number of feminist thinkers, Irigaray calls for a reinterpretation of transcendence in this-worldly, immanent, or materialist terms: a sensible transcendental. Specifically, Irigaray wishes to locate transcendence in the irreducible difference between female and male sexuateness. By "materializing" transcendence, the expectation is that there can be a certain spiritualizing or divinizing of materiality and bodiliness, in other words, an avowal of material immanence. This materialist reconception of transcendence is believed to overcome the denigration of the material said to result with any acknowledgment of traditional understandings of transcendence.

Against the grain of much feminist reflection on transcendence, I have, in this chapter, wanted to show that the theistic idea of divine transcendence need not be viewed as necessarily opposed to, and discrediting of, the material world; particularly given the customary identification of women with nature and materiality. I hope to have shown that the transcendence of divine mind can be construed as endorsing material immanence in its very creation, thus positively valuing it.

The passage to divine mind, and so to a theological materialism, that I have traced in this chapter is through an analysis of the metaphysics of the material object. In response to the disenchantment of the world described by Adorno and Horkheimer in *Dialectic of Enlightenment*, I turned to Adorno's negative dialectics, which seeks to release the object from the spell of immanence so perfectly cast by instrumental reason. With its insistence on the primacy of the object and an axial turn in cognition, whereby the utopic moment of thought is nonidentity rather than identity, I suggested that Adorno's philosophy presents a fruitful resource for feminists rethinking transcendence. I maintained that with Adorno we can advance an immanent or materialist transcendence that can both fund a critique of inequitable social conditions (a prerequisite for transformative action) and offer redemptive hope. However, I argued that upon scrutiny Adorno's materialism is unable successfully to maintain the nonidentity between subject and object because his view of the object—as sedimented history—assumes what could be labeled a "social idealism." I then concluded that realism about material objects is needed if the transcendence of the object in its sensuous particularity is not to be collapsed into the immanence of thought. I proposed that such realism is best formulated by affirming divine mind as the creative and loving intellect that desires that each thing may be for its own sake and so not as a fungible token of some universal type.

While the theological materialism that I have began to delineate here is only emergent, and would need to respond to some difficult metaphysical issues (for example, how the forms of divine mind are concretely individuated), I hope to have offered at least an opening for feminists who wish to affirm both material and bodily immanence *and* the divine transcendence of theism. To admit divine transcendence need not call us out of this world. Instead divine transcendence can invite recognition of the material world's intrinsic meaningfulness as the tangible expression of God's love. As Julian of Norwich puts it "everything exists through the love of God" (11). In view of this, the reenchantment of the world would entail a mode of thinking that does not seek to dominate the object but, rather, in Adorno's words, to save in it "something of the calm of its day of creation" (*Minima Moralia* 76). That is to say, to preserve in the object God's desire for it to be for its own sake: a sensuous particularity in praise of the divine.

It may be feared that a theological materialism can at best offer a nice mystical vision of the world that is nevertheless politically vacuous, and so of no use to feminists seeking social transformation. To this I would say that one way in which a theological materialism is politically significant is that (as a realist ontology, but not a naïve realism) it demands we acknowledge that the world cannot be construed just any which way we please; indeed, to do so only leads to suffering.[15] Moreover, a politics informed by a theological materialism will aim for the transformation of the world so that it may be in praise of the divine, and as such a world where each thing exists *with* the other in love and justice.

NOTES

1. See also Nancy Frankenbury, who writes, "contemporary women's articulation of a relation between God and the world depicts the divine as continuous with the world rather than as radically transcendent ontologically or metaphysically. Divine transcendence is seen to consist in total immanence" (11); "Philosophy of Religion in Different Voices," in *Feminist Philosophy of Religion: Critical Readings*, ed. Pamela Sue Anderson and Beverley Clack (London: Routledge, 2004), 11.

2. See Sallie McFague, *The Body of God: An Ecological Theology* (London: SCM, 1983), and *Models of God: Theology for an Ecological, Nuclear Age* (Philadelphia: Fortress, 1987); Carol P. Christ, *She Who Changes: Re-imagining the Divine in the World* (Hampshire: Palgrave Macmillan, 2003); and Sharon Welch, *A Feminist Ethic of Risk* (Minneapolis, MN: Fortress Press, 1990), 172–78.

3. In his introduction to his translation of Adorno's work on Kierkegaard, Robert Hullot-Kentor says, "Theology is always moving right under the surface of all Adorno's writings"; Theodor W. Adorno, *Kierkegaard: Construction of the Aesthetic*, trans. Robert Hullot-Kentor (Mineapolis: University of Minnesota Press, 1989), xxi. For the only extended study (to my knowledge) on Adorno and theology, see Hent de Vries, *Minimal Theologies: Critiques of Secular Reason in Adorno and Levinas*, trans. Geoffrey Hale (Baltimore: John Hopkins University Press, 2005).

4. "She [Woman] became the embodiment of the biological function, the image of nature, the subjugation of which constituted that civilization's title to fame"; Theodor W. Adorno and Max Horkheimer, *Dialectic of Enlightenment*, trans. John Cumming (London: Verso, 1997), 248. For an analysis of "woman" and "the feminine" in Adorno and Horkheimer's *Dialectic of Enlightenment*, see the classic paper, Andrew Hewitt, "A Feminine Dialectic of Enlightenment: Horkheimer and Adorno Revisted," in *Feminist Interpretations of Theodor Adorno*, ed.

Renée Heberle (University Park: Pennsylvania State University Press, 2006). Hewitt argues that while Adorno and Horkheimer are critical of the patriarchal subjugation of women (both discursive and material), they, nevertheless, also end up instrumentalizing "woman" as a figure that could provide a way out of the masculinist philosophical system.

5. Also, "Leaving behind nothing but what merely is, demythologisation recoils into the mythus; for mythus is nothing than the closed system of immanence"; Theodor W. Adorno, *Negative Dialectics*, trans. E. B. Ashton. London: Routledge and Kegan Paul, 1973, 402.

6. We should note that for Adorno the natural and social world are inevitably intertwined; this will become apparent in the forthcoming discussion of the question of realism in Adorno. On the relationship between nature and history in Adorno, see also Theodor W. Adorno, "The Idea of Natural History," trans. Robert Hullot-Kentor. *Telos* 60 (1984): 111–24; and Deborah Cook, "Adorno's Critical Materialism." *Philosophy and Social Criticism* 32, no. 6 (2006): 719–37.

7. For a critique of the way in which Adorno and Horkheimer fail adequately to acknowledge sexual difference in *Dialectic of Enlightenment*, see Christine Battersby, *The Phenomenal Woman: Feminist Metaphysics and the Patterns of Identity* (Cambridge: Polity Press, 1998), 125–47); and Marsha Hewitt, *Critical Theory of Religion: A Feminist Analysis* (Minneapolis, MN: Augsberg Fortress, 1995), 77–80.

8. The subject "is the How—never the What" of mediation. Theodor W. Adorno, "Subject and Object," in *The Adorno Reader*, ed. Brian O'Connor (Oxford: Blackwell, 2000), 142.

9. "Thought need not be content with its own legality; without abandoning it, we can think against our thought"; Adorno, *Negative Dialectics*, 141.

10. I remain agnostic on the question concerning the nature of the causal relationship between identity thinking and the capitalist exchange principle. As I read Adorno, it seems that there are certain features of thought—for example, the tendency toward instrumentality and abstraction—that encourage certain forms of social organization, such as capitalism. Equally, capitalist societies intensify and facilitate instrumental reason and identity thinking. What is clear is that, for Adorno, a transformation of consciousness is possible within the social context of capitalism, but this transformation is not an end in itself, but rather the basis for initiating the transformation of social relations.

11. Adorno rejects any positive, constructive program for political transformation since "the right consciousness in the wrong world is impossible": quoted in Marsha Hewitt, *Critical Theory of Religion: A Feminist Analysis* (Minneapolis, MN: Augsberg Fortress, 1995), 85.

12. For an excellent discussion on how Adorno's negative dialectics can enable feminists to expose the social interests and cognitive practices at work in the identification (and determination) of actual women, see

        Gillian Howie, "The Economy of the Same: Identity, Equivalence and Exploitation," in *Feminist Interpretations of Theodor Adorno*. ed. Renée Heberle (University Park: Pennsylvania State University Press, 2006).

13.   For an instructive commentary on Adorno's understanding of the object, see Brian O'Connor, "Adorno and the Problem of Givenness," *Revue Internationale de Philosophie* 63, no. 227 (January 2004): 85–99.

14.   Feminists have rightly criticized the gendered nature of the distinction between mind and body, where "mind" is aligned with maleness, and "body" with femaleness. I certainly recognize the risk involved in my supporting the idea of divine mind as the foundation of the material world, namely, that my ontology will continue to encode and (unwittingly) promote sexist depictions of women. This is a real concern; however, I do think feminist philosophers and theologians should challenge the idea that the concept of "mind" is simply "nonfeminist" and instead begin to engage with this concept in ways that need not be hostile to feminist concerns.

15.   For feminists who underpin their political vision with a metaphysical realism, albeit conceived nontheistically, see Alison Assiter, *Enlightened Women: Modernist Feminism in a Postmodern Age* (London: Routledge, 1996); Sally Haslanger, 'Feminism in Metaphysics: Negotiating the Natural," in *The Cambridge Companion to Feminism in Philosophy*, ed. Miranda Fricker and Jennifer Hornsby (Cambridge: Cambridge University Press, 2000); Tony Lawson, "Feminism, Realism, and Universalism," *Feminist Economics* 5, no. 2 (July 1999): 25–59; and Kate Soper, *What Is Nature?* (Oxford: Blackwell, 1995).

BIBLIOGRAPHY

Adorno, Theodor W. "The Actuality of Philosophy." In *The Adorno Reader*, edited by Brian O'Connor, 23–39. Oxford: Blackwell, 2000.

———. "The Idea of Natural History." Translated by Robert Hullot-Kentor. *Telos* 60 (1984): 111–24.

———. *Kierkegaard: Construction of the Aesthetic*. Translated by Robert Hullot-Kentor. Minneapolis: University of Minnesota Press, 1989.

———. *Minima Moralia*. Translated by E. F. N. Jephcott. London: Verso, 1999.

———. *Negative Dialectics*. Translated by E. B. Ashton. London: Routledge and Kegan Paul, 1973.

———. "Subject and Object." In *The Adorno Reader*, edited by Brian O'Connor, 136–51. Oxford: Blackwell, 2000.

Adorno, Theodor W., and Max Horkheimer. *Dialectic of Enlightenment*. Translated by John Cumming. London: Verso, 1997.

Assiter, Alison. *Enlightened Women: Modernist Feminism in a Postmodern Age*. London: Routledge, 1996.

Battersby, Christine. *The Phenomenal Woman: Feminist Metaphysics and the Patterns of Identity*. Cambridge: Polity Press, 1998.

Beauvoir, Simone de. *The Second Sex*. Translated and edited by H. M. Parshley. London: Vintage Classic, 1997.

Christ, Carol P. *She Who Changes: Re-Imagining the Divine in the World*. Hampshire: Palgrave Macmillan, 2003.

Clark, Stephen. R. L. *Biology and Christian Ethics*. Cambridge: Cambridge University Press, 2000.

———. *God, Religion and Reality*. London: SPCK, 1998.

———. *God's World and the Great Awakening*. Oxford: Clarendon Press, 1991.

Cook, Deborah. "Adorno's Critical Materialism." *Philosophy and Social Criticism* 32, no. 6 (2006): 719–37.

Coole, Diane. *Negativity and Politics: Dionysius and Dialectics from Kant to Post-Structuralism*. London: Routledge, 2000.

De Landa, Manuel. "Deleuze and the Open-Ended Becoming of the World." Dialogues. http://www.watsoninstitute.org/infopeace/vy2k/delanda.cfm.

De Vries, Hent. *Minimal Theologies: Critiques of Secular Reason in Adorno and Levinas*. Translated by Geoffrey Hale. Baltimore: John Hopkins University Press, 2005.

Frankenbury, Nancy. "Philosophy of Religion in Different Voices." In *Feminist Philosophy of Religion: Critical Readings*, edited by Pamela Sue Anderson and Beverley Clack, 3–27. London: Routledge, 2004.

Hampson, Daphne. *Theology and Feminism*. Oxford: Blackwell, 1990.

Haslanger, Sally. "Feminism in Metaphysics: Negotiating the Natural." In *The Cambridge Companion to Feminism in Philosophy*, edited by Miranda Fricker and Jennifer Hornsby, 107–26. Cambridge: Cambridge University Press, 2000.

Haynes, Patrice. "Transcendence Matters: Rethinking Transcendence, Materialism and the Divine in Philosophical Context." PhD thesis, University of Liverpool, 2005.

Hewitt, Andrew. "A Feminine Dialectic of Enlightenment: Horkheimer and Adorno Revisted." In *Feminist Interpretations of Theodor Adorno*, edited by Renée Heberle, 69–96. University Park: Pennsylvania State University Press, 2006.

Hewitt, Marsha. *Critical Theory of Religion: A Feminist Analysis*. Minneapolis, MN: Augsberg Fortress, 1995.

Howie, Gillian. "The Economy of the Same: Identity, Equivalence and Exploitation." In *Feminist Interpretations of Theodor Adorno*, edited by Renée Heberle, 321–41. University Park: Pennsylvania State University Press, 2006.

Irigaray, Luce. "A Bridge between Two Irreducible to Each Other." In *Why Different?* translated by Camille Collins, 57–62. New York: Semiotext(e), 2000.

———. *An Ethics of Sexual Difference*. 1984. London: Continuum Books, 2004.

———. *Sexes and Genealogies*. Translated by Gillian C. Gill. New York: Columbia University Press, 1993.

Jones, Serene. *Feminist Theory and Christian Theology: Cartographies of Grace*. Minneapolis, MN: Augsberg Fortress, 2000.

Lawson, Tony. "Feminism, Realism, and Universalism." *Feminist Economics* 5, no. 2 (July 1999): 25–59.

McFague, Sallie. *The Body of God*. London: SCM Press, 1983.

———. *Models of God: Theology for a Nuclear Age*. Philadelphia: Fortress Press, 1987.

Miles, Rebekah L. *The Bonds of Freedom: Feminist Theology and Christian Realism*. New York: American Academy of Religion and Oxford University Press, 2001.

Murdoch, Iris. *Metaphysics as a Guide to Morals*. London: Penguin Books, 1992.

Norwich, Julian of. *Revelations of Divine Love*. Edited by Halcyon Backhouse and Rhona Pipe. London: Hodder and Stoughton, 1987.

O'Connor, Brian. "Adorno and the Problem of Givenness." *Revue Internationale de Philosophie* 63, no. 227 (January 2004): 85–99.

Pohier, Jacques. *God in Fragments*. London: SCM Press, 1985.

Rose, Gillian. *Hegel Contra Sociology*. London: Althone Press, 1981.

Sanford, Stella. *The Metaphysics of Love: Gender and Transcendence in Levinas*. London: Althone Press, 2000.

Smith, James K. A. *Introducing Radical Orthodoxy: Mapping a Post-Secular Theology*. Grand Rapids, MI: Baker Academic, 2004.

Soper, Kate. *What Is Nature?* Oxford: Blackwell, 1995.

Welch, Sharon. *A Feminist Ethic of Risk*. Minneapolis, MN: Fortress Press, 1990.

CHAPTER 4

TRANSCENDENCE AND IMMANENCE

COMING OF AGE IN PHILOSOPHY

Claire Colebrook

Transcendence might appear to be the most philosophical of issues. Critical approaches to philosophy have taken this to be the case. How is it that thought goes beyond itself, and how do we establish legitimate ways of relating to that which transcends thought's own acts? Before defending transcendence *as ethics,* this essay will consider two of the most profound late twentieth-century arguments that urge us to free ourselves from the burden of transcendence: Gilles Deleuze's ethics of "impersonal and pre-individual" singularities (*The Logic of Sense* 145) and Michel Foucault's call to think "the being of man and the being of language" (*The Order of Things* 338).

For Deleuze and Guattari, transcendence is *the* illusion that enslaves thought to notions of a foundation, ground, or presence that would be other than the becomings of life. *Only* philosophy can cure us of this illusion. Philosophy is, or ought to be, a commitment to, and an affirmation of, immanence.[1] Transcendence is not simply an accident or error that befalls thought. On the contrary, the tendency toward the subjection to transcendence is at the heart of thinking, a thinking that has for too long been assumed to be motivated by a "good will" (Deleuze, *Difference and Repetition* 134). That is, as long as we assume that thought is naturally directed to discover truth, and that there is ultimately a single truth toward which all thinking is directed, then we will fail to recognize the constructive, productive, and desiring positivity of thought, wherein desire brings relations into being rather than being determined by already existing terms. To live and make its way in the world, the human organism—the body with organs that folds what the eye sees, the ear hears, and the hand touches around its own point of view—lives the sensibility that affects it as the sensibility *of being* (Deleuze, *Difference and Repetition* 254). Intensities (or the vibrations, pulsations, differences, and becomings of life that are events of variation) are lived as differentiations *of* an extended world. For Deleuze and Guattari, this commitment to the transcendence in intentionality—that experience is always experience *of* a world—is just the error of phenomenology. Insofar as it begins with phenomena, or the appearing of a world to a subject, phenomenology's initial commitment to immanence always places immanence within a subject (*What Is Philosophy?* 171). But, for Deleuze and Guattari, the failure of phenomenology, which began with immanence but ultimately ascribed that immanence to a horizon of "the lived," is not an error that can be contained within philosophy. Even before philosophy commits the error of transcendence by regarding the world of intensities as grounded on a "One," or an "in itself," history tends toward a laziness, stupidity, and violence that cannot live without the solace of foundations. This capacity for thought to enslave itself to grounds or axioms reaches its highest pitch in capitalism, which is at once a refusal of transcendent bodies—such as the king or state—but a return of thought's enslavement to what is not itself in the logic of exchange. With the axiomatic of capitalism, we have arrived at immanence, for we have stopped believing in the world (Deleuze, *Cinema* 2) and cynically subject ourselves to the fatalism that there is nothing more than the circulation of one global system. But this mode of capitalist immanence, while it frees itself from a directly transcendent ground, nevertheless precludes radical immanence. With the resignation that there is nothing other than the system of exchange, and the acceptance that nothing is or has a proper territory, we once again subject thought to a single logic (if not a single transcendent substance; Deleuze and Guattari, *Anti-Oedipus* 245).

According to Deleuze and Guattari, there is a tendency within thought to abandon its own force and subject itself to transcendent figures and axioms. This is neither tragic nor specifically human. Indeed, they provide a general logic (applicable to all life) that would account for the emergence of transcendence. Life organizes itself through territorialization, or the production of relations and terms; deterritorialization occurs when that field or distribution is subordinated or subjected to another term or terms; language is, for example, a deterritorialization that allows the sounds of the voice to be taken as signs of some intent. Transcendence is the illusion that occurs through metalepsis. Instead of beginning with territorialization, or the production of relations and terms through difference, and then seeing how those relations can enter into relation with other systems, we regard one term as foundational, and see all systems as emanating from that privileged point. Thus, with language, we could center sounds, gestures, bodies, and intentions on "man" as a signifying animal, who would then be seen as the cause of all systems of relations and would, therefore, reterritorialize difference onto some ultimate ground. Deleuze and Guattari describe territorialization in the "art" of the Australian *Scenopoetes dentirostis* bird, whose ongoing life and individuation take the form of assembling sensation into a distinct dwelling;[2] thus territories, or the creation of relations from "formed matters" are the essential art of life—the "refrain," or point of view, that allows the virtual potentiality of life to take on some form of actuality. If the bird's song could be repeated by a composer or another animal, then it would have been liberated from its territory. All art is, or should aim for, "higher deterritorialization," which is the liberation of sensations from any specific body. But reterritorialization is transcendence: a single point of view or body is not situated in relation to sensations but is seen as the eminent cause, ground, or author of sensation. The figure of man as a representational animal is therefore the transcendent figure par excellence and comes to the fore with an accompanying politics of late liberal capitalism: we have no being, essence, or transcendent law *other than* our capacity to exchange (sounds, words, money, commodities, women, images, etc.).

According to Deleuze and Guattari, philosophy has missed a series of historical opportunities to express the intensity that is life. Philosophy, they argue, fails to realize its highest potential as long as the intensity of life—the experience or events from which subjects and objects are constituted—is regarded as immanent *to* some already constituted or constituting subject. There was, Deleuze suggests, a radical potentiality in Platonism's positing of Ideas as pure potentials from which actual experience and the given world were effected (*Difference and Repetition* 127). That power was abandoned when Aristotle grounded the differences of life on categories of ordering (categories that accorded with the subject of common sense). There was a later possibility in the history of philosophy for a thought of radical immanence with Kant. The synthesized world that transcends "us" cannot be grounded on some knowable subject within the world. However, Kant's "fracturing" of the self who can no longer be the substance that precedes experience is again lost when the transcendental subject is claimed as the necessarily presupposed origin from which synthesis proceeds (*Difference and Repetition* 87). Finally, with phenomenology and its refusal of the transcendental subject who would be prior to or other than "the lived," there is still a failure to release thought from transcendence. For the lived is the flowing, synthesized world as given to an active and intentional humanity (even if the human is no longer a body "in" the world but a lived body that is the ultimate horizon of all experience).

Notoriously, Deleuze and Guattari begin the liberation from being with "becoming-woman." Although closely affiliated with becoming-child, becoming-animal, becoming-imperceptible, and even a becoming-East (away from the occident) or becoming-West (toward the frontier), their creation of the concept of becoming-woman indicates that the problem of transcendence is sexed (*A Thousand Plateaus* 276). That is, with capitalism and the representing "man" subjected to the laws of language and the oedipal triangle, it is woman—as some seemingly prohibited beyond—that functions as the contemporary fantasy of transcendence. Although Deleuze and Guattari consider modes of territorialization that are nonhuman, it is the modern advent of man (who regards himself as the conjunction of all the syntheses of life) that allows all difference to be referred back to one seemingly immanent flow (while that immanence is always the immanence *of* capital, the system of labor and bodies that opens exchange in general). The sexed nature of transcendence is apparent in the ways in which all differences are related back to an organizing principle, be it the economic principle of exchange, the psychoanalytic principle of desire, or the philosophical principles of reason and good sense. That subjection to transcendence is not a solely philosophical error but is lived in the nightmare of oedipalism, with subjects neurotically subordinated to one matrix of desire beyond which is supposedly the chaotic night of the undifferentiated. Modern man is coupled to a world now lived as known only through the signifier—a transcendence that can be desired but never attained. Philosophy, however, can create concepts, such as becoming-woman, which liberate thought from its bourgeois figures of upright reason and common sense. Indeed, 'becoming-woman' is both a *created concept* and a concept required by thinking in order to become creative. Woman, as Lacan reminds us, "does not exist." Deleuze and Guattari take this up critically; all we know in modernity is oedipal man, with woman as that unthinkable prohibited beyond.

Because she is not yet actualized, because we all live the neurosis of Oedipus and the signifier (we are all reasoning men), she is the "key to all becomings." As long as philosophy subjects itself to one actualized figure—the man of reason who recognizes a common world there for us all—it will be enslaved to the illusion of transcendence. This is the illusion that the force of thought, the force of life, might be grounded upon a norm that guides the will (such a will would be reactive, rather than actively affirming itself as that which is nothing other than will to power; Deleuze, *Nietzsche and Philosophy*). Becoming-woman is a *concept* because it does not name an already existing grouping of bodies (bodies as substantive beings that then have the attributes of being female), for becoming-woman operates *intensively*: creating a new orientation or sense. If the *cogito* was a concept because it linked thinking with doubting, with objectifying one's body, with imagining oneself as mad, becoming woman is linked with imagining what it might be to perceive as an animal or as a child and ultimately what it might be to perceive from the point of view of the eternal. Becoming-woman is a movement, or infinitive, connected to becoming-animal and becoming-child, both of which are indications of styles and manners of perception that are not perceptions *of* this one common world to be communicated by one mutually recognizing man.

Philosophy, then, creates becoming-woman to realize its highest potential. And becoming-woman, alongside the molar movement of feminist politics, enables life to be released from disjunctive gendered coordinates (man *or* woman) and then opens the way to "a thousand tiny sexes." Becoming-woman requires a liberation from transcendence, entailing a style of thought that encounters events as intensities, not as beings *for* a recognizing, representing, signifying man. Equally, though, release from transcendence requires becoming-woman: no longer thinking the world as it is there *for me*, as necessarily synthesized from the point of view that represents and judges.

If philosophy, becoming-woman, and immanence are intensively intertwined in Deleuze and Guattari, they are no less insistently placed in mutual exclusion by Michel Foucault. In *The History of Sexuality*, volume 1, Foucault regards the interpretation of the self through sexuality and desire—or the idea of a preceding substance that the self might interpret—as a specifically debilitating mode of selfhood. Although they did not appeal to sexuality as an underlying normality, Deleuze and Guattari nevertheless insist that attention ought to be paid to *desire* (or the force from which relations emerge), rather than *power* (the grid of relations; Deleuze and Guattari, *A Thousand Plateaus* 531). For all their similarities, it was Foucault's commitment to the immanence of relations that marked his difference from Deleuze and Deleuze and Guattari. Power is known as distributed through bodies and events; indeed, power is just this distributive field, not a substance that exists in itself. Foucault does not only not inquire about power or life "in itself," for there is no "in itself," only a series of relations. Foucault does not posit any desire from which such distributions would be actualized. Desire, for Deleuze and Guattari, would not transcend or be prior to relations but would also never be exhausted by relations. Although Foucault does not target Deleuze's transcendental empiricism—a transcendental that does not exist outside the given but nevertheless remains as a virtual opening within the given (Deleuze, *Difference and Repetition* 38)—he does argue that the transcendental tradition is one more endeavor in a history of the subjection to transcendence, an "ethics of knowledge," and a "logophobia" (a resistance to thinking language in its own distinction (Foucault, *The Archaeology of Knowledge*) Foucault relates, in a critical and effective genealogy, a shift from a time when the force of speech and language was not referred to some external criteria of truth. Foucault also suggests that a time may come when we might overcome "man" (the being who at once recognizes himself as empirically determined but who can also discern the historical conditions from which that determination unfolds). The animal who is at once located within the world, yet who also functions as the point of view from which the logic of the world emerges—the man of phenomenology—may recede. And this would allow for an immanent ethics of experimentation. Philosophy, or the transcendental enterprise of tracing the conditions of experience from a given human experience, would be transformed and possibly surpassed by modes of writing no longer subordinated to anything other than the force of utterance. Unlike other normalizing and transcendent grounds (such as our sexual or living being in modernity), the experimentations of language would, for Foucault, be liberated from foundationalism, precisely because language occurs as an ongoing, dynamic, and forceful series of relations, never directly reducible to a substance.

Man, then, would appear to be at the heart of the logic of transcendence in its modern form. Liberation from normative images of man would open us to the immanence of the superman (Deleuze, *Foucault*). Man would not be this or that specified, delimited, and worldly being but that strange animal who at once regards himself as a potentiality for self-creation and whose very being as this pure potentiality cannot be grounded on any normalizing or transcendent end. The turn to immanence, or the liberation of potentiality and becoming from anything other than itself, would appear to be compatible with, and perhaps necessary for, a feminist politics. But feminist politics, as becoming-woman, or as the overcoming of man, would be the destruction of transcendence, a tirelessly critical reaction against the normalizing figure of humanity.

Let us summarize then before moving on: Both Deleuze and Foucault regard transcendence as thought's subjection to its own created images, while forgetting the status of those images *as created*. In this respect, Deleuze and Foucault continue a history of philosophy that has been critical of transcendence, or thought's tendency to emasculate and passify itself before its own productions. Transcendence, as a moment of inert, unthinking, and malevolent stupidity, has been figured as a mode of stupidity both within philosophy and as a charge against philosophy. For Foucault, it is the institutionalization of philosophy's notion of transcendent truth, rather than truth as an event of active and explicitly forceful rhetoric, that is tied to a steady process of normalization. This does not mean that Foucault is a straightforward or simple relativist, for the "games of truth" that allow for true and false statements are constrained by the order of bodies and relations at any given time and are inflected by the various relations between the history of truth practices and its relations to an "outside" (which, in turn, varies according to the "historical a priori"). Although history is far from being a unified passage toward an increasingly restrictive modernity, it is the subjection to transcendence, or the idea that thought directs itself to some ground from which truth issues forth, that must be overcome by thinking the *being* of language. Far from language being the expression of, label for, or mediation of some already given outside world, we need to examine the ways in which the relation between thought and the unthought, the interior and exterior, or "man" and the world he represents, unfolds from events and styles. Such an examination is necessary for Foucault, precisely because as long as we maintain the illusion of transcendence we will see ethics as a question of knowledge and not—as it really is—as an ongoing series of practical and productive procedures. Philosophy, as the enterprise that would master or tame language as some vehicle for the expression of truth, must yield to a confrontation with literature and games of truth: both of which no longer strive to recognize, to discover, or to unveil the true but begin from the relations from which truth is effected.

Thus, with both Deleuze and Guattari and Foucault, transcendence is targeted as at once the symptom of thought's capacity for self-enslavement but also—through the diagnosis of transcendence—

as a means by which thought can come into its own power. Whereas Foucault would liberate thinking from philosophy as a transcendental enterprise and instead focus on immanent practices and the concomitant production of selves, Deleuze and Guattari regard philosophy as the true path for thinking the plane of immanence. For Deleuze and Guattari, philosophy's proper mode as creator of concepts must liberate itself from opinion and from actualized states of affairs. Concepts do not name sets of extended objects but are intensive lines of flight, manners, styles, or "arrows" that allow thought to move once again, not in some natural or normative milieu, but in a "higher deterritorialization" that extends the potential for thinking beyond any given end or actualized body. Philosophy therefore bears within its own history both glimpses of its proper potential—those moments when philosophers *think* by creating orientations or possibilities that are not merely continuations of some perceived nature—and a constant fall into stupidity, opinion, and transcendence. The latter occurs philosophically as a subjection to an "image of thought," or the notion that we must begin thinking from some idea of reason, recognition, or rightness.

This notion of transcendence as the submission of thought to images not of its own explicit and self-inaugurating power may arrive at its clearest articulation in Deleuze and Guattari but has a long-standing history (as Deleuze and Guattari acknowledge) within philosophy. In *Difference and Repetition*, Deleuze seizes on Duns Scotus, Spinoza, and Nietzsche as philosophers of univocity: against a notion that we know actual beings only as expressions of, or modes of, some prior or preeminent substance we need to think that all being is said in the same voice (38–39). There is as much reality in a smile, a color, a mood, or a potentiality as there is in an atom, a table, a sound wave, or a quark. The idea that we can speak of being or substance *only* with regard to that which requires no other being in order to be, and that we should speak of secondary and dependent qualities as having being only by *analogy* is an idea that Deleuze regards as properly overcome only with Nietzsche's move toward prepersonal singularities. This, in turn, has ethical implications, for Deleuze regards the recognition of immanence as the first step toward a new pragmatics. This would not be a pragmatism in which truth was determined by its fit or suitability for "us" but would place fidelity to events and intensities as the primary aim of all life and thought. Philosophy ought to be fashioned in accord with its capacity to mobilize this desiring and trans-human life.

Despite a series of important differences, we can note a move away from transcendence toward immanence both in contemporary theory and in popular culture. Giorgio Agamben has, in a number of ways, insisted that potentiality needs to be liberated from the notion that the political space is the realization or actualization of some governing human norm and that "man" unfolds most authentically in those moments of pure potentiality wherein he is nothing other than the opening of political space in general: politics not as the realization of what man properly is *in* this world but man as the unfolding of world, as one who emerges as human only in the creation in common of a world (*Means without End*). Jean-Luc Nancy, less concerned with pure potentiality and more attentive to the radical finitude and singularity of each and every being, nevertheless marks out a project of thinking that is freed from the notion that there is anything like being in general, or being as such, which would reveal itself in beings but always be radically other than any given being. Perhaps the most significant "hybrid" form of the critique of transcendence would be Michael Hardt and Antonio Negri's *Empire*. Although *Empire* is heavily indebted to both authors' weighty philosophical writings and hardly a blockbuster best seller, it does effect a transition from the philosophy of immanence to political programs and slogans. The most telling of the latter would be Hardt and Negri's call to the multitudes to become "homo homo humanity squared." There should be no idea of humanity other than that which emerges from production, and production itself ought to be oriented today not toward the creation of external goods but to nothing other than relations among producers. A key example of such an opportunity of immanent production for Hardt and Negri would be what they refer to as "affective labour": liberated from material production, the service industries (and particularly those now operating through the internet rather than locatable factory floors) enable forms of collective self-definition and communication that ought to be liberated from the axioms of capital.

Hardt and Negri's emphasis on multitudes, on political communities, and on collective action taps into a much broader rhetoric, tradition, and imagery of emancipation that allows us to consider the sex and gender of immanence and transcendence. For it has always been the case that the figure of "man" has at once been identified as the proper site for the return to immanence: "man" is that being who creates and constitutes the world from himself but then forgets that creation and enslaves himself to his own imaginative productions. This is certainly the case in all forms of philosophical humanism but even in popular traditions that would free humanity of sexual stereotypes and gender norms. Hardt and Negri's *Empire* is at once a sophisticated metaphysical critique of transcendence (and its notion of a grounding substance) and a populist call to liberate ourselves from all imposed images. Hardt and Negri's intervention allow us to consider immanence and transcendence not as philosophical but as popular political problems, allowing in turn a passage from the critique of metaphysical transcendence to the problem of imposed and alienating images. Transcendence, as philosophy has defined it, takes the form of subjection to norms, to givens, to opaque figures, or to unthought assumptions. But the capacity for thinking subjects to be governed by alien or alienated motivations has formed a central strand of feminist thinking. Unless we assume a radically liberal mode of feminism—where all subjects are recognized as nothing other than a formal capacity for decision making, with the body as the vehicle or site for the mind—then we need to explain how criticism can at once appeal to the presently unjust nature of social relations without assuming that individuals will necessarily decide to be free. That is, can we appeal to revolution or a mode of life *other than the present* if we do not have transcendent criteria? If we do assume that thinking should not be marked, invaded, or subjected to anything other than itself—if thought is self-inauguration with no reference beyond itself—then we at one and the same time arrive at radical immanence, pure potentiality, and (I would argue) a highly masculinist conception of the subject. That is, the turn to immanence—so often seen as a rejection of the subject as a ground or foundation, becomes a heightened form of subjectivism in its refusal to recognize *any* otherness that would deflect thought from its own self-making. And this self-making subject has always been, as Luce Irigaray argued in *Speculum of the Other Woman*, a masculine subject who recognizes no mediation or body in its capacity to give birth to and originate itself. To understand how immanence, as it operates at a popular, political, and moral level has both a sex and gender, let us consider three "problems" from the current terrain of sexed ethics: beauty, religion, and pornography. To give some indication of my conclusion, I will suggest now that these three problems concern transcendence. At least, they *ought* to concern transcendence. However, the way in which these problems are debated and defined has all too often already assumed an immanent approach. That is, beauty is a tyranny or "myth" for women today *because* beauty is a relation to an ideal that is not one's own. The striving for beauty can only be acceptable, not if it is a transcendent ideal, but if it is an immanent practice. Religion, similarly, is defined as a negation of the self's powers if it is a subjection to transcendence but acceptable and enabling if we look at the positive practices, groupings, and styles of selfhood that religious activity enables. Finally, pornography, as it is figured in feminist antiporn discourse, is targeted as a medium in which women are objects, not subjects, and in which male desire is reified by being oriented toward clichéd images of women. Sexuality proper, it is assumed, must not be governed in advance by images or norms; instead, sexuality should unfold in relation to nothing other than the relation to the other, without being determined in advance or deflected by anything other than the coupling of desire. The increasingly shrill insistence that the self's submission to images or figures is a form of alienation should prompt us to ask: Is there not something profoundly *infantile* in this refusal of transcendence? The idea that the self ought to be subjected to no image or power other than that of its own choosing, the idea that one's world is always already one's own, and that others occur as nothing more than occasions for unfolding relations with no prior or impeding determinant: is not this refusal of that which is radically other than the self a denial of contingency, risk, and exposure?

First, beauty: Mary Wollstonecraft was one of the first to argue for the political, and politically sexed, problem of beauty. As long as women defined themselves according to physical criteria of attractiveness, and in relation to men's desire for submissive, weak, and emotional women, they would not only be precluded from the genuinely political processes of education, reason, and improvement, but also from the production of properly rational social bonds. Instead of two individuals negotiating decisions in concert, marriages would be made up of domineering masters and unthinking slaves; the primary social unit would have tyranny at its heart. One might suggest that prior to Wollstonecraft the great meditations on beauty did not concern themselves with self-definition and social relations; beauty had, from Plato's *Symposium* to the formulation of aesthetics as a discipline, been a necessarily transcendent ideal. That is, beauty would figure, intimate, or express a pureness, harmony, or accord that transcends any worldly particular. Beauty is either some ideal toward which desire is directed, *or* beauty occurs when we encounter that which seems to express the perfect harmony of the world in relation to our finite experience. Even after Wollstonecraft, the great Romantic meditation on beauty, John Keats's "Ode on a Grecian Urn," couples beauty with truth *and* with a certain impossibility: Fleeting experience intimates beauty only in its imminent decay, and it is only with the freezing of such evanescence in a timeless figure or representation that we can grasp beauty as such.

For Wollstonecraft, beauty becomes a problem precisely because her liberal feminism demands that women *not* be passively submitted to norms and relations beyond their own reason. As long as women are valued for being beautiful, they will be objects, not subjects, of desire; and as long as men objectify women, they too will relate their desire to reified bodies, not to reasoning individuals. We can note, then, that it is with the liberal insistence on the self-inaugurating subject (and rational immanence) that any norm or ideal beyond the self becomes necessarily alienating. This allows us, I would argue, to see the ways in which the problem of beauty, as played out in popular culture, presupposes an increasingly intense turn to immanence. According to the increasingly intense refusal of transcendence, the self ought not to be defined or subjected to any ideal other than its own praxis; *if* the desire for beauty is at all legitimate or permissible, then it is so only to the extent to which it is not a passively incorporated ideal—the self orienting itself to some higher idea of what it might become—but an actively managerial process. As any series of makeover programs or beauty campaigns have artfully insisted, beauty practices can be seen either as imposed ideals that rob the self of its autonomy or as ways in which the self recreates and makes itself, with reference to nothing other than its own self-fashioning. In the popular media, much is often made of increasingly stringent ideals of beauty: This is nowhere clearer than in the increased attention paid to body images, with the assumption that the body is now, more than ever, subjected to images and ideals not of its own *and* that such ideals are increasingly alien and unattainable. But was it ever the case that beauty was immanent/imminent and attainable? Is the incantation that Marilyn Monroe was a size 16, or that Rubens's females were fleshy, really any help in bridging the distance between ideals of beauty and the everyday bodies we inhabit? Is it really the case that beauty has become tyrannical because its ideals are stringent? Doesn't the tyranny lie in refusing all relation to ideals, insisting that whatever images of beauty are set before us they must also be nothing other than what we already (potentially) are?

The feminist criticisms of the "beauty myth" that would have us return to an authentic mode of self-definition against the beauty industry presuppose immanence as an unquestioned ethical ideal. The same applies to antiporn discourse, both in its radical feminist mode, in which porn is attacked because it depicts (dominating) male desires for women rather than women as they define themselves (see Dworkin) *and* in the more sophisticated philosophical accounts. Rae Langton and Caroline West have used a complex combination of Kantian ethics and David Lewis's philosophy of language to argue that pornography objectifies women, first by presenting the unchallenged assumption of women as passive objects and then allowing that conversational maneuver to proceed without comment and without women as interlocutors. The problem with pornography is its unquestioned and passively assumed presupposition that women are objects, not subjects, of discourse. But what such a criticism of pornography *in general* assumes is that our relations to images always ought to be one of immanent and self-critical conversation and that relations among persons ought not to be deflected by any figure or transcendence that cannot be claimed by reason. One other criticism of pornography is not its treatment of persons as objects but its focus on objects—body parts—at the expense of persons. But such a critique once again assumes that something like a relation to persons as such is possible, *without* something like a defining or marking trait. To return to Irigaray's insistently transcendent approach to ethical relations, we might note that Irigaray is not simply critical that a certain part of the body—the phallus—has defined bodies in general; her criticism is directed at the exclusion of other bodily modalities, such as the notorious lips that in touching each other without active and passive division allow for a different consideration of bodily relations. But women's bodies here would possess a genre, a way of considering their own being beyond each individual body, and that genre would be defined less through the general notion of the person and more through each body's forming of itself through figures. It is this recognition of transcendence in relation that would allow us to consider beauty, not as a necessarily alien imposition so much as an ideal that allows bodies of women to recognize themselves in relation, and to also allow for erotic discourses that would not see an attention to bodies and their differences as reifications of some properly disembodied subject.

Finally, in debates over secularism and rights, an opposition is frequently assumed between rights on the one hand, where one appeals to the ideally inalienable self whose desires ought not to be determined or delimited by arbitrary particularity, and religious respect on the other. Even the complex work of Judith Butler assumes that one must *both* submit to some form of normativity or transcendence to be recognized as human *and* suffer from the loss or mourning that such a subjection to norms requires. In response to such a logic that would regard submission to transcendent norms as an infraction on the self's potentiality, Saba Mahmood has argued for the positivity of religious ethics. Looking at the ways in which religious practices enable modes of subject position, she insists that we should see religion less as a transcendent imposition upon subjects whose autonomy ought to be effected through performances that destabilize the enabling matrices that allow for recognition and, instead, regard piety as a mode of positive subject production. What Mahmood's defense of piety brings to light, I would argue, is that there has been a certain horror directed toward transcendence, evidenced in Butler's highly influential account of the self as being enabled by the very transcendent structures that also account for its ultimate and inevitable subjection. Mahmood's defense of some versions of Islam as *immanent*—as having less to do with subjects who believe and repeat than it does with styles of life that enable subject formation—indicates just how completely immanence has become not so much a norm as the only possible way of approaching normativity.

The overwhelming assumption both in contemporary theory and in popular culture is that immanence is not just the only critical, responsible, justifiable, and *mature* approach to ethics but also that such a refusal of transcendence would be necessarily feminist or antimasculinist. Since Kant, philosophical maturity has been aligned with "freedom from imposed tutelage." What follows from the Kantian model of enlightenment is a critical approach that recognizes that in the absence of given norms or foundations one is required to give a law to oneself. In recent approaches to normativity, this Kantian emphasis on the refusal of assumed or imposed figures has devolved upon the self: "the only normativity to which I am subject is the ongoing norm of selfhood" (see Korsgaard with Cohen). If I were not to act according to *who I am*, then I could no longer claim to be a self; indeed, I could no longer claim. We are postmetaphysical, today, only insofar as we have the courage to act and speak without any support beyond ourselves. Such a maneuver might at first be seen as tantamount to feminism: If there is no law of humanity to which ethics might appeal, if there is no *man of reason* but only reason as an ongoing and communal procedure that can appeal to nothing other than itself, then we are liberated from implicitly gendered accounts of human normality. For, as many feminists have noted, appeal to humanity has always been an appeal to *man*. Accordingly, if we abandon such normative and substantive concepts of the subject, we are also, through processes of community and interaction, brought closer to all those ideals that have often been associated with "the feminine." For, it might be argued, women have been defined both ideally and empirically as more oriented to negotiation, care, and otherness and less inclined to follow transcendent rules or procedures (see Gilligan). Although feminism might appear, then, to be essentially immanent—in its resistance both to images of "man" and to strict moral logics—even those relational ethics of care, or ecofeminist returns to the nurturance of the earth, rely on the respect and recognition of what exceeds the self, as transcendent.

I wish to conclude by taking up my earlier claim that this seemingly mature, immanent, and protofeminist approach to the ethical actually suffers from an inability to deal with that which is radically resistant to, yet undeniably constitutive of, the self and that such a refusal of transcendence is a form of infantilism. By infantilism, I refer to the mythic image of the infant, perhaps best described by Freud's phrase of "his majesty the baby" (Freud 48–49). The ideal child is at once fully open to the world—for the infant is not yet subjected to all the clichés, conventions, and repressions of maturity—but is also a world unto himself, for he is not yet aware of all the frustrations of contingency, others, and temporality. The infant, we might say, is pure existence, pure potentiality, not yet determined as this or that located, delimited, or identified being.[3] If we no longer believe in a God who would at once be capable of creating a world from himself while also remaining radically free from the necessity of the world, we nevertheless harbor the idea of the child: that prelinguistic, presocial microcosm whose loss and seduction in adulthood we constantly mourn. The yearning for immanence, as is made explicit in the work of Deleuze and Guattari, is a yearning for becoming-child. But the links between immanence, childhood, *and* a certain notion of the feminine are also common in popular culture. It was in Romantic poetry that the idealization of childhood was celebrated as a moment when one was not yet burdened with the inauthenticity of social convention, and it was this moment of unselfconscious being-at-one with the world that was also tied to a notion of feminine plenitude. Freudian psychoanalysis is at once an expression and a critique of this striving for immanence, this desire that one's world be nothing other than one's own world.

To gesture toward what might be other than this infantilism, we might return to two of the scandalous charges brought against the philosophy of Irigaray: essentialism and heterosexism. First, let's deal with essentialism, as it is this supposedly unthinking commitment to an ideal of the feminine that marked Irigaray's radical attempt to write and think through an entirely different modality from Western subjectivism (see Moi 126–48). The subject—translated from the Latin *subjectum*—is that which grounds, precedes, and underlies all thought and difference; when man becomes "the subject," he becomes the sole point from which representation and relations can be thought. While there have been a number of sophisticated defenses and nuanced readings of the way in which Irigaray redefines her supposedly essential feminism, I would like to consider the attack on her putative essentialism as symptomatic and see her philosophy as a way of thinking beyond a knee-jerk antiessentialism. Why would essentialism necessarily be a problem? By what right does one assert the prima facie value of antiessentialism and regard essentialism as an *essentially* unphilosophical endeavor? If philosophy has always been a subjectivism this is also because, as Irigaray's readings note, the trajectory of the philosophical text has been one of incorporation: all the figures, media, and times through which the thinking of the text takes place must be regarded as nothing more than actualization of the subject's own potentiality for self-making. What cannot be considered or encountered is that which remains radically resistant to the self's existence.

To consider that selves might not be pure existence, that they might have a weight or potentiality that is not absolutely subject to the pure event of becoming, is to consider difference. It was Jean-Paul Sartre who, in *Being and Nothingness*, diagnosed the condition of bad faith as one in which the self denies aspects of its being, *including* one's facticity. Sartre famously declared that existence precedes essence and that one's actual relations to situations and others were the means for, rather than determined by, one's unfolding identity (see *Existentialism Is a Humanism*). But Sartre also noted that the desire to be a being for-itself and in-itself, to be both absolutely freely self-determining *and* not subjected to the burdens of decision and contingency, was a desire to be God. Such a desire was impossible (according to Sartre) and, I would argue, *infantile* insofar as it is a desire for omnipotence and relations that are ultimately nonrelations. Irigaray's attention to the difference of the sexes, to the ways in which one's autonomy or notion of self required recognizing that one differed from another in genre, was a way of acknowledging that the self is not a world unto itself. Relations to others, to time, to the sensible, and to being, do not unfold from an undetermined point of pure decision but take place through different modalities of becoming.

Essentialism, then, can only be thought of as the enemy of thought, if thinking and existing are defined as properly immanent; for, in such cases, the appeal to essence—to that which persists and insists beyond nominalism—would be an appeal to that which transcends thought. If, however, we begin thinking not with ontology (with the self that is pure existence and is the site for the unfolding of all that is), but with ethics, or the place, locale, and relations of bodies, then we also have to acknowledge that thinking is traversed by powers not its own. It may still not be the case that thinking unfolds from essence: that there is some already given logic—a transcendent norm—that one must follow. But it may nevertheless be possible to consider the encounter with essence—with that which is, which is not yet thought's own—as the relation to transcendence that is the very possibility of the ethical. Irigaray's definition of the divine, as a genre or mode of one's being that is at once not yet oneself but nevertheless an ideal toward which the self might be oriented, offers a new ethics of transcendence and a new mode of essence. First, essence is not an appeal to what one is, or even what one properly is, but to an ideal. The self oriented to the divine is a self in becoming, but that becoming is not a "becoming-woman" or "becoming-child" that *counters* all actuality; instead, it is a recognition of the weight of being, of the ways in which our relations to our selves are always already made possible through figures, styles, and transcendent images.

Second, we might conclude by thinking the problem of heterosexism in Irigaray's work and why such a notion should be so immediately regarded as blind to the properly open potentiality of sexualities. Now, of course, any ethics or philosophy that regarded the only proper and authentic relation to others as necessarily heterosexual would not only be limited, it would also have failed to take on board Irigaray's criticism of subjectivism. The ethics of sexual difference stresses that one recognizes that all recognition or relations to others are inextricably bound with a certain intransitivity: it is not just the case, as in liberal ethics, that conversations must respect the other's freedom as much as my own. What is more important is that my openness to an other, my relation to any other, must consider that the other has an entirely different mode of relation. Thus, we are neither a fraternity of fatherless self-legislators, liberated from all ground, past, and determination beyond our own being; nor are we the standard heterosexual couple of complementarity, where one sex's rationality is tempered by another's compassion. On the contrary, every relation to an other is a relation to a self who is oriented to a transcendence, who understands their own being through a genre, a mode, a style, or a divine sense of that which is other than their self-present immediacy. This is why Irigaray begins with *at least two* sexes. Sexual difference cannot be absolutely and infinitely divisible because sexual difference is transcendence—that mode or genre of my being that marks the style of relations to others. To preclude sexual difference is to deny that the self's relations are not inflected by determinations, decisions, and rhythms that are beyond the subject's pure potentiality.

NOTES

1. "Whenever there is transcendence, vertical Being, imperial State in the sky or on earth, there is religion; and there is Philosophy whenever there is immanence, even if it functions as arena for the agon and rivalry." Gilles Deleuze and Felix Guattari, *What Is Philosophy?* trans. Graham Burchill and Hugh Tomlinson (London: Verso, 1994), 43.
2. "This emergence of pure sensory qualities is already art, not only in the treatment of external materials but in the body's postures and colors, in the songs and cries that mark out the territory"; ibid., 184.
3. This is the sense in which Giorgio Agamben has recently appealed to the ideal of childhood and play, an ideal in which events and actions are not yet subjected to some end or function beyond their pure present (*Profanations*).

BIBLIOGRAPHY

Agamben, Giorgio. *Means without End: Notes on Politics.* Translated by Vincenzo Binetti and Cesare Casarino. Minneapolis: University of Minnesota Press, 2000.

———. *Profanations.* Translated by Jeff Fort. New York: Zone Books, 2007.

Butler, Judith. *Giving an Account of Oneself.* New York: Fordham University Press, 2005.

Deleuze, Gilles. *Cinema 2: The Time-Image.* Translated by Hugh Tomlinson and Barbara Habberjam. Minneapolis: University of Minnesota, 1989.

———. *Difference and Repetition.* Translated by Paul Patton. New York: Columbia University Press, 1994.

———. *Foucault.* Translated by Sea?n Hand. Minneapolis: University of Minnesota Press, 1988.

———. *The Logic of Sense.* Translated by Mark Lester with Charles Stivale. Edited by Constantin V. Boundas. London: Continuum, 2001.

———. *Nietzsche and Philosophy.* Translated by Hugh Tomlinson. London: Athlone, 1983.

Deleuze, Gilles, and Felix Guattari. *Anti-Oedipus.* Translated by Robert Hurley, Mark Seem, and Helen R. Lane, London: Continuum, 2004.

———. *A Thousand Plateaus.* Translated by Brian Massumi. Minneapolis: University of Minnesota Press, 1987.

———. *What Is Philosophy?* Translated by Graham Burchill and Hugh Tomlinson. London: Verso, 1994.

Dworkin, Andrea. *Pornography: Men Possessing Women.* New York: Perigee Books, 1981.

Foucault, Michel. *The Archaeology of Knowledge.* Translated by A. M. Sheridan Smith. New York: Pantheon Books, 1972.

———. *The History of Sexuality*. Vol. 1, *An Introduction*. Translated by Robert Hurley. New York: Pantheon Books, 1978.

———. *The Order of Things: An Archaeology of the Human Sciences*. New York: Random House, 1970.

Freud, Sigmund. "On Narcissism." In *Collected Papers*, edited by Joan Riviere and James Strachey, 4:48–49. New York: Basic Books, 1959.

Gilligan, Carol. *In a Different Voice: Psychological Theory and Women's Development*. Cambridge, MA: Harvard University Press, 1982.

Hardt, Michael, and Antonio Negri. *Empire*. Cambridge, MA: Harvard University Press, 2000.

Irigaray, Luce. *Speculum of the Other Woman*. Translated by Gillian C. Gill. Ithaca, NY: Cornell University Press, 1985.

Kant, Immanuel. *Foundations of the Metaphysics of Morals and, What Is Enlightenment?* Translated by Lewis White Beck. 2nd ed., rev. ed. New York: Macmillan, 1990.

Korsgaard, Christine M., with G. A. Cohen. *The Sources of Normativity*. Edited by Onora O'Neill. Cambridge: Cambridge University Press, 1996.

Langton, Rae, and Caroline West. "Scorekeeping in a Pornographic Language Game." *Australasian Journal of Philosophy* 77 (1999): 303–19.

Mahmood, Saba. *Politics of Piety: The Islamic Revival and the Feminist Subject*. Princeton, NJ: Princeton University Press, 2005.

Moi, Toril. *Sexual/Textual Politics: Feminist Literary Theory*. London: Routledge, 1995.

Nancy, Jean-Luc. *Being Singular Plural*. Translated by Robert D. Richardson and Anne E. O'Byrne. Stanford, CA: Stanford University Press, 2000.

Sartre, Jean-Paul. *Being and Nothingness*. Translated by Hazel Barnes. New York: Philosophical Library, 1956.

———. *Existentialism is a Humanism*. Translated by Carol Macomber. Edited by John Kulka. New Haven, CT: Yale University Press, 2007.

Wollstonecraft, Mary. *A Vindication of the Rights of Woman*. Edited by Miriam Brody. Harmondsworth: Penguin Books, 2004.

CHAPTER 5

WOMEN, SACRIFICE, AND TRANSCENDENCE

Morny Joy

To achieve a different social order, women need a religion, a language and a currency of exchange, or else a non-market economy. These conditions are in fact closely linked.

—Luce Irigaray, *An Ethics of Sexual Difference*

The Western tradition typically represents living energy as sacrificed to spirit, to a truth assimilated to immutable ideals, beyond growth, beyond corporeality; celestial ideals imposed as models so that we all become alike—our sensible, natural and historical differences neutralized.

— Luce Irigaray, *I Love To You*

We've generally located transcendence between the "sky" and us. We should learn to lay it between us. Each one of us is inaccessible to the other, transcendent to him/her.

—Luce Irigaray, *"Why Different?"*

The relationship of women to the divine has been a troubled one in the majority of traditional religions. Women have been denied right of entry to the superior destiny that is associated with transcendence. They have also not been granted, until quite recently, and then only rarely and reluctantly in certain denominations, access to what I term "symbolic status." By symbolic status, I intend to signify a parity of esteem that pertains either to being respected as a religious authority, or to being invested with a mode of religious agency that is most revered in a particular religion. The term, with its symbolic reference, has both psychoanalytic and religious resonances.[1] The pertinent forms of access and religious agency would include the right to study, interpret, and teach sacred texts in their original languages, to officiate at sacred rituals, and to make decisions of a deliberative nature that would have practical applications for adherents of that religion. Such attributes and activities have been mainly the prerogative of men, and many religions still forbid women the means to attain such accomplishments and their accompanying recognition.

This exclusion of women has occurred in the religions affiliated with the Bible, in both its Hebrew and Christian variants, despite the creation story of Genesis 1: 27, where both male and female are made in the image of God. These religions have chosen instead to focus on Genesis 2: 22. Here woman is formed from the rib of Adam and is thus deemed inferior or less perfect in the order of creation. In addition, though there is no scriptural basis for associating the expulsion of the first couple from Eden with a sin of sexuality, especially its seductive or promiscuous aspects—it was women who, in time, were held responsible for the fall from original innocence. Women's purported willful prodigality—whether of body or emotions—has, as a result, been deemed as in need of control. Rules and regulations have been designed by mortal men whose pronouncements even came to have the authority of a divine imperative. In this context, it is not my intention to rehash this unfortunate history, because its consequences are all too evident. My aim is to examine contemporary developments that challenge this perspective.

I will appeal to the phenomenon of sacrifice as a paradigmatic example of the type of exploitative economy that has been imposed on women, and I will examine certain suggestions that are being made today to remedy this situation. My belief is that women have been refused almost uniformly not only symbolic status, but also an ontological integrity. By this I mean that women have been denied both a form of self-determination and affirmation of their own self-worth. In such a sacrificially based economy, women are manipulated in the service of appeasing men's fears or fulfilling their fantasies, which are represented as having resulted from traits specific to women. In my analysis, I will investigate various notions of this sacrificial economy as it is presided over by male control that derives its power from an omnipotent and transcendent God of the same gender. As a principal support in these explorations, I will turn to insights that have been provided by the work of Luce Irigaray. I do realize that unfortunately, due to space constrictions, I will tend to be dealing mainly in generalities. Irigaray's own tendencies in this direction make a more nuanced approach somewhat difficult. I want to make it clear, nonetheless, that I do not agree with her idea that patriarchy, even in the "West," has operated in an identical fashion over the course of history. In responding to Irigaray, I will try to focus specifically on the way the contemporary situation is understood by a number of Western scholars from anthropological, philosophical, and religious backgrounds.

SACRIFICIAL ECONOMIES

At a basic level, one of the main thematic ways to understand the sacrificial role played by women is to focus on the fact that she is often given as an object of exchange in arrangements that are decided without her consent. Women thus represent a medium in transactions that sustain an economy of bartered objects—sacred or otherwise. Since they have not had a say in these negotiations, women are neither in control of their bodies nor their destiny. A dramatic illustration of this phenomenon can be found in the work of the French anthropologist, Claude Lévi-Strauss, who posits that the commercial exchange of women in certain societies is necessary to the latter's smooth functioning. Yet there is a certain irony in his description of the sacrifice that is demanded of women, especially when he rationalizes it as a consequence of the incest prohibition. This is because the realization that it is only women, rather than men, who are asked to make such a sacrifice lurks just beneath the surface of his consciousness. As a good anthropologist, however, he accepts this phenomenon as a given, describing it as if the women themselves had agreed to the arrangement. "The prohibition of incest is less a rule prohibiting marriage with the mother, sister or daughter, than a rule obliging the mother, sister or daughter to be given to others. It is the supreme rule of the gift, and it is clearly in this aspect, too often unrecognized, which allows its nature to be understood" (Lévi-Strauss 481). The problem is that nobody, neither Lévi-Strauss nor his later commentators, seems inclined to identify, let alone begin to question, the origin of this apparently necessary sacrifice that is demanded of women.

Irigaray refers to Lévi-Strauss in "Women on the Market" (Irigaray, *This Sex Which Is Not One*). In this essay, she details the exploitation of women, whom she describes as providing the unacknowledged infrastructure of the entire sociocultural-economic apparatus of patriarchy. Though she specifically faults Lévi-Strauss, Irigaray views the problem as symptomatic of an ingrained masculine disposition to control and manipulate women. Irigaray asks a rhetorical question: "Why exchange women?" She responds herself in a subversive manner, mimicking the voice of Lévi-Strauss: "Because they [women] are 'scarce [commodities]' . . . essential to the life of the group." She then continues her interrogation: "Why this characteristic of scarcity, given the biological equilibrium between male and female births?" In answering this time, Irigaray quotes from Lévi-Strauss: "Because of the 'deep polygamous tendency,' which exists among all men, [and which] always makes the number of available women seem insufficient" (Irigaray, *This Sex Which Is Not One* 170). Irigaray finally poses a number of ironically tinged questions to which again she provides her own countercommentary: "Are men all equally desirable? Do women have no tendency toward polygamy? The good anthropologist does not ask such questions. *A fortiori*: why are men not objects of exchange among women?" (171). Irigaray then concludes by describing this attitude of Lévi-Strauss as indicative of the unfolding of "History" and its universal exploitation of women.

In this analysis, Irigaray adopts a Hegelian custom of referring to "History," though she understands the term from a quite different perspective. This chapter will explore the way Irigaray posits that History must be reconceived so that an acknowledgment of women in their own right will contribute to establishing a new era of History. This new era will not be so one-sided. "We have to acknowledge that official History is partial and slanted. So, it often involves only half of humanity: the men . . . It's important to see how the role of women has been erased in relation to the role of men in the unfolding of History" ('*Why Different?*' 65). Her actual depiction of the unfolding of traditional History reinforces her diagnosis of a sacrificial economy. "All the social regimes of 'History' are based upon the exploitation of one 'class' of producers, namely, women. Their reproductive use value (reproductive of children and of the labour force) and their constitution as exchange value underwrite the symbolic order as such, without any compensation in kind going to them for that 'work'" (*This Sex Which Is Not One* 173; translation amended).

As a consequence, for Irigaray, women cannot "go to market on their own." Her protest against this restriction is to urge women to react and to set up a new economy of their own. "*But what if these 'commodities' refused to go to the 'market'?* What if they maintained 'another' kind of commerce, among themselves?" (196). Such an impetus informs Irigaray's further question: "How, within this society, can women initiate certain rites that allow them to live and become women in all dimensions? How are systems of exchange to be set up *among women?*" (*Sexes and Genealogies* 80). These questions mark the beginning of a constructive phase where Irigaray will encourage women to undermine the present symbolic system and its management of them. In developing this position, Irigaray will thus begin to move away from her earlier criticisms of a patriarchal order, with its deeply embedded male-centered symbolic values, to explore ways that women can reclaim their subjectivity or ontological integrity. In an interview, Irigaray describes what she posits as the three phases of her work that mark this exploration. The first demonstrates "how a single subject, traditionally the masculine subject, had constructed the world according to a single perspective. . . . The second phase . . . [defines] those mediations that could permit the existence of a female subjectivity. . . . The third phase . . . corresponds . . . to the construction of an intersubjectivity respecting sexual difference" (Hirsh and Olson 96–97). The basic issue in this process, which is relevant to my chapter, concerns the liberation of women from this imposed construction of their promiscuity, and their consequent exclusion from parity of symbolic status in religious matters.

These two issues, of man-made attributions and symbolic inferiority, are inherently interrelated, and it is by appreciating their mutual reinforcement that the beginnings of a solution to the problem can be discerned. This is because the notion of women's status as sexual beings who are spiritually imperfect, and thus in need of guidance and control, has permeated all levels of our Western heritage from its origins in ancient religious sources. It has been reinforced by later scriptural depictions and commentaries. This is an area where I believe that secular feminists have underestimated the magnitude of the problem. By simply advocating the outright rejection of religion as outmoded, such feminists fail to appreciate the intensity of the archaic symbolic forces that remain at work graphically depicting women solely as sexual objects. These deeply embedded symbolic mechanisms spring back, like an automatic reflex-action, even in a secular society, whenever women fail to directly confront such basic assumptions. These mechanisms are only too visible in many commercial activities with their proprietary organizations that dominate contemporary culture. Prominent examples include the following:

1. The actual trafficking in women's bodies in the aptly named "sex-trade."
2. The commodity fetishism that controls and regulates the cosmetic, fashion, and plastic surgery industry.
3. The rapes, sexual violence, and murders of women, especially by outraged former partners or spouses, when women end or try to escape from a relationship.
4. The hostile reaction from religious authorities in particular when women assert their own "body-right." This term, coined by Christine Gudorf, a Catholic theologian, refers to the fact that women should be able to make decisions for themselves about their own bodies—a move that has wide-ranging implications, of which freedom to exercise reproductive choice is an important item.[2]

Given the deep-seated nature of these prevailing obsessions, it does not appear to be enough to attempt to rectify the present situation by legal and political means alone, although Irigaray is correct when she declares that women cannot reclaim their subjectivity in a social vacuum. Laws must be enacted to safeguard women's rights on these issues. For Irigaray, such rights would include rights to moral and physical inviolability and rights to voluntary marriage and motherhood. Irigaray also supports the right to distinctive forms of cultural expression in the areas of language, economics, and the sciences.[3] These rights are necessary to protect and foster women's initiatives as they free themselves from the dominant symbolic order that has dictated the terms of their existence, and begin to formulate intimations of a new identity or subjectivity, which amounts to an ontological integrity.

Irigaray's describes her vision of this new culture and its economy:

> It would entail, beyond the enslavement to property, beyond the subject's submission to the object . . . becoming capable of giving and receiving, of being active and passive, of having an intention that stays attuned to interactions, that is, of seeking a new economy of existence or being which is neither that of mastery nor slavery but rather of exchange with no preconstituted object—vital exchange, cultural exchange, of words, gestures etc., an exchange thus able to *communicate* at times, to commune . . . beyond any exchange of objects. What we would be dealing with, then, is the establishment of another era of civilization, or of culture, in which the exchange of objects, and most particularly of women, would no longer form the basis for the constitution of a cultural order. (*I Love to You* 45)

Yet—and this is a crucial issue for all feminists to recognize in their attempts at reform—because the majority of the symbolic constraints imposed on women have had their beginnings in religious orientations, this ingrained religious symbolic system needs to be strongly challenged. In Irigaray's view, this can only be done by proposing that women create an alternative symbolic mode that will avoid both the intransigency and exclusions of the male model of God and his directives. Before beginning to explore the groundwork for alternative forms of symbolic expression that would promote both women's agency and ontological integrity—including that of body-right—certain core attitudes based on religious constraints that have restricted women are in need of further investigation.

THE ROLE OF SACRIFICE

A further and deeper analysis of sacrifice as it implicates women belongs, according to Irigaray, to an even more primordial level than that of woman as object. This sacrifice has to do with the suppression of the natural world, and of the body, especially its sexual dimensions—both of which Irigaray identifies with women. In this connection, Irigaray places the blame for these problematic, even invidious attitudes, on religion: "The religion of men masks an act of dispossession that has broken the relation to the natural universe and perverted its simplicity. Clearly, religion is a figure for a social universe organized by men. But this organization is founded upon a sacrifice of nature, of the sexed body, especially of women. It imposes a spirituality that has been cut off from its roots in the natural environment. Thus it cannot fulfill humanity" (*An Ethics of Sexual Difference* 191). In such a comparison, women's exclusion is dependent on an association of their bodies with the natural world, which is regarded as fertile, though untamed, and therefore in need of supervision and appropriate measures of control. A corollary of this position is the notion, particularly prevalent in Christianity, that to be spiritual, one has to sacrifice the body, which is deemed, because of its affinities with nature, to be similarly reprobate: "It is strange that the philosopher, like the devout man, should have imagined for centuries that thinking or praying have to be sacrifices. It is also significant in our cultures man thinks or prays by estranging himself from the body, and that thinking or praying does not assist him in becoming incarnate, becoming flesh. Yet if thinking means becoming aware of one's natural immediacy, that does not mean that it has to be sacrificed" (*I Love to You* 40). For Irigaray, any relation to the natural world is not something to be rejected but a connection to be celebrated. As I will describe later in this chapter, she will nonetheless propose her own remedy of a discipline that is non-sacrificial to modify the basic instinctual reactions that she associates with an unreflective natural immediacy (*I Love to You* 46–47).

In addition to this repudiation of woman because of her connection to nature, another indication of her lack of symbolic status can be detected in religious rituals that are concerned with the literal, as opposed to the figurative, domain of sacrifice. To gain some insight into this phenomenon, it is again necessary to turn to a male author. This time, it is the work of René Girard and his study of the scapegoat figure that provides an appropriate entrée to the topic. Girard's work allows at the outset that there is a basic human propensity to ward off the potential malevolence of gods or powerful figures/spirits by a sacrifice of a propitiatory or expiatory nature. Girard is more interested, however, in embellishing this rudimentary gesture of placation by grounding it in more complex motivations. In Girard's delineation of an originary act of violence, it is guilt or appeasement for the murder of a victim that instigates this immemorial compensatory response. In his scenario, however, it is not the primal father, as in Freud's *Totem and Taboo* study of ritual obsession, who is murdered. Instead, it is a scapegoat.

Girard situates the source of this sacrificial propensity in what he posits as a desire for the fullness of being. Yet this desire does not seem to be satisfied by self-love or other acts of self-gratification. Rather than fulfilling his own desires, an individual becomes fixated instead on another person, who seemingly manifests the plenitude that he lacks. A form of mimetic behavior, as well as cupidity of the other's goods, ensues. Unfortunately, this desire can escalate out of proportion, unless it is contained by the sacrifice of a substitute figure—the scapegoat—that defuses this covetous impulse. As with Freud's murder/sacrifice of the primal father, this archaic projection seems an implausible explanation on many counts as an explanation for the origin of religion.[4] In Girard's script, however, in contrast to Freud's secular conclusions, there is the intervention of the Christ figure, the ultimate innocent victim. Christ, with his own act of self-sacrifice on the cross, inverts and thus revolutionizes the established order by revealing the mercenary machinations involved in all previous sacrifices. As a result, Girard believes that Christ, by this gratuitous sacrifice as a manifestation of God's love, changes forever the former violent and destructive drive at the root of religion.

Girard's theories, however, exhibit a distinct bias in favor of male behavior, which becomes the basis of Irigaray's telling criticism of his work. Not once does Girard refer to women's participation, or lack of it, in this ritual of immolation—except for a casual, even dismissive reference to ecstatic and murderous Dionysian maenads. This reference is featured simply as an aside that serves to reinforce the need to restrain women. Though ultimately Girard is concerned with a vindication of Christianity as the ultimate solution to this dilemma of passions gone awry, where love replaces envy, he will nevertheless fundamentally claim that: "All religious rituals spring from the surrogate victim (scapegoat), and all the great institutions of mankind, both secular and religious, spring from this [substitutive sacrificial] ritual" (*The Scapegoat* 306).

While Luce Irigaray is in agreement with Girard that: 'Most of our societies have been built on sacrifice' (*An Ethics of Sexual Difference* 75), this does not necessarily mean that she accepts the situation. In her reaction to Girard, Irigaray regards his theory as simply one more illustration of the suppression or sacrifice by men of the female of the species—both theoretically and practically. In the context of sacrifice, however, Irigaray is especially concerned to stress that beneath Girard's foundational speculations regarding the scapegoat—the sacrifice of whom restores equilibrium—there exists another more primordial unacknowledged victim—woman (76). Irigaray has stated elsewhere: "This offense against women will be systematically revealed and repeated through the designation and sacrifice of the scapegoat that belongs to the social body in a more visible way than women do. Periodically, throughout history, men will designate a guilty person or persons and will wage war on them. Beneath this cyclical time scheme lurks the offense that has already been against another gender" (*Sexes and Genealogies* 134). For Irigaray, this female figure does not feature as necessarily a scapegoat nor an overt offering on an altar. This is because her sacrifice is a more latent one—she has been the victim since time immemorial of covert deprivation and repression. Her flesh, her integrity, her place in the natural order have all been effaced by the male emphasis on his gender's role not just as primary in the religious sphere, with a direct access to transcendence, but also as presuming precedence in the social scheme of things.

Basically, it would appear that many of the mechanisms involved in sacrificial observances, particularly in the substitutive remnants that feature in many Western religions, are geared to protecting the boundaries, or to safeguarding the limits within which the requisite public, male-dominated rituals can be observed. The fact that women are placed as external to such exercises of power, rather than as participants, appears to result from deeply rooted psychological prejudices.

Certain defensive measures connected to these prejudices have been thoroughly investigated in Mary Douglas's work, *Purity and Danger*. Douglas tellingly demarcates the bifurcation of purity and pollution, sacred and profane, nature and culture. In these binary oppositions, women have consistently been identified with the less valued side of the pair. Both the subsequent theoretical and practical applications of such binary divisions and their resultant female subordination have also been amply described by other women scholars.[5]

Irigaray argues that societies that operate according to this system, with its deliberate displacement of women, need to become aware of their originary sacrifice of women, rather than continue to repeat protective rites of substitution that reinforce this repression. She poses a number of disturbing questions that indicate her own possible solution: "Is it impossible for a community to gather together morning, noon or night without needing a sacrifice? The meeting could ritually celebrate our joy in seeing one another and exchanging greetings. Why could a collective not be formed on the basis of social and cosmic goals without feeling a need to sacrifice, or eat the sacrificial object, etc.?" (*Sexes and Genealogies* 76).

In addition to her criticisms of the displacement of women, Irigaray also makes another observation that is profoundly significant regarding with regard to the institution of sacrifice. In this instance, her insight is particularly incisive in its implications for contemporary Western religions. Irigaray reports that women have rarely, if ever, been involved in either the preliminary protocols of sacrifice, let alone in their execution, even in their contemporary "tamed" or substitutive versions. As she observes: "One other thing is obvious: in the religions of sacrifice, religious and social *ceremonies are almost universally performed by men*. Men alone perform the rite, not women or children (though male children can sometimes act as acolytes). Women have no right to officiate in public worship in most traditions, even though that worship serves as the basis and structure for the society" (*Sexes and Genealogies* 78). This is indeed a denial of symbolic status to women. Irigaray provides a rebuke for such a narrow appreciation of the contribution of women to society, and even to life itself. Irigaray remarks: "And yet, when the minister of that one and only God, that God-Father, pronounces the words of the Eucharist: 'This is my body', according to the rite that celebrates the sharing of food and that has been ours for centuries, perhaps we might remind him that he would not be there if our body and our blood had not given him life, love and spirit" (*Sexes and Genealogies* 21).

It is not as if Irigaray is advocating that women become ritual specialists in the art of sacrifice. What she wants to bring to the reader's attention is that this exclusion of women from officiating at rituals is emblematic of the principal form of sacrifice of women—her exile from what I have termed the source of symbolic status. Nonetheless, Irigaray does provide a different scenario for such a ritual if ever a woman were to preside: "If a woman were to celebrate the Eucharist with her mother, giving her a share of the fruits of the earth blessed by them both, she might be freed from all hatred or ingratitude toward her maternal genealogy, and be hallowed in her identity as a woman" (*Sexes and Genealogies* 21–22). Irigaray's final emphasis in this essay is on the fact that even today women are still inevitably forced to participate in a society that reenacts and demands sacrifices of them without any consultation.

A remarkably similar judgment on the subject of women and the enactment of sacrifice has also been made by Nancy Jay in an essay that previews her major study *Throughout Your Generations Forever: Sacrifice, Religion and Paternity.* Jay's observations are even more striking than Irigaray's: "Sacrifice may be performed for many reasons. But it is beautifully adapted for integrating patrilineal descent groups, a goal that can only be accomplished by differentiation from all other lines of descent. Sacrifice can both expiate descent from women (along with other dangers) and integrate the 'pure and eternal' patrilineage . . . There is necessarily an either-or about lineage membership . . . This either-or requires transcending descent from women. This is one way to understand why child-bearing women must not sacrifice and also why the pollution of childbirth so commonly needs to be expiated sacrificially" ("Sacrifice as a Remedy" 296–97). Both Jay and Irigaray see the rubrics governing sacrifice as still alive and well today, with Jay, in particular, analyzing their controversial implications for contemporary women who desire ordination: "In the sacrificing churches, resistance to ordination of women is not just psychological . . . Both sides of the controversy over women's ordination appear to share an understanding with sacrificing patrilineage members around the world: recognition of the power of sacrifice as a ritual instrument for establishing and maintaining an enduring male-dominated social order" (304). While initially such statements by Irigaray and Jay might seem somewhat simplistic in their explanatory power, they nonetheless strike a chord with many women who have struggled against what seem to be inflexible and insuperable obstacles in their quest to become ordained ministers or rabbis.

It becomes all too apparent that such sacrificial operations and their sanctions have continued to function as an unconscious prohibition that has also served to exclude women until quite recently from access to appropriate education. Their belated admission to selected institutions of learning has since provided women with a self-reflexive consciousness, as well as the requisite knowledge to articulate their grievances. It is such a move to consciousness that marks for Irigaray the founding act that is necessary for women to enter a new order of creation. Such a new order will entail women's claiming for themselves a different form of divinity, or of becoming divine. For Irigaray, this development will not exactly correspond with what has conventionally been named "transcendence," or employed with reference to a supreme male God.

BECOMING A DIVINE WOMAN

Irigaray provides a number of suggestions for ways that a woman can become divine, but I will concentrate on two examples that have particular relevance for changing the symbolic status of women from that dictated by a sacrificial economy. The first will involve women themselves attaining a sense of their own subjectivity; the second will result from their being engaged in an ethical relationship. In her essay "Divine Women," Irigaray states that "divinity is what we need to become free, autonomous, sovereign" (*Sexes and Genealogies* 62). The basic challenge, however, will be to rethink a way by which women can become divine, so that they do not imitate the masculine mode of transcendence and hierarchical ordering of the world, specifically in religion. While Irigaray has described God as the "Other of men" who is made in their image, she wants women to relate to: "Their Other without capital letters" (*An Ethics of Sexual Difference* 115). Irigaray gives an intimation of the direction she will take in defining this notion of the divine when she states: "It [religion] has not been interpreted as the infinite that resides within us and among us, the god in us, the Other for us, becoming with and in us" (*Sexes and Genealogies* 63). To implement this vision, Irigaray proposes that God should no longer be cast as a distant figure, exterior to the process of achieving integrity. Irigaray further qualifies this position when she states: "If she is to become woman, if she is to accomplish her female subjectivity, woman needs a god who is a figure for the perfection of *her* subjectivity" (64).[6] In this sense, becoming divine need not necessarily imply that one has a relation to a transcendent God, but to the evocation of a god that inheres in the process of attaining a sense of self integrity or, as Heidegger would term it, "one's ownmost possibilities."[7]

According to Irigaray, the change to such an appreciation of god and of religion can only be achieved by a transformation of consciousness. Perhaps her most graphic description of this transformation occurs when she depicts her own process that involved training in "an art of perception" (*Sexes and Genealogies* 144), which effected "an inversion of an imposed femininity" (*I Love to You* 63). Irigaray characterizes this as a process of interiorization or *recueillement* (*I Love to You* 40).[8] In this practice: "Perception can be trained as a spiritual method. As such, it becomes a means for respecting what exists" (*To Be Two* 50). In addition, "perception should not become a means of appropriating the other, of abstracting the body, but should be cultivated for itself, without being reduced to a passivity or to an activity of the senses" (*To Be Two* 43).

Irigaray portrays this process as at once a demanding but gentle discipline, involving a conscious curbing of needs and desires—of what she calls "natural immediacy," or instinctual gratification (*I Love to You* 64). It involves an act of conscious sublimation rather than repression. "Sublimating my sensible immediacy seems to be a condition of my authority to speak truth. I must recognize that I am a woman and, remaining such, I must also be able to differentiate myself from my immediate sensibility" (*To Be Two* 105). Irigaray believes that the knowledge of sublimation is a skill that has been lost by women. "We women have either forgotten or we never learned the art of genital sublimation, perhaps of the historic gap between the culture that corresponds to female genealogies and the culture produced by the social foundations of patriarchy" (*Sexes and Genealogies* 165). Such a cultivation of sensibility nurtures an enhanced sensitivity to the natural world. It marks an attempt to move beyond narcissistic and acquisitive desires so that a self-reflexive awareness can emerge. Irigaray describes this procedure of self-differentiation as: "Mastering oneself without sacrifice, amputation or self-annulment" (*To Be Two* 72). She appreciates this discipline as distinct from the abrupt severance from nature and the body that has sustained the predominant masculine model of both rationality and religious asceticism. Irigaray continues: "Here, human becoming unfolds in a way that is different from the becoming of Western man, who 'with violence leaves his dwelling and ploughs up, captures and tames'" (72). This cultivation of the senses and consciousness also sustains the development of a spiritual dimension that, for Irigaray, is intimately related to her notion of the divine.

At the same time, such an attentiveness will also foster a growing insight that questions received definitions of God, with their hierarchical values and transcendent attributes that have served to exclude women from any offices associated with such a deity. This will, in time, free women to pursue a state of self-realization that is not dependent on imposed norms or external religious regulations. Such a process will also promote an affirmation of the body, particularly of the senses that are now expressed in a nonimpulsive way. Because of this inclusion of the body in an integrated process, Irigaray understands her proposed model as introducing a "truly sexualized thought." The achievement of an identity by women that incorporates mind and body in an interdependent equilibrium is another articulation of what Irigaray understands as becoming divine. It would also amount to attaining a state of ontological integrity. This process can also be understood as a reformulation by Irigaray of the integration of the forces that have been traditionally designated as "culture" and "nature"—though Irigaray refuses to position them in either a movement of progressive development whereby nature is supplanted, or a false dichotomy, where the two are opposed. She thus tries to avoid Freud's stark dualism that describes the acquisition of civilization as demanding the mastery of nature that leads to adverse repressions.

The most fascinating aspect of this undertaking of becoming divine is that it does not recommend that women have to become gods or goddesses in the traditional understanding of these terms. "It is not a matter of returning to the goddesses of the earth, even if this were in our power" (*Sexes and Genealogies* 81). Yet certain theological critics have nonetheless taken Irigaray to task for her Feuerbachian reclamation of idealized "feminine" qualities that resonate with attributes of goddesses.[9] In one sense, they do have a point, in that Irigaray can certainly be interpreted in a humanistic way, especially her definition of divinity as: "What we need to become free, autonomous, sovereign" (*I Love to You* 62). She also does advocate the adoption of certain characteristics that she regards as "feminine," for example, tenderness, peace, that she associates with a prepatriarchal gynocracy when women were worshiped as goddesses (*Sexes and Genealogies* 129). In addition, it does seem that she wants to put aside the issue of the actual existence of God (*"Why Different?"* 173). When critics further imply, however, that such a process leads to self-aggrandizement or even idolatry, I believe that this is a misinterpretation of Irigaray. This can be rectified by reading "Divine Women" (in *Sexes and Genealogies*, 1993) in the light of *I Love to You* (1996) and *To Be Two* (2001). These later works exhibit definite Buddhist resonances. Irigaray often refers to an example of Buddha regarding a flower as an illustration of nonattachment. "Buddha's contemplation of the flower suggests that we learn to perceive the world around us, that we learn to perceive each other between us: as life, as freedom, as difference" (*To Be Two* 23).[10] While the particular process that Irigaray supports, however, is not identical to the strict Buddhist path of a monk or nun's meditative discipline and sexual abstinence, there are similarities. This is especially evident in Irigaray's insistence on a deepening insight into psychological states that aids in overcoming addictions, instinctual desires, and any attachment to a false sense of self (*I Love to You* 24–25).

Such a process of cultivating awareness is, of course, never finished. It marks a state of constant development where the task of becoming a divine woman, and thus fulfilling the potentialities of her being, is an infinite one. Irigaray believes that it is only by living in this state of heightened perception—and this is not to suggest that there have not been individual women in the past who have achieved such states of consciousness—that a woman can achieve a measure of integration and autonomy. It will not necessarily be easy, as the apparatus of cultural conditioning still attempts, at every turn, to deprive her of what Irigaray understands as a divine birthright. This new level of consciousness on the part of women, however, will promote a change so that women need no longer function simply as dependent entities in a cosmic scheme where a transcendent God regulates compulsory gradations in the order of creation. Yet, ultimately, Irigaray will not associate this achievement of integrity by women with any sense of finality or complete self-sufficiency. It is as if the self-discipline and inner contemplation that she has recommended constitute the preparatory phase for a more demanding endeavor. And it is here that her work takes a somewhat unexpected turn, though Irigaray herself views it as a natural progression.

DIVINE RELATIONSHIPS

To understand this development in Irigaray's thought, it is perhaps necessary to first situate her work within a revised Hegelian framework, particularly the idea of "History." As noted earlier, Hegel's interpretation of History, in Irigaray's view, has been the prerogative of men. As such, the dialectic progression of history, in which spirit has been disclosed, has instigated violent conflict. "The history constructed by man resembles a history of enduring violence, of appropriation, of dominance and not a contribution to what is" (*To Be Two* 73). It has also denied women access to the universal and due recognition of their distinct identity (*I Love to You* 26, 61). Irigaray wants to conceive of another mode of the unfolding of spirit that will allow for a certain cultivation of humanity based on an ethics that depends neither on an imposed divine mandate nor on paternalistic directives of appropriate conduct for women. For this to occur, women, once they have achieved their own subjectivity, must not fall into the same snare of self-sufficient narcissism as Irigarary believes men have done (118).

This change will entail a radical revision of the dynamics of the dialectic that will take as its ethical exemplar a renegotiated love relationship between a man and a woman. Irigaray charges that Hegel himself was incapable of portraying the type of love that she envisages because he reduced love to a transaction where the male dictated the terms (63). In addition, Hegel also described a man's love for a woman as a reverting to the "natural immediacy" of the private domain of women and family. This marked a withdrawal from his primary public duties (82). In Irigaray's estimation, Hegel's depiction amounts to a graphic portrait of marriage as it exists in a patriarchal culture. In this context, the only way that the natural immediacy of family life can be overcome in a dialectical movement is by defining man and woman as conflicting entities. "Man and woman are thus in opposition to one another in the labor of love, according to Hegel" (21). Irigaray attests that love cannot exist, let alone flourish in such circumstances. The new era of History, which Irigaray wishes to introduce, will be based on the sharing of love between a man and woman who respect each other as equals and affirm each other's integrity (130). Irigaray's intention is to transform what has been accepted as sexual love between a man and a woman. She understands that this can only happen once women have come into their own. Yet, in Irigaray's view, this will also only occur if men, predominantly male philosophers, also begin to question why male culture has tended to seek objective knowledge outside of the self in conceptual formulas, principally of their own devising. They regard these abstract concepts more highly than any appreciation of existence itself. The following question that she poses summarizes Irigaray's principal protest to this rejection of the body and natural world: "Why do they [male philosophers] define and impose as objectivity what is a product of their auto-reflection, a necessity of their consciousness, and place it before knowledge of existing reality?" (*To Be Two* 91). Such questions inaugurate Irigaray's own vision of an alternative orientation that is founded on sexual difference.

In *An Ethics of Sexual Difference*, Irigaray first depicted thematically the dynamics of a mutually enhancing relationship as a way of encouraging a revolution in the relations between the two sexes.[11] As she continues to develop her advice for cultivation of love, Irigaray introduces the controversial notion of sexual difference as an intrinsic element of her position. She states: "Human nature is two: each gender having its own characteristics that are irreducible to *one* nature . . . Men and women are corporally different. This biological difference leads to others: in constructing subjectivity, in connecting to the world, in relating" (*"Why Different?"* 173). Or again, as she has expressed elsewhere, "Between man and woman, there really is an otherness, biological, morphological, relational" (61). This distinctness provides the basis for a renegotiated relationship between the two sexes that becomes the core of an ethical program promoting heterosexuality. As she later observes in *To Be Two*: "Belonging to a gender represents a destination to the other more than it represents a biological destiny. To be born a woman, before signifying to be humanity's reproducer, means to incarnate woman's to be with the other-man, together with man's to be" (*To Be Two* 33). To emphasize that this idea of sexual difference is the major element in her modification of Hegel, Irigaray describes it as "the most powerful motor of a dialectic without masters or slaves" (*I Love to You* 51).

Irigaray concluded that neither Western philosophy nor religion could supply adequate resources to portray a genuine loving encounter where the women partner was not diminished. In an essay entitled "The Universal as Mediation" (*Sexes and Genealogies* 125–50), Irigaray began to examine the work of Hegel in detail and propose her new understanding of his dialectic. She sought to discern a way where the negative, or differentiating moment of the dialectic, could convey an interaction that would be neither enveloping nor sacrificial. Irigaray further asks: "How can we ensure that the negative does not entail martyrdom?" (*I Love to You* 13). In this reconfiguration, she also sought to renegotiate Hegel by turning "the negative, that is, the limit of one gender in relation to the other, into a possibility of love and creation" (*I Love to You* 11). Finally, Irigaray did not wish to remain within the customary categories of the Hegelian dialectic insofar as they culminate with the abstract postulate of a transcendent Spirit/God. "The lack of definition of the alterity of the other has left all thought, the dialectical method included, in a state of paralysis, in an idealistic dream appropriate to a single subject (male), in the illusion of a unique absolute" (*I Love to You* 61).

In rethinking the Hegelian dialectic structure and its inevitable encounter with difference or negativity, Irigaray presumes each person has previously cultivated their consciousness with specific mediations that are appropriate to each gender (*I Love to You* 27, 47).[12] As a result, neither partner would try to make the other conform to either their fantasies of fusion or of conquest. In this reconfiguration of the dialectic, Irigaray's intention is to conceive of the negative movement as preserving a difference between the two participants. "My way uses the negative as a path which permits, at each moment, dialogue between subjects in respect of singularities, in particular of gender. Here, the negative is therefore insurmountable and the absolute can never be unique nor universally shared. The negative real and the living *dialegomai* between subjectivities which, beyond appearing to self, and to other, must speak to one another in order to be and become self" [*sic*] (*"Why Different?"* 156–57). As a result, any encounter with another will be based on a recognition of a person that confirms him or her in his or her separate integrity (*I Love to You* 103). This is a rejection of the previous rules of exchange, from "the sacrifice of sexed identity to a [neutral] universal defined by man with death as its master" (*I Love to You* 26).

Irigaray's previous recommendations for a woman to become divine for herself can now be appreciated as providing the initial steps towards a form of divinity that is to be realized in a heterosexual relationship. Nonetheless, it needs to be noted hat Irigaray appears to be placing an incommensurable demand to produce this revolution on women, who still seem to carry the burdens of reforming the world, even having achieved integrity: "She [woman] should not comply with a model of identity imposed upon her by anyone, neither her parents, her lover, her children, the State, religion or culture in general. That does not mean she can lapse into capriciousness, dispersion, the multiplicity of her desires, or a loss of identity. She should, quite the contrary, gather herself within herself in order to accomplish her gender's perfection for herself, for the man she loves, for her children, but equally for civil society, for the world of culture, for a definition of the universal corresponding to reality" (27).

For Irigaray, however, the foremost achievement is that a woman can now participate in a relationship of fully equal and finely attuned people. This will culminate in an apprehension of the divine by both participants. "Love . . . carnal love is thereby cultivated and made divine" (139). Insofar as woman and man, according to Irigaray, belong to different genders, and have each carried out distinct forms of sexual differentiation, their task now is "to bring one another to the revelation of an ontic and ontological difference" (146).[13] In *To be Two*, Irigaray virtually rhapsodizes: "We give birth to it [the divine], adults at last. Arriving at another stage of our history, God reveals himself as the work of man and woman. It always awaits us, like a horizon between memory and alliance" (13). Human sexual love here achieves its plenitude, or divine status, where both the body and human nature are vindicated as integral elements of a divine realization that is revealed in the flesh. Irigaray also appreciates that this process would allow religions to revise their relations to the flesh and love, so that they need not be sacrificed to attain spiritual perfection: "Renouncing love, including carnal love, for 'God' would lose its meaning since amorous relations would be transformed into weddings and festivals, both spiritual and divine" (59).

RETHINKING TRANSCENDENCE

It is in the context of this renegotiated relationship between men and women that Irigaray has also undertaken a significant revision of the notion of "transcendence" that could have important consequences for the understanding of transcendence. Here any resonances of a triumphant or autocratic God are left behind. This is because the notion of "becoming divine" as a human couple not only brings about definite benefits, but also involves certain responsibilities. One of these is the acceptance of one's own limitations. Such a movement can be considered as an ethical responsibility in that it introduces a mode of respect that requires a recognition of the "irreducibility of the other" (*To Be Two* 13). The negative in sexual difference thus inculcates both an acceptance of the limits of my own gender and a responsibility towards protecting the other's integrity. It is in this move that the influence of Emmanuel Levinas can be detected in Irigaray's thought.[14] Irigaray's own position, however, will ultimately differ from both Hegel and Levinas because the intersubjectivity that she supports expects equal responsibility from both partners.

Such a combination of personal negation/limitation and the irreducibility of one's partner constitute for Irigaray what she terms the "transcendence" of the other. "Transcendence is thus no longer ecstasy, leaving the self behind toward an inaccessible total other, beyond sensibility, beyond the earth. It is a respect for the other whom I will never be, who is transcendent to me and to whom I am transcendent" (*I Love to You* 104). This mode of transcendence as irreducibility has very different implications from either Hegel's Absolute Spirit or the utterly remote Otherness associated with the traditional model of God. Such a transcendence will nevertheless have connotations of mystery—insofar as the other of sexual difference represents something that I acknowledge as beyond my control or manipulations. "The other, whose mystery will never be a shared secret, the other who will always remain a mystery, is the other of sexual difference" (*To Be Two* 111). Irigaray brings her ideas together in a vision that she believes has definite repercussions not just for gender relations and human consciousness but for the way that rationality itself has previously been conceived in terms of spirit. Spirit no longer operates in accordance with the machinations of the Hegelian dialectic's *Aufhebung*—whether in the service of God or human consciousness—but is manifested in an ethical relationship where the recognition of another's integrity is essential to one's own ontological affirmation: "These dimensions of the negative, of the mystery, of the invisible are fundamental in the philosophy of subjectivity that I try to construct. They represent a questioning of the foundations of what we call intelligible, epistémé, reason, idea, concept, etc. But they signify one more step in the becoming of human consciousness, liberty, ethics, a stage where ethics is not separated from ontology but remains linked to it as access to the world of another light where the 'mystery of the of the other illuminates' on the path of a new rationality" (*Why Different?* 165–66).[15]

CRITICAL RESPONSES

In the contemporary world, where the notion of gender has undergone a remarkable theoretical revision in the last decades, Irigaray's appeal to a mode of heterosexuality, even if a renegotiated one, appears as something of an anomaly, if not distinctly naïve in its naturalistic presuppositions. Irigaray own response to criticism is always along the lines that she is challenging what has been, and continues to be, the site of the most intimate yet most misconstrued of human relationships. She believes that unless this fundamental form of human contact is reformed and becomes an expression of love that recognizes the intrinsic worth of each partner, women will be unable to assume their proper role as co-creators and guardians of both society and the cosmos. From a historical perspective, Irigaray's observations certainly have merit. This is because a survey of Western history specifically illustrates how the institution of marriage has been perhaps the site of the most flagrant exploitation, if not abuse of women.

It would seem nonetheless that the crucial issue today is the potential efficacy of all modes of consciously conducted relationships, including those that are not heterosexual, and their recognition of the integrity of another human being. Sex and gender, while extraordinarily important, do not necessarily always represent the most extreme kind of discrimination. Intersubjective relations that foster an acceptance of those rejected on the grounds of age, class, ethnicity, income, race, and religion would also appear to be particularly compelling ways of challenging ingrained prejudices. Irigaray, however, resists any such concessions: "The whole of humankind is composed of men and women and nothing else. The problem of race is, in fact, a secondary problem—except from a geographical point of view, perhaps?—which means we cannot see the wood for the trees, and the same goes for other cultural diversities—religious, economic and political ones. Sexual difference probably represents the most universal question we can address" (*I Love to You* 47). Irigaray does not present any detailed argument in support of her position, apart from a basic and seemingly intuitive appeal to a form of natural law. She states that: "*Nature has a sex*, always and everywhere" (*Sexes and Genealogies* 108), as evidence of her promotion of sexual difference as taking priority of place in relations of difference that needs to be renegotiated. The labor of love, as it instantiates love, is indeed a serious issue with the potential to intimidate or abuse another human being. Yet surely many instances of exploitation, expropriation, extermination of other people, especially as evidenced in recent incidents of ethnic cleansing, could prove just as potent a stimulus to scrutinize the impulses driving such behavior and thus initiate ethical reform. In-depth analysis of these other human examples of misconduct could prove equally appropriate a means for reworking exclusivist or xenophobic fixations.

It is not as if Irigaray's revised model of intersubjectivity, which endorses recognition, and which rules out any diminution or effacement of one person by the other, would be inapplicable to all such modes of human interaction where hierarchical standards or teleological controls have previously dictated the terms of engagement. In all human relationships, a constant process of becoming could now operate, where every person is encountered in a space of respect and recognition that fosters mutual support. Neither person involved is regarded an object in a transaction. No sacrifices need occur. It is a matter of relating to another in a way that enhances particular differences as well as individual integrity. Consequently, it is particularly ironic that Irigaray's following words can be used in defense of such a position, although she is actually addressing them solely to participants in heterosexual relationships: "Interdependency between subjects is no longer reduced to questions of possessing, of exchanging or sharing objects, cash, or an already existing meaning. It is, rather, regulated by the constitution of subjectivity. The subject does not vest its own value in any form of property whatsoever. No longer is it objecthood, having or the cost of having that governs the becoming of a subject or subjects and the relation among them. They are engaged in a relationship from which they emerge altered, the objective being the accomplishment of their subjectivity while remaining faithful to their nature" (Irigaray, *I Love to You* 127).

Finally, Irigaray's redeployment of Hegel's dialectic seems something of an anachronism. One contemporary commentator has referred to Hegel's grand synthetic maneuver as the tricks of a magician that no longer work. While Irigaray is not investing her energy in a similarly idealist panoramic perspective, her optimistic vision depends for its success on an appeal to separate sexual (or gendered) mediations that are of a dubious naturalistic provenance. This strategy risks reinforcing existing stereotypes of respective male and female qualities and conduct. The main problem is that Irigaray does not even mention the continuing debates on the extent of the interactive effects of biological and cultural influences.[16] Nature and culture are accepted by Irigaray as distinct spheres of influence that operate independently yet need to be integrated by means of a renegotiated dialectic. Such a model does not even begin to address the major contentions on this topic in contemporary scholarship, especially the contributions made by many feminist theorists.

Nevertheless, Irigaray, by thus reframing human sexual relationships, has endeavored to change the basic forms of encounter between a man and a woman in ways that refuse co-optation by either a traditional reading of the dialectic as antagonism, or a mercantile model of exchange motivated by gain. Her work thus poses a major challenge to previous theories of sexual intersubjectivity that refused to acknowledge women in their own right, and thus their ontological integrity or divinity. In addition, she establishes the basis for a constructive argument that can challenge the subject/object dichotomy, as well as the dualism of body and spirit—both models that are predominantly associated with the inferiority of women and their flesh. It is by effecting this momentous change in attitudes towards women—where the body no longer deemed sinful, and women can no longer be excluded as profane—Irigaray's work has made its finest contribution. As a result, certain barriers that have denied women symbolic status have been breached, and there can be no further excuses for the refusal by religious authorities to exclude women on such grounds. In the meantime, however, many women have abandoned organized religion as a lost cause that remains a male preserve. There are, however, certain other scholars who, while they may not agree with all of Irigaray's suggestions, are inspired by her ideas and continue to foment symbolic rebellion that would recast the traditional forms of divine transcendence that have excluded women.

CONCLUSION

Irigaray's critical analysis is a strong indictment of many Western male theologians' and philosophers' propensity to either neglect women or to appropriate their identity and consequently pronounce the terms of their functioning in both church and state. This has been nowhere more evident than in the assignment of women to the sphere of sacrifice. If they have not been ignored entirely, women appear to have been sacrificed in two ways. First, women have been accorded the suspect achievement of providing the resources which fuel the economy, but denied any authority in the allocation of those resources. Alternatively, they have remained largely a pawn in the services of various schemes devised by men—of either purported divine or merely human provenance—that not only determine their value, but also organize the rules that preclude their participation in men's rituals and organizations. This has been based on a projection that women's bodies, minds and emotional tendencies have rendered them both deviant and erratic. The consequences of this projection are the continuing, unjust denial of symbolic status.

Irigaray's analysis would seem to have a particular applicability to orthodox, established religions and their societal applications. Her work is extremely helpful in providing insights into many of the major obstacles that have been placed in women's way. But there are some problems both in her diagnosis and her prescription. As I noted earlier, I believe it is false to assume such patriarchal restrictions as she describes have been ubiquitously imposed throughout all histories and cultures.[17] Also, from a secular perspective, many do not think Irigaray's remedy for women attainment of the universal firstly, as a specific gendered identity—even if this interpreted from a humanistic perspective as being "sufficient unto oneself"—is an adequate strategy to reorder political and societal abuses. Her further emphasis on heterosexuality is also regarded as both narrowly focused and subjectively biased. Thus, while I believe Irigaray's work has been extremely helpful in indicating the stereotypical sexual constructions that have been evident particularly in mainstream Eurocentric religious traditions, her major solution, with its emphasis on sexual difference, does not satisfy those who are concerned with other modalities of gender identity or even other modes of difference, specifically those of race,

ethnicity, class, and religion affiliation. As a result, although Irigaray's
proposals may not find a ready acceptance with all feminist theorists,
she has provided invaluable assistance in delineating the symbolic categories derived primarily from religions that have both denigrated
women and denied them recognition. In Irigaray's judgment this has
been tantamount to sacrifice. For this vital insight, many of us are in
her debt. We may prefer, however, to envisage other ways of channel-
ing women's energies and imagination in the search for more equitable relations with those of different persuasions, as well as in the
acquisition of a symbolic status that is our rightful inheritance.

NOTES

1. In one sense, the word "symbolic" has traditional religious conno-
    tations as representative of ideas/ideals that command veneration
    because of their auspiciousness, eminence, or might. The term is also
    used by the French psychoanalytic theorist, Jacques Lacan, to refer to
    the received social and political conventions that one assumes by resolv-
    ing the oedipal crisis. On both scores, Irigaray regards the Western
    tradition as irrevocably patriarchal. See Irigaray, *Speculum of the Other
    Woman*, trans. G. C. Gill (Ithaca, NY: Cornell University Press, 1985a
    [1974]), 337–42.

2. Christine Gudorf has written on the topic of "bodyright": "I would
    argue that one of the most serious negative consequences of the heritage
    of mind/body dualism in the Christian West is the failure to recognize
    bodyright"; *Body, Sex, and Pleasure: Reconstructing Christian Sexual
    Ethics* (Cleveland, OH: Pilgrim Press, 1994), 162. She continues, plac-
    ing it in a context similar to that of Irigaray: "The purpose of women
    in patriarchies is both sexual and reproductive—as sexual object for the
    male, and as reproductive source of his heirs. To this end, women have
    historically not been allowed to control completely either their sexual
    or reproductive functions. In our society until very recently, there was
    no recognition of marital rape, since sexual consent was permanently
    conferred with a woman's consent to marriage" (165).

3. Irigaray expands on these rights in a number of her works. One succinct
    summary can be found in *I Love to You*, trans. A. Martin (New York:
    Routledge, 1996 [1992]), 132.

4. Martha Reineke provides a critique of this aspect of the work of Girard
    in *Sacrificed Lives*. She states: "He explains how conflict emerges
    among humans when humans are caught up in processes of mimetic
    desire that attend emergent subjectivity. He describes how conflict is
    elaborated within a signifying economy when persons who are beset by
    multiple trajectories of mimetic conflict invoke substitutionary violence

or surrogate victimization to bring an end to conflict. But Girard is less successful in establishing why persons who are beset by escalating levels of violence kill each other. A full theory of *sacrifice* turns on this third point; in its absence, Girard has a theory only of cultural violence, not of sacrifice"; *Sacrificed Lives: Kristeva on Women and Violence* (Bloomington: Indiana University Press, 1997), 87.

5.   Julia Kristeva is also in agreement with this primordial erasure of women as a form of matricide. For Kristeva, this movement involves not simply the erasure/sacrifice of women from a significant place in the symbolic order but also extends to rituals of purification that serve to protect a society from pollution associated with their destructive or contaminating influences. One of the most powerful agents of such pollution in Western cultures has been the female body—with its menstrual blood and other bodily fluids; *Powers of Horror: An Essay on Abjection*, trans. Léon S. Roudiez (New York: Columbia University Press, 1982).

6.   Irigaray believes that in the prehistoric period women did have access to the energy and powers that are inherent in symbolic representations of a god, and that women need to reclaim such properties. "Moreover, the religious aspect has had in the past, and in certain traditions still has, a feminine specificity. It's important for women to remember this and reappropriate it for themselves. If God is the keystone of our tradition, I think that the most decisive act of sovereignty is to become ware of all the energy, all the representations invested in him"; Luce Irigaray, *"Why Different?" A Culture of Two Subjects*, interviews with Luce Irigaray, trans. Camille Collins (New York: Semiotext(e), 2000), 173. Irigaray is not necessarily supporting belief in either a traditional understanding of God or in goddesses. I have addressed this issue in my book *Divine Love: Luce Irigaray: Women, Gender and Religion* (Manchester: Manchester University Press, 2006), 26–29.

7.   There is a subtext of Heidegger throughout much of Irigaray's work, besides the two books where she engages specifically with his work; Luce Irigaray, *The Forgetting of Air in Martin Heidegger*, trans. M. B. Mader (Austin: University of Texas Press, 1999 [1983]); and *The Way of Love*, trans. Heidi Bostic and Stephen Pluháček (London-New York: Continuum, 2002). There is not the space to explore her thoughts on Heidegger in this essay. Though she never develops her intimations of the divine/God in any comprehensive way, in *The Way of Love*, Irigaray comes as close as possible to providing a Heideggerian influenced definition: "The gods are far away—in us. It is not by searching for them far outside that we will discover them. To be sure, we will perhaps discover in foreign lands traces of gods that we are lacking. But, without a journey in ourselves, to celebrate with them will not be possible . . . It is in the intimate of ourselves that a dwelling place must be safeguarded for them, a dwelling place where we unite in us sky and earth, divinities and mortals" (Irigaray, *The Way of Love*, 51).

8. "*Recueillement*" is variously describes as a "form of recollection" or a "return to the self." It indicates a practice of self-analysis that Irigaray views as an undertaking necessary to curb instinctual reactions. She also views it as an antidote to sacrifice. "Rather, sacrifice is a sign of a lack of contemplation (*recueillement*) and thought" (Irigaray, *I Love to You*, 40).

9. I have dealt with Irigaray's use of Feuerbach and the charge of idealization in some detail in my book. See *Divine Love*, 24–26.

10. There are a number of problems in Irigaray's references to Buddhism. As one instance, I am not sure that there are any scriptural references to Buddha contemplating a flower. He is often depicted, however, as holding the lotus in his hand as an emblem of enlightenment. Again, a more developed discussion of Irigaray's reflections on eastern religions can be found work can be found in my book *Divine Love*, 124–41.

11. Irigaray clarifies her usage of the terms "sex" and "gender" accordingly: "I often use the word 'sex' for the sexed identity. This doesn't designate the sexual per se, in particular genitality, rather the woman being and the man being [*sic*]. The word 'gender' is often used as already codified by language and culture; it thus runs the risk of perpetuating the existing hierarchy between men and women" ("*Why Different?*" 190). That said, in her most recent work Irigaray tends to used the term "gender" often when she is referring to the innate sexual difference that she posits between the "man being" and the "woman being."

12. Irigaray will also describe specific tasks as appropriate for each gender, in addition to the discipline of the senses. "Woman has to seek out the values of exchange and communication, as does the man, but for different reasons. He has to overcome the priority he gives to accumulation, possession, or at best exchange of objects, while she must avoid the risks of hierarchy and submission, of fusion between persons, of losing her identity in the impersonality of the *one*" (*I Love to You* 76).

13. This individual form of self-differentiation is not something that occurs in Hegel. But then Hegel had not heard of Freud. The mode of Irigaray's differentiation has much in common with psychoanalysis where the engagement with the other takes the form of separation from one's parents or their substitute. The difficult task is that the daughter must not neither identify solely with her mother, nor reject her mother to earn her father's love, but differentiate herself in a way that allows her autonomy as her own woman. As such, there is no reproduction of mothering, as the girl will not necessarily consider her only role to be that of mothering.

14. For Irigaray's own estimation of Levinas's position on the role and place of women, see Irigaray, *Sexes and Genealogies*, trans. G. C. Gill (New York: Columbia University Press, 1993a [1984]), 185–217. I have also addressed this assessment in a chapter of my book, *Divine Love*, 56–82.

15. This modification of rationality also involves an alteration in Hegel's understanding of s/Spirit. It is no longer simply associated with a unitary Absolute Spirit, which Irigaray describes as a neutral totalization. Instead, it is depicted as a form of energy that supplies "the means for matter to emerge and endure in its proper form" (*I Love to You* 25). This achievement, in Irigaray's view, is gender specific, so that spirit is realized in two discrete modes "within or according to one's gender"; *An Ethics of Sexual Difference*, trans. C. Burke and G. C. Gill (Ithaca, NY: Cornell University Press, 1993b [1984]), 110. There is also a fascinating slippage that is never clarified in Irigaray's work between the actual manifestation of spirit in its revised Hegelian form and the type of spiritual achievement that Irigaray aligns with becoming divine.

16. A good overview of the various debates on the topic of gender can be found in Sherry Ortner's *Making Gender: The Politics and Erotics of Culture* (Boston: Beacon Press, 1996). I have also attempted to account for the various meanings of gender as they have been used recently in religious Studies. See Morny Joy, "Gender and Religion," *Temenos* 42, no. 1 (1996): 7–30.

17. Irigaray does make mention of purported prepatriarchal gynocracies, but there is no appreciation that cultures other than Western may not have subscribed to a patriarchal model.

BIBLIOGRAPHY

Douglas, Mary. *Purity and Danger: An Analysis of the Concepts of Pollution and Taboo*. Boston: Ark Paperbacks, 1966.

Freud, Sigmund. *Totem and Taboo*. Translated by A. A. Brill. New York: Random, 1918.

Girard, René. *The Scapegoat*. 1982. Baltimore: Johns Hopkins University Press, 1986.

———. *Violence and the Sacred*. Baltimore: Johns Hopkins University Press, 1979.

Gudorf, Christine E. *Body, Sex, and Pleasure: Reconstructing Christian Sexual Ethics*. Cleveland, OH: Pilgrim Press, 1994.

Hirsh, Elizabeth, and Gary A. Olson. "'Je—Luce Irigaray': A Meeting with Luce Irigaray." *Hypatia* 10, no. 2 (1995): 93–114.

Irigaray, Luce. *An Ethics of Sexual Difference*. Translated by C. Burke and G. C. Gill. Ithaca, NY: Cornell University Press, 1993.

———. *The Forgetting of Air in Martin Heidegger*. Translated by M. B. Mader. Austin: University of Texas Press, 1999.

———. *I Love to You*. Translated by A. Martin. New York: Routledge, 1996.

———. *Sexes and Genealogies*. Translated by G. C. Gill. New York: Columbia University Press, 1993.

———. *Speculum of the Other Woman*. Translated by G. C. Gill. 1974. Ithaca, NY: Cornell University Press, 1985.

———. *To Be Two*. Translated by M. M. Rhodes and M. F. Cocito-Monoc. New York: Routledge, 2001.

———. *The Way of Love*. Translated by Heidi Bostic and Stephen Pluháček. London-New York: Continuum, 2002. From the French La Voie de l'amour (not yet published in France).

———. *"Why Different?" A Culture of Two Subjects*. Interviews with Luce Irigaray. Translated by Camille Collins. New York: Semiotext(e), 2000.

———. "Women on the Market." In *This Sex Which Is Not One*, translated by C. Porter, with C. Burke, 170–91. Ithaca, NY: Cornell University Press, 1985.

Jay, Nancy B. "Sacrifice as a Remedy for Having Been Born of Woman." In *Immaculate and Powerful*, edited by Clarissa Atkinson et al., 283–309. Boston: Beacon Press, 1985.

———. *Throughout Your Generations Forever: Sacrifice, Religion and Paternity*. Chicago: University of Chicago Press, 1992.

Joy, Morny. *Divine Love: Luce Irigaray: Women, Gender and Religion*. Manchester: Manchester University Press, 2006.

———. "Gender and Religion." *Temenos* 42, no. 1 (2006): 7–30.

Kristeva, Julia. *Powers of Horror: An Essay on Abjection*. Translated by Léon S. Roudiez. New York: Columbia University Press, 1982.

Leacock, Eleanor Burke. *Myths of Male Dominance: Collected Articles on Women Cross-Culturally*. New York: Monthly Review Press, 1981.

Lévi-Strauss, Claude. *The Elementary Structures of Kinship*. Translated by J. H. Bell et al. Boston: Beacon, 1969.

Ortner, Sherry B. *Making Gender: The Politics and Erotics of Culture*. Boston: Beacon Press, 1996.

Reineke, Martha Jane. *Sacrificed Lives: Kristeva on Women and Violence*. Bloomington: Indiana University Press, 1997.

CHAPTER 6

THE RETURN OF THE GODDESS

FEMININITY AND DIVINE LEADERSHIP

Beverly Metcalfe

Respect for God is possible as long as no one realizes that he is a mask concealing the fact that men have taken sole possession of the divine, of identity, and of kinship. Once we give this whole issue the attention and serious consideration it deserves, however, it becomes obvious that God is being used by men to oppress women and that, therefore, God must be questioned and not simply neutered in the current pseudoliberal way.

—Luce Irigaray, *Sexes and Genealogies*

INTRODUCTION

This chapter is concerned with becoming, specifically feminine becoming. By "becoming," I mean towards a state of transcendence beyond dominant masculinist knowledge, allowing all human beings to take their place as embodied living subjects in their own right, and without recourse to dualistic constructions of sex/gender. Drawing on the poststructuralist writings of Irigaray and the Divine, and feminist scholars I show how a rereading of feminine wisdom and leadership can help us move towards a location of transcendence, and to become sexed subjectivities. The investigation of feminine becoming will not draw on contemporary female leaders, but heroines in the tales of human morality and spirituality contained within the Hebrew Bible. Focusing specifically on Deborah in the Book of Judges, one of the earliest recorded female leaders, the aim is to contribute to a process of reimagining new readings of ancient leadership knowledges so as to further advance leadership theorizing by inscribing a feminine logic.

If one examines critical discourses of management and organization, it will reveal that leadership theory is not neutral. Since its early conceptualization and subsequent developments, leadership theorizing has been underwritten from a male perspective (Metcalfe and Rees; Billing and Alvesson; Calás and Smircich, "Voicing Seduction"). Texts have drawn heavily on masculinist assumptions when discussing leadership qualities such as decision making and visionary power; we can generally conclude that when critiquing managing and leading we are defining male characteristics and attitudes (Calás and Smircich, "Dangerous Liaisons"; Wacjman; Billing and Alvesson). Feminist sociologists note that the leaders we read about, the leadership activity we read about, and the theory we read about, are forms and relations of "idealised masculinity even when the pronoun is she" (Oseen 170).

The association with men and leadership and masculinity and leadership is especially important when one considers the way in which leaders, whether political, organizational, or spiritual, are perceived as having special and unique qualities; we often set them part, differentiate them. And of course leadership characteristics are not just to be nurtured and capitalized upon in organization contexts; they help constitute power relations in the fabric of our social economy.

In response to the concerns relating to dominant cultural values about masculinity and leadership in society, scholars have examined the specificities of feminine leadership knowledges and sought to explore the ways in which women may have a special feminine advantage (for example, Helgeson; Eagly and Carli). However, critical scholars have stressed that the language of femininity and feminization has not been explicitly named in many organization writings; rather, descriptions of leadership work increasingly use characteristics that are culturally associated with females and "not named"; these texts therefore function as "carriers of a feminine ethos" (Fondas 359). The recognition by scholars of the gendering of theory formulation is important because it evidences forms of subordination and domination and of subsequent hierarchies in knowledge construction (Irigaray, *This Sex Which Is Not One*). As Irigaray argues, within Western philosophical traditions we have inherited approaches to knowledge formation that recognize sexual difference as male sameness, with male mastery of knowledge embedded within, and outside, of social reality (*Speculum of the Other Woman*). Knowledge structures and women's ways of knowing can only be articulated through masculine language systems.

Given these tenets of Western philosophy, how can we as feminist scholars transcend the binary hierarchies and come to be recognized as equal leadership subjects? This chapter tackles this question by exploring how women can become, connect with their feminine power, and claim their status as equal subjects to men. Following Billing and Alvesson, the subsequent feminist investigation reimagines leadership as intrinsically feminine. In essence, I return to the Goddess. In focusing on the feminine, my aim is not to recreate essentialist binary classifications of women and leadership but to unveil the gendered nature of leadership theory through mimetic appropriation of the feminine (see also Irigaray, *This Sex Which Is Not One; Speculum of the Other Woman;* Schor; Braidotti). I tackle these theoretical considerations by proposing two alternative readings of leadership theorizing based on one of the earliest accounts of a woman leader in Western human civilization, Deborah, and her female supporter Jael, in the Book of Judges.

Firstly, I unveil how traditional feminist critiques portray the Bible as a text used to undermine women's identity and social status (see Bird; Farley; Ruether, *Sexism and God-Talk*). In this account, I relate how Deborah (and Jael) are subjected to, and conditioned by, their gender. Hence, in spite of Deborah's great achievements and the magnitude of her figure, she is portrayed as a "lesser" leader. I highlight how leadership is inextricably related to maleness and reveal how the feminine other is repressed. I relate this reading to the work of Irigaray, who argues that women's identity can never be spiritually complete because their emotions and passions are controlled by men: so much so that women have failed to become "*inside as well as outside of [themselves]*" (*Sexes and Genealogies* 67; emphasis original). I suggest that Christianity, by oppressing women, by taking sole possession of the "divine, identity, and kinship" (Irigaray, *Sexes and Genealogies* 5), limits and controls the way women can exercise priestly (Godly?) and leadership power.

In my second reading, I articulate humanity's rejoicing in the feminine divine and female power. I return to the Goddess. In this account biological sex and gender constructions do not distract from Deborah or Jael's female qualities. On the contrary, their female essence serves to highlight the qualities of leadership—determination, bravery, charisma—as universal virtues irrespective of how sexual identity is constructed. The analysis draws on Goddess feminism (see Ruether, *Sexism and God-Talk*; King; Raphael, *Thealogy and Embodiment*; Christ), which is perceived as an emancipatory religion and is seen as a symbol for the realization of women's collective and individual potential—"womanpower" (Raphael, "Truth in Flux" 200). This is not to suggest that Goddess religions are universalized; rather there is an emphasis on fluid formation. The key point to note is that Goddess religions are transformatory. The Goddess represents a useful symbol of rebellion and transcendence against patriarchal religions' construction of femininity. It focuses on female images of power and helps deconstruct patriarchal images in the scriptures (Goldenberg). In Goddess religion woman's reproductive power is sacralized. Resources for returning to the Goddess can be identified in some of the more ancient writings on biblical interpretation. I refer specifically to the early philosophers Clement of Alexandria (in McVey) and Pseudo-Philo (in Brown), whose retranslations of the Hebrew Bible reenergize and upgrade women.

GENDER, RELIGION, AND LEADERSHIP

Feminist theological inquiry has revealed the way many religions have been shaped and formulated by masculinist interpretations and ensured male dominance in the prevailing social organization (see, for example, Anderson; Ruether, *Sexism and God-Talk*; Stanton; Farley). According to Hampson, the structural arrangements of the Christian Church reinforce the superiority of men via their placement in the majority of senior religious positions. The Bible's tales recall the story of one of humanity's most revered, moral and spiritual leaders, the male Christ: his divine male power, his male goodness and how HE is the redeemer of humanity (Hampson, "On Power and Gender").

Hampson (*Theology and Feminism*) thus argues that women's positioning as the subjugated other is largely because the Bible is a collection of stories depicting men's experiences; it is a story written by men using "man's language" that largely represents the interaction of men with one another and their God. More recently commentators have argued this exclusion is not however ignoring women in the Bible's tales, since they are still bound by the moral framework, but in positioning women as "different," sexual hierarchies have been constituted. A key concern for feminist theologians has been to examine the way in which God is seen to embody stereotypical masculine traits. A common reason proposed is that, historically and socially, conceptions of authority and power are deemed as properly invested in the male (Hampson, "On Power and Gender"; McLaughlin). The association between men, masculinity and authority in religious organizing and organization parallels the work of feminist scholars of leadership, who stress the symbolization and embodiment of masculinist power in leadership roles and process (Calás and Smircich, "Dangerous Liaisons"; Collinson and Hearn; Metcalfe and Rees).

God's powerfulness is related to the fact that God is seen as separate, different and alone. He is said to have aseity: "he is entire unto himself, and did not to have to create anything to be complete" (Hampson, "On Power and Gender" 235). God's power is vested in his very being, and through his divine leadership he may intervene in the human world. Irigaray argues that there has been a socially constructed religious hierarchy that depicts humanity in a male form, so that the female represents the subordinate other in relation to both man and God (Irigaray, *This Sex Which is Not One; Sexes and Genealogies*).

The exclusion and subjugation of women is further revealed by drawing on "Christological" accounts of God and his Divine power. "Christology" refers to doctrines concerning the nature and person of Christ.[1] This is potentially problematic for women and feminists since Jesus was a male human being; therefore, as a leadership symbol, as the Christ, or as the second person of the Trinity, it may appear that God becomes in some way male (despite orthodox assertion that God is in essence genderless). The key question is whether the male figure of Christ can be seen to represent the holistic view of humanity since the figure of Christ is not inclusive of female passions and sensibilities (Ruether, *Religion and Sexism*; Ostriker). A number of feminist theological scholars thus argue that Christianity cannot be inclusive and incorporate the sensualities of all humankind, since women have somehow been seen to be included in the concept male.

However, conservative Christologies hold that the maleness of Christ is central to understanding Christianity. The Anglican Bishop Leonard makes his position very clear:

> I believe that the Scriptures speak of God as Father, that Christ was incarnate as a male, that he chose men to be his apostles . . . not because of social conditioning but because in the order of creation headship and authority is symbolically and fundamentally associated with maleness. For the same reason the highest vocation of any created being was given to a woman, Mary, as representative of mankind in response to God because symbolically and fundamentally, the response of sacrificial giving is associated with femaleness . . . For a woman to represent the

> Headship of Christ and the Divine Initiative would, *unless her feminine gifts were obscured or minimised*, evoke a different approach to God from those who worship. (quoted in Hampson, *Theology and Feminism* 66; emphasis original)

A woman's role and status are thus not historically and culturally constructed; she exists as part of the "order of creation" under male humanity. These theological accounts support tenets of Western philosophy which have tended to theorize maleness and femaleness in terms of a dualistic hierarchy, whereby women's social identity is premised on her body, incorporating the aesthetic and her reproductive powers, with male social identity symbolizing reasoning and intellectual powers (Grosz; Butler; Jackson and Scott). Yet this sex/gender hierarchy is further extended within theological interpretations. Maleness is not only characterized as intellectually superior; there are also clear indicators that man's material physicality is also imbued with greater strength and power:

> In its origin [Christianity] presents to man and woman a glorious picture of sexual integrity: the Son of God who has become man and flesh, knowing from inside his Father's work and perfecting it in the total self-giving of himself, not only of his spiritual but precisely also of his physical powers, giving not only to one individual but to all. What else is his Eucharist but, at a higher level, an endless act of fruitful out-pouring of his whole flesh, such as a man can only achieve for a moment with a limited organ of his body. (Balthasar, quoted in Hampson, *Theology and Feminism* 67)

In the above statement, the strength and power of men's bodies are displayed as important in shaping man's natural energy, virility and thus intellectual (leadership) supremacy. The gift of creation was a power given to woman, but the womb is ultimately barren without man's sperm to fertilize it. It might be concluded therefore that for Balthasar the process of ejaculation is symbolic not only of fertility and life-giving power, but also spiritual power. Women's position in the natural order is therefore to support men. Women cannot hold an equivalent place to male figures within Christianity as a deeply masculine religion. For Balthazar it is precisely femaleness that is a barrier to women's ordination and in taking on spiritual leadership roles.

In contrast, Kiesling argues: "It does not appear that femaleness, femininity, womanhood *as such* is the barrier to receiving woman's holy orders, but femaleness *in a state of subjection*" (quoted in

Hampson, *Theology and Feminism* 69; emphasis original). This is highlighted by Irigaray, whose discussion of the Divine suggests that female subjectivities have been entombed within masculinist constructions of the divinized power. It is to this debate I now turn.

DIVINE WOMEN?

Irigaray develops the idea that female imaginary and identity are held under patriarchal religious power by discussing women's exclusion from the divine. In *Sexes and Genealogies*, her detailed chapter on "Divine Women" succinctly recounts the main trope running throughout her work, namely, that forms of knowledge and knowing can only be uttered with recourse to masculinist symbolism and imagery, and that the dominance of the masculine subject renders women's subject position as lacking so that "They lack, we still lack, the affirmation and definition of values *of our own*" (*Sexes and Genealogies* 72; emphasis original). Irigaray notes that theological formulations are based on the father-son relation in religion and life. Feminine roles and theological presence on the other hand are ignored and impoverished. The absence of a female divinity paralyzes the capacity for women to "become whole" in a totally sexually embodied and spiritual sense. She states: "To posit a gender, a God is necessary: *guaranteeing the infinite* . . . In order to become, it is essential to have a gender or an essence (consequently a sexuate essence) as *horizon*. Otherwise, becoming remains partial and subject to the subject. When we become parts or multiples without a future of our own this means simply that we are leaving it up to the other, or the Other of the other, to put us together" (Irigaray, *Sexes and Genealogies* 61; emphasis original).

In other words, by relying on, rather than challenging, the dominance of the masculine subject, women's relationship to God will be materialized through the male, so that women come to be positioned as a receptacle for male completeness. In developing her analysis she draws on woman's relationship to her body, in particular the maternal body, as a way of exposing the debt patriarchy owes to the maternal. According to Irigaray, women have served as an excess for male experiences of the divine. She argues that when theorizing about women's consciousness and identity it must always be determined as a loving mother or a prostitute lover (Irigaray, *Sexes and Genealogies* 63). She states that woman's body was eaten at the Eucharist since it is through the body of a woman that God becomes man. Irigaray thus subverts the original reading of the Eucharist by claiming that the male priest and male minister would not be alive if the female body had not given him "life, love and spirit" (Irigaray, "The Bodily Encounter with the Mother" 45). The male other entombs women so that the most perfect goal women can aim for is to become a man (Irigaray, *Sexes and Genealogies* 64). Thus, male sameness and masculine divinity repress sexual difference, while the female other bolsters (male) identity and (masculine) divinity. Irigaray uses the mirror as a metaphor to explain the act of looking at herself, which represents a "screen" between the other and woman. She claims "women have rarely used their beauty as a weapon for *themselves*, even more rarely as a *spiritual* weapon" (*Sexes and Genealogies* 64, emphasis original; see also *An Ethics of Sexual Difference* 170–71). The mirror and the gaze are "tools" and "weapons" which injure and suppress women's true sensibilities and desires; the mirror "freezes our becoming breath, our becoming space" (Irigaray, *Sexes and Genealogies* 64–65). The mirror makes possible male sameness. Woman's reflections reflect the masculine; she cannot become divine except through her son—there is no equal female trinity representing mother, daughter and spirit (see Daly). Woman is thus relegated to the position of the other—she is denied a feminine spirituality: "The God we know, the Gods we have known for centuries, are men; they show and hide the different aspects of man. He (they) do(es) not represent the qualities or predicates of the *female* made God. Which explains, perhaps, why *women who have grown used to the God/s of men will have no more to do with Him/them* (as men do?) and are ready to give up their on divinity" (Irigaray, *Sexes and Genealogies* 71–72, emphasis original).

To change woman's position, Anderson argues it is not enough that patriarchal religions owe their life to the maternal; it is also necessary to "transform the rationality of religious belief so that the maternal, and the maternal content she desires, does not merely bolster the paternal as formal and rational" (115).

If a woman is to become she must "accomplish her female subjectivity," because a "woman needs a god who is a figure for the perfection of *her* subjectivity" (Irigaray, *Sexes and Genealogies* 64; emphasis original). Without a God they are not able to "communicate or commune with one another" (62). What we discern from Irigaray's writings is that "divine identity," as it is presently constructed within dominant modes of philosophical reasoning, its sacral power, has intellectually, morally, and spiritually closed off feminine sensitivities, feminine knowledges, and feminine wisdoms.

However, I will argue that Irigaray's reinterpretations can offer new insights into ways we can "unveil" the feminine in biblical texts via conceiving of God in terms both male and female, and immanent and transcendent. This is an important advance for feminist scholarship since, as the preceding discussion revealed, the Bible, as a major "truth" and "power" symbol, has laid bare the foundations for dominant understandings of human knowledge and existence. And, as we briefly outlined above, when we come to examine leadership theory and leadership theorizing, the female and the feminine appear silent, absent, written out. Following the outline of my feminist research approach in the first reading, I show how the feminine has been entombed within masculinist constructions of knowledge and leadership. I then, following Irigaray's affirmative mimesis (Braidotti 47) as a way of empowering embodied constructions of the feminine, proceed to offer a rewriting of leadership knowledge in the Hebrew Bible.

RESEARCH APPROACH: FEMINIST INTERPRETATIONS OF THE BIBLE

The revision of scriptures is part of the process of raising and articulating a truer feminine subjectivity. Adrienne Rich comments: "Revision—the art of looking back, of seeing with fresh eyes, of entering an old text from a new critical direction—is, for women more than a chapter of cultural history: it is an act of survival" (quoted in Ostriker 31).

Recent feminist scholarship has tended to take a transdisciplinary approach to women's experiences. Since 1980 June O'Connor has grouped together questions and studies of women and religion in terms of the three Rs: rereading, reconceiving and reconstructing religious traditions. By "rereading" the traditions she means reexamining religious materials "with an eye attuned to women's presence and absence, women's words and women's silence, recognition and denied women" (O'Connor, "Rereading, re-reconceiving and reconstructing traditions" 102). Reconceiving women in the different religious traditions requires the retrieval and the recovery of lost sources and suppressed visions. Through this process it is argued we can reclaim women's heritage and unveil the women as agent as well as object (see King). Theoretical reconstruction involves unraveling and deconstructing the past on the basis of new information and employing new paradigms for thinking, seeing and understanding (O'Connor, Rereading, re-reconceiving and reconstructing traditions," "The Epistemological Significance of Feminist Research in Religion").

DEBORAH AND BARAK IN THE BOOK OF JUDGES

Among the many figures whose histories and deeds are portrayed in the Hebrew Bible, Deborah stands out as a unique figure. Deborah is the first and arguably only woman leader of the Old Testament. She is a judge, to whom people would turn for settling disputes and legal counsel; a leader of a military campaign who rallies her people to the flag; a prophetess, touched by God; and finally, a notable poetess. Alongside Deborah another female figure—Jael—plays a crucial leadership role in the victory of the Israelites over their enemies.

IN PRAISE OF FEMININE LEADERSHIP?

"The only diabolical thing about women is their lack of a God and the fact that, deprived of God, they are forced to comply with models that do not match them, that exile, double, mask them, cut them off from themselves and from one another" (Irigaray, *Sexes and Genealogies* 64).

The figure of Deborah stands out as a unique woman who heralded power and status. She is presented, to start with, as someone's wife, which is the proper naming in the Bible of women in a patriarchal society (and, in that respect, is no more than a naming). The careful reader will note that Lappidoth, Deborah's husband, is mentioned only once in the text. Significantly, the expression "a Lappidoth's wife" has in Hebrew become synonymous with a resourceful and outgoing wife. Other translations of `esheth lappidoth* suggest the phrase means a fiery or spirited woman (Exum 84). Stanton suggests that Deborah was not even married and that the text is referring to Lappidoth a name place, since her character, wisdom and self-reliance indicate it is unlikely she was ever able to fill the role of a Jewish wife. She is presented clearly as a "woman prophet"; Deborah did not judge as a princess by any civil authority conferred upon her, but as a prophetess, as a mouthpiece of God. The people of Israel appealed to her not to resolve controversies amongst the population but to learn what was amiss in their service to God. This is significant because it demonstrates that she was the divinely chosen leader. Deborah is the only biblical figure who assumes a prominent position by virtue of her divine status—even Miriam, the only other female equal to her in status and who challenges Moses, is discussed often in relation to her sons (Exum).

Deborah is also unique in that she is the only woman in the Old Testament to call her people into battle. She heralds the war against the

Jabin and commands it strategically, through the assistance of Barak, although it is he who is required to execute the actual battle plan. It is significant though as a "woman leader" that she commissioned Barak to battle. As a messenger of the Lord, Barak appears accountable to Deborah in the same way that Samuel holds accountable to the Lord (see Exum 84). This is presented as a state of symbiosis in what becomes a key phrase of the narrative: "Barak said to her, 'If you will go with me, I will go; but if you will not go with me, I will not go.' And she said, 'I will surely go with you; nevertheless, the road on which you are going will not lead to your glory, for the LORD will sell Sisera into the hand of a woman'" (Judges 4: 8–9; RSV). Yet examination of the subtext reveals that Deborah's leadership role is constructed along gender lines. She is portrayed as "the mother of Israel" and provided her country and its people with appropriate nurture and support. The image of the "mother" figure is of particular importance. She is not depicted as a mother in the same maternal sense that other matriarchs are, since their identity and role is shaped by giving birth to famous sons (for example, Sarah mother of Abraham and Rachel mother of Jacob). Indeed, some mothers of famous sons are not even named, for example, the mother of Samson. Nevertheless, the imagery that is used to describe her leadership skills and virtues draws on stereotypical models of femaleness. The mother label can be seen to represent fertility, growth, sensitivity, and warmth:

> The peasantry prospered in Israel,
> they grew fat on plunder,
> because you arose, Deborah,
> arose as a mother in Israel. Judges 5: 7–9 (RSV)

She offers liberation from oppression, provides protection, and ensures the well-being and security of her people and her land (Exum). Her leadership style is depicted as participatory and supportive; she "listens"; she was appointed by the Lord God of Israel. In direct contrast, the persona of Sisera is perceived as dictatorial and hard—his reign was characterized by pain and misery. Sisera uses cruelty and violence (Judges 4: 3) to rule the land. We can draw some comparisons to the work of feminist scholars who articulate men and women's different leadership styles by reference to stereotypical descriptions of male and female behavior (Vecchio; Collinson and Hearn; Billing and Alvesson). Deborah can lead and help rebuild a nation, acknowledging women's reproductive and self-renewal qualities, but in more tough, competitive times she must submit to the strength and authority of a man, in the same way that women can be managers today, but the battles in the boardroom must typically remain the place for men. This gendering of leadership is further exposed when we consider the tale from a feminist theological perspective. Critical feminist scholars, as already noted, highlight how biblical texts are underwritten from a male perspective. Farley, for example, stresses that in the scriptures the male Christ represents a figure of humanity—with both men and women "in Christ." I would argue that this is problematic enough but, to allude to our analysis of leadership, it is important to highlight again the relationship between the male figure of Christ and the authority to yield "priestly power" (Hampson, "Power and Gender"; McLaughlin). Following Irigaray's reasoning, because women are denied access to the divine, because men have possessed spiritual kinship and identity, the heritage of sacerdotal powers is aligned to men of the Church. This dominant construction of the interconnecting relationships of men, masculinity, religion and power has positioned women as historically and socially subordinate to men in all spheres of public and private knowledge.

Deborah as a woman, then, will always be positioned as entombed within traditional malestream notions of leadership knowledge and action.

Femininity, Seduction, and Leadership

Turning now to the story of Sisera's assassination and the role of Jael in defeating him, it will be seen that the text is equally alive with sexualized and traditionally (stereotypically) feminine imagery. Early feminist interpretations suggest that when Sisera was slain he fell at her feet but the Hebrew word *raglaim* knows an alternative euphemistic meaning of the word feet as genitals or legs. Various feminist theologians (for example, Niditch, quoted in Sakenfield, "Deborah, Jael and Sisera's Mother") translate between her legs rather than at her feet:

> Between her legs he knelt, he fell, he lay
> Between her legs he knelt, he fell
> Where he knelt, there he fell, despoiled. (20)

Sisera's manly prowess is lost by seeking refuge in a woman's tent and hiding behind a curtain: his cowardly behavior is manifested by association with a woman's world; inversely, thus empowering Jael to command strength and be his match. Jael, by seducing Sisera ("Turn aside, my lord, turn aside to me; have no fear"; Judges 4: 18) enchants

him with her female allure. The reference to how Sisera fell "between
her legs" communicates powerful sexualized messages of how women
can be successful if they use their beauty weapons and sexual talents
to win over men. The way Sisera "sank" to his knees and "fell down"
emphasizes how men are enchanted and seduced by female sexual
power. Her role is that of seductress, stressing her female sexual
energy and vitality.

Calás and Smircich ("Voicing Seduction") link leadership knowledge to maleness and masculinity by tracing the homosocial system
prevalent in leadership theorizing. Their deconstruction of leadership
and seduction is appropriate to the analysis of Jael's role in the battle over the Israelites. The concepts of leadership and seduction are
clearly interwoven. They state that: "Leadership . . . is only capable
of articulating a form of seduction which thrives on *sameness*. That
is, leadership as leadership seduces only those who are of the same
kind—masculine or masculine identified—and promotes, as 'leadership knowledge', only a homosocial system of organization, i.e. based
on the values of masculinity, including masculine values of *femininity*"
("Voicing Seduction" 571, emphasis original).

Thus, Jael as supporter to Deborah draws on her sexually charged
"physical" and "seductress" power as defined within masculine systems of leadership knowledge. Jael is a sexually specific subject: Her
seductress capital is not afforded the same status as leadership power,
and this is shaped by homosocial systems of organization that link
leadership strength and vitality with men, and seduction as leadership
gone wrong, somehow lesser than, with women and femininity: "One
who seduces, lures, induces, entices, presents an attraction so strong
that it overcomes restraints. One who seduces is a seductress: a feminine seducer. Seductors (male seducers) no longer exist. Thus many
can be a 'leader' but only a woman can be a 'seductress'. No need for
the term 'seductor' when 'leader' will do" (Calás and Smircich, "Voicing Seduction" 573).

Organization writers have argued that sexual power is the most
defining feature of women's presence in organizations; their place
is of aesthetic accessory or indeed, through her sexedness, a femme
fatale (Burrell; Hearn and Parkin). This sexualized "positioning" of
course reaffirms the dominance of sex/gender knowledge hierarchies
in organizational and social contexts.

Even where female talents are valued and praised, the story of
Deborah and Barak does so in a way that positions women in a sexual
hierarchy under men. Deborah is strong in a supportive sense; she
assists but does not direct Barak's war plan. Jael is presented as a

sexual commodity. Through creating feminized/sexualized imagery, the biblical tale of Deborah and Barak succeeds in essentializing the differences between men and women and supports gendered stereotypes of men and women and of their leadership capabilities.

In this sense, how is woman to become, how can she can gain access to the divine, and how can she be seen as an equal power-bearer to men? The art of raising feminist consciousness cannot rewrite the biblical message but it can offer new interpretations by revealing the masculine mask and by attempting to touch the feminine divine and female power. Irigaray argues we can reimagine a feminine subjectivity, through destabilizing tenets of phallocentric philosophy, and through mimetic appropriation of the feminine: "There is, in an initial phase, perhaps only one 'path', the one historically assigned to the feminine: that of *mimicry*. One must assume the feminine role deliberately. Which means already to convert a form of subordination into an affirmation, and thus begin to thwart it. Whereas a direct feminine challenge to this condition means demanding to speak as a (masculine) 'subject', that is, it means to postulate a relation to the intelligible that would maintain sexual indifference" (Irigaray, *This Sex Which Is Not One* 76, emphasis original).

One way of valuing and naming the feminine is to interpret Deborah and Jael's sensitivities from the standpoint of the Goddess, which acts as a psychotherapeutic device for the revalorization of the female self and resists any sort of canonical process (Raphael, "Truth in Flux" 202). This reimagining exalts the qualities of women's reproductive powers and sexedness, to which I now turn.

REIMAGINING THE FEMININE IN LEADERSHIP: THE RETURN OF THE GODDESS

"What was the special character of Deborah that she, too, judged Israel and prophesied . . . ? In relation to her deeds, I call heaven and earth to witness that whether it be a heathen or a Jew, whether it be a man or a woman, a manservant or a maidservant, the holy spirit will suffuse each of them in keeping with the deeds he or she performs" (*Midrash Eliahu Rabba*, chap. (9) 10, quoted in Bronner 173). This quotation implies that woman is also imbued with God's feelings and energies and (his?) divine power. It clearly highlights that the "spirit" is embodied within both men and women; there is no sexual hierarchy. Feminist theologians have begun to reconstruct the scriptures and reject the interpretations of the Bible that insist on woman's subordination to patriarchal Christianity (Sakenfield, "Feminist Uses of

Biblical Material"; O'Connor). They question whether the process of "reimagining" God should rightly refer to the father and the son. The National Council of Churches in the 1970s sought to reject Christological phraseology and changed the phrase "Son of Man" to the "Human One" and the "Son of God" to "Child of God" (Miller 3). It can be argued that these translations stand both theologically and linguistically, since the message of the scriptures was premised on the humanity of Jesus and was not to be interpreted as gender referential (Miller 3). However, the Council of Churches still acknowledges that Jesus was male and "masculine." It is these beliefs by leading Church council members that have led many feminists to engage in debates concerned with the process of unveiling the feminine character in the scriptures by reimagining God. This analysis can be linked with images of wisdom and leadership associated with the feminine, outlined in the work of Clement of Alexandria and Pseudo-Philo, and subsequent analyses labeled more broadly as Goddess feminism exemplified in the writings of Melissa Raphael and Carol Christ. These accounts of women's position pay special significance to the feminine in the Divine. Specifically with and through Goddess feminism, women's embodied spirituality and the rejuvenating qualities of woman's earthly power are emphasized (Raphael, "Truth in Flux").

Unlike the patriarchal symbolism in the Old Testament that undermines female sexuality, Goddess feminism rejoices in the self-authenticating of women's natural body. Raphael argues, "She *is* nature: the earth is her body, or she is immanent in the cyclic processes of nature, women and in all sexual energies. Above all, female embodiment replicates (either symbolically or actually) the cosmogonic or regenerative activity of the Goddess. Where female reproductive organs were cast as more or less profane in patriarchal religions, they are now sacralized" (Raphael, "Truth in Flux" 200).

There is debate about what Goddess feminism hopes to achieve: whether to revive an ancient religion; supplant patriarchal religions; or to reveal that Goddess power can be interlocked with God's power, thus offering revisionist feminists with the opportunity of rewriting women into biblical texts (Christ). There is not space in this chapter to debate this, save to say that as I have stressed my approach here is concerned with reimagining new interpretations of the Divine. I would argue that Deborah as "Mother of Israel" represents all the rejuvenating aspects of growth and harmony, but also significantly she symbolizes a device for the revalorization of the female self. Aspects of this line of reasoning can, indeed, be discerned in the early writings of both Clement and Pseudo-Philo, as briefly explored below. In the following, I argue that Deborah and Jael can be seen to represent figureheads for Goddess feminism.

FEMININITY, LEADERSHIP, AND WISDOM

Clement's[2] analysis is significant since his interpretations draw on feminine imaginary when describing the philosophical power and wisdom of God. He draws on the Alexandrian Jewish Wisdom tradition, in which Sophia is personified in feminine terms:

> Her I loved and sought from my youth, and longed to
>   make her my bride, and I became a lover of her beauty.
> She magnifies her noble birth by enjoying intimacy with
>   God,
> and the Master of All loved her. For she is initiate in the
>   knowledge of God,
> and chooser of his works. (Wisdom of Solomon 8: 2–4,
>   quoted in McVey 39)

Here we see feminine intellectual power interweaved with God's knowledge, raising the question whether all forms of knowledge can be necessarily constructed in relation to the masculine. The image of Sophia (a female name for wisdom) embodies the wisdom of God in both theological and devotional contexts. A feminist rereading would thus see Deborah as a prophetess, Judge, and poet embracing not only a female imaginary and knowledge but also one that embraces the full wisdom of humanity, albeit expressed via the use of female metaphors.[3] This linking of femininity with knowledge and reason is further revealed in Clement's use of maternal imagery: "God, out of His great love of humankind, comes to the help of humanity, as the mother-bird flies to one of her young that has fallen out of the nest; and if a serpent open its mouth to swallow the little bird, 'the mother flutters round, uttering cries of grief over her dear progeny' [Iliad 2: 315]; and God the Father seeks His creature, and heals its transgression, and pursues the serpent, and uncovers the young one, and incites it to fly up to the nest" (Clement, *Protrept.* 10, 91: 3, quoted in McVey 40).

These images of God as nursing mother and as Mother Bird mirror Deborah's divine status as "Mother of Israel." Within Clement's work, then, the symbol and role of the mother is not subordinated within masculine patriarchal structures, it is associated with the totality of human knowledge, spiritual transformation and human development.

This linkage of the feminine with wisdom is further elaborated upon in the work of Pseudo-Philo to which I now turn.

FEMININITY, POWER, AND WISDOM

Pseudo-Philo's[4] interpretation of the scriptures also reconstructs women's status and, in particular, his translation of Deborah's leadership role links leadership skills to the embodiment of the feminine. The readings clearly afford Deborah an authority both in terms of "ruling" and also "enlightening." Pseudo-Philo reaffirms the authority of Deborah's position by claiming all will be made well now a "woman will rule over them and enlighten them for forty years" (*Biblical Antiquities* 11: 2, quoted in Brown 43). The fact that Pseudo-Philo uses the terminology "enlighten" is significant, since in his interpretations this is a phrase that is only linked to Moses, and of course according to Hebrew lore it was Moses who first delivered God's divine wisdom to all of humanity. Further, light is seen to represent a metaphor for wisdom, so that both Moses and Deborah, as "enlighteners" are symbolic of human and divine wisdom. It is not only that wisdom is seen as vested within the female, but that she has the sacerdotal power to administer and guide on the laws of God: "The primal light of creation [which is] symbolized by the number seven [and which] gives true Sabbath rest to those who *follow her*" (Aristobulus, *Fragment* 5, quoted in Brown 44; italics my insertion)

Deborah is sent on the seventh day as the number seven is identified in some Jewish texts to be connected with wisdom and primordial light, thus again emphasizing energy and enlightenment. Although the biblical scriptures do not mention it, Pseudo-Philo records that Deborah served for forty years, and for all that time the land was free of war, the harvest bountiful, and humankind was not remiss in their service to God. This again could be read as a sign that female leadership, through divine understanding and wisdom, is rejuvenating and nurtures harmony.

Turning now to the role of Jael in overcoming the Israelites' enemies, it was previously noted that within traditional feminist critiques of the scriptures she relies on her sexedness to lead (seduce) and conquer. Pseudo-Philo's account does mention Jael was "beautiful" and that she "adorned herself," and that these represent "beauty weapons"; however, he notes significantly that she was pious, and it was this religious conviction that was her strength, not her sexedness. Pseudo-Philo stresses that when Sisera asks for water and Jael gives him milk, this communicates a strong symbolic gesture, since milk is seen to represent nurturing under the care of God, and food for wisdom (Brown 48; see also McVey). Moreover, he moves away from the sexualized connotations and claims that Sisera fell from the couch onto the ground, and not between Jael's legs. Thus, Pseudo-Philo's interpretations reconstruct the images of frailty, weakness and sexuality and their association with women, and of warrior and physical strength, culturally linked with men, by suggesting that power is that which comes through one's devotion to God.

It would also be worth noting Pseudo-Philo's reassessment of Deborah's song, which I have ignored until now. In his rereading, Deborah is not just a Judge, poet and prophetess: he also bestows on her the powers of a visionary, and command over the cosmic and natural elements. This is acknowledged by the way in which Deborah speaks in the shadow of the stars and moon. In doing so he envisions the female in God, and with God. Deborah's authority and ruling position is highlighted by Pseudo-Philo. Brown lays out the series of analogies Pseudo-Philo uses to emphasize the authority of Deborah's words:

1. "I am warning you as a woman of God."
2. "I am enlightening you as one from the female race."
3. "Obey me like your mother" (Brown 66).

Perhaps the association of leadership, femininity, and wisdom in our reimagining can be discerned from the following quote: "For example, Ben Sirah states that "She [Wisdom] will come to meet him like a mother" (Sirah. 15: 2), and Philo of Alexandria declares that Wisdom is "the mother and nurse of the All" (Brown 66). From the preceding discussion, it can be seen that in using Clement and Pseudo-Philo, my thealogical reconstructions are significant in advancing further the debates about the gendering of leadership theory. The portraits reveal the positive valuation of women and the roles that they could perform in Israel.

Drawing on Irigaray's conception of divine generation and the union of man and woman, we can envision a leadership dynamics as both embodied, and in transcendence of the human. By refiguring the human and divine as both immanent and transcendent, Irigaray has collapsed the distance between the human and the divine. Deborah does symbolize a "closeness to God"; she does embody a feminine subjectivity, since the female voice has been reintroduced into conceptualizations of leadership and wisdom. The feminine has become. Deborah has fulfilled the full range of leadership activities.

As Irigaray argues: "To become means fulfilling the wholeness of what we are capable of being" (*Sexes and Genealogies* 61). Deborah symbolizes spirituality and wisdom. Power and authority are not vested in the female as such; women "do not have to comply with "masculine models," or reside unnoticed behind the "masculine mask"; rather, the unveiling of the feminine is a signature of that which is holy and divine, embracing rejuvenating and cosmic processes.

This resonates with dominant themes in Goddess feminism literature. Goddess feminism has no wish to reproduce a masculine account of divine sovereignty and ruling power in a feminized form. Starhawk claims that a feminist reinterpretation of divine power is not about "power over" but "power from within" or "power for" (Raphael, "Truth in Flux" 202). Goddess feminism thus rejects the androcentric hierarchalism of patriarchal religions, since it blurs the distinction between humanity and divinity. Although Irigaray's work does not specifically advocate this position on power, this feminine reasoning strongly relates to her own philosophical concerns to reappropriate the feminine for herself, thereby destabilizing masculine logic so as to include the female and the feminine (see Butler; Schor).

CONCLUSIONS: REWRITING THE FEMININE DIVINE INTO LEADERSHIP THEORIZING

The aim in this chapter has been to unveil female sensualities in the scriptures and reimagine the female in order further to elucidate and advance our conceptualizations of leadership. I feel that this reconstructive approach is a powerful tool to aid both feminist and theologian scholars with opportunities to further the critique of theological foundations that had excluded them (Harrison).

I wanted to challenge the existing phallocentric versions of leadership and power and inject feminist ideas as a way of reconceiving and reconstructing male knowledge and power. In focusing on the feminine in leadership, I would like readers to bear in mind that I did not want to replace a male-centered lens with a female-centered lens. My aim was to draw attention to the feminine in leadership theorizing as an expansion, alternative, or corrective to the historically male biased lenses (see Calás and Smircich, "Voicing Seduction," and Fondas, who take this position also). Men can use feminist perspectives to illuminate their own lives by critically examining the religious institutions and practices in which they think, believe, and behave (O'Connor, "The Epistemological Significance of Feminist Research in Religion").

The story of Deborah and Barak, and Jael, raises important issues regarding women's experience of leadership and management. In the first reading although the women are clearly represented as courageous, and as such heroines, the tale highlights the limits of women's leadership roles. Deborah and Jael clearly do not challenge the conventional malestream and hierarchical notions of leadership. A woman can become a leader in her own right—she may assume most, but not all, of a man's leadership roles: the domain of war, however, is an all-male domain. Is there much difference if we draw parallels between the male executives' senior positions in contemporary organizations? Can we ever expect women to be equal when theorizing about leadership ability and effectiveness? The assertion of male heterosexual power in most organizations communicates cultural images of gender identity and competence (Billing and Alvesson). There is an inference that Barak, by virtue of his manly strength, has appropriate characteristics associated with leadership success, and in the modern corporation and Christian Church the persistence of organizational power relations reinforces dominant workplace masculinities, as well as the continued dominance of men in public, private and religious institutions (see Billing and Alvesson). Indeed, in both organization and religious writings there has been a recurrent association between gender, hierarchy and organization on the one hand, and militarism and warfare on the other (Collinson and Hearn; Vecchio). Barak's warrior profile is a prime example of how organization writers have tended to draw on military experience and language when formulating leadership theory reasserting the dominance of masculinist constructions in leadership theorizing (Bass and Avolio).

The case of Deborah and Barak reinforces sex role stereotypes and the unequal power relations between men and women by positioning Deborah as an accessory to man and Jael as a sexual object. As Wajcman and Vecchio both argue, although the symbolic representation of management is male, there is substance to sex role stereotypes because they appear to have such an enduring force. Attempts to undo these stereotypes have primarily focused on the special (and different from men) qualities that women leaders possess (Eagly and Carli; Helgeson). Where feminine qualities and skills are given preeminence, it is done so under the veil of patriarchy (Fondas).

In the second rereading I drew on Goddess feminism and sought to reimagine feminine leadership. In this version I highlight that the feminine has become, she has achieved a closeness to God, and she can represent a transcendent position. In injecting the concept of a divine leadership status for women I make a step towards opportunities for political and social transformation. Although I have sought to reveal a female sacral power embodied via the spirit of Deborah, I would never claim that the divine only manifests itself solely in femaleness: only that *she* be noticed. As noted at the beginning of this paper, in trying to unveil the feminine I wanted to try and unsettle malestream notions of leadership and leadership activity. While the female body and feminine characteristics, as expounded by maternal symbolism, might provide particularly apt metaphors for divine generativity and transcendence, and also become a medium for divine generativity (as Irigaray argues), this is not the only thing to do so. And certainly this configuration over time has shaped social values and organizational systems that privilege men and masculinity in discourses of leadership. In reasserting the power of the feminine I have shown how this perspective can be destabilized.

Although I have offered an alternative reconstruction of women and leadership in the Bible, the repression of a hierarchical duality and the reaffirmation of the female voice will not be easy. It will be an ongoing and constantly negotiated and renegotiated process: "Patriarchal religion is built on many millennia of repressed fear of the power of female body processes. Any effort to admit the female in her explicit femaleness as one who menstruates, gestates and lactates, will create psychic time-bombs that may explode with incalculable force. One can expect cries of 'witchcraft', 'blasphemy', 'sacrilege' and 'idolatry' to be directed at those who seek to resacralize the female body" (Ruether, quoted in Raphael, *Thealogy and Embodiment* 21).

In this vein, I would like readers to reimagine with me, and recreate a state of transcendence. Within and through Goddess feminism, the social world is (re)opened to new levels of consciousness and possibility. In thealogy, a woman's embodied finitude is holy in that it belongs to the processes of divine creativity (Irigaray, *Sexes and Genealogies*). The Divine and feminine in leadership helps women to explore women's potentiality, their strength, imagination and creation "which exists for us both within and beyond, as our possibility of a present and future" (Irigaray, *Sexes and Genealogies* 72). As Raphael states, quoting Zsuzsanna Emese Budapest, there is "no division of the spiritual and the profane; all is related in the universe, and none stands part from nature. All is nature" (*Thealogy and Embodiment* 23).

When nature is impregnated with the numinous the feminine sacred cannot simply be entombed within man. In this respect, I would argue that the patriarchal construction of female otherness need not be reversed into sameness but into a positive celebration of otherness as a mark of holiness. Thus, while feminists have used female otherness as a term against women, I support spiritual feminists who have revised and reclaimed the phrase for themselves (Raphael, "Truth in Flux"; Harrison). The female otherness is no longer subjugated but marks the numinous power of a female being (Daly; Raphael, "Truth in Flux"). Deborah as the Mother of Israel symbolizes this feminine passion and vitality.

Now to bring my feminine writings to a close. We cannot speak with a female voice because it can only be heard within, and under, masculinist discourses (Irigaray, *This Sex Which Is Not One*; *Speculum of the Other Woman*): but, in interrogating phallocentrism, and invoking the feminine (as Irigaray does), I have for a fleeting moment articulated resistance, and made a space possible from which to reimagine a feminine transcendent identity as part of leadership theorizing, as well as begin to represent woman's closeness to God. As Calás and Smirch suggest we can only move forward when we begin to understand female sexuality (whether in organization or theological contexts) by theorizing it in its own right, not in relation to men, so that we may take the steps of: "Recognizing that gender no longer equals women—*therefore the implicitly male gendered organizational theorizing practices get noticed*—and recognizing that the implicitly male gendered organizational theorizing has kept women's voices silent—*therefore women's voices begin to be written into organizational theorizing*" (Calás and Smircich, "Rewriting Gender" 235, emphasis original).

NOTES

1. It is generally agreed among feminist theologian scholars that the reluctance to accept women into service with God as ordained is related to the view that God himself was male and that power is naturally vested within the male human being. See, for example, D. Hampson, *Theology and Feminism* (Oxford: Blackwell, 1990); and P. S. Anderson, *A Feminist Philosophy of Religion* (Oxford: Oxford University Press, 1998).

2. Clement of Alexandria lived in the second and third centuries. His key work was the trilogy *Proptreptikos*, *Paedagogus*, and *Stromateis*, which sets forth the doctrine of God, his formulation of the goal of human life, and the manner of reading scripture to attain that goal. He is attributed as one of the first Christian writers to use female metaphors in theological contexts, especially Sofia. See K. E. McVey, "In Praise of Sophia: The Witness of Tradition," in *Women, Gender and Christian Community*, ed. J. D. Douglass and J. F. Kay, 34–35 (Louisville, KY: Westminster/John Knox Press, 1997).

3.   Some have argued that Miriam also held a leadership role but that this was suppressed; we thus end up with "Miriamic fragments." See P. Trible, "Subversive Justice: Tracing the Miriamic Traditions," in *Justice and the Holy*, ed. D. A. Knight and P. J. Paris. Atlanta: Scholars, 1989).

4.   Pseudo-Philo's key text was *Biblical Antiquities*, which is his own account of the scriptures. What is significant is that the Bible's tales tend to be quite short; Pseudo-Philo's accounts, however, tend to be more detailed and lengthy. For example, in the story of Deborah and Barak in the Bible it is recalled that the Israelites had suffered and sinned, whereas Pseudo-Philo evidences in detail what this suffering was—inter alia, ignoring the word of Moses; they have lost their heart. I draw on the interpretations of Clement of Alexandria—cited in C. A. Brown, *No Longer Be Silent, First Century Jewish Portraits of Biblical Women* (Louisville, KY: Westminster/John Knox, 1992)—who uses Pseudo-Philo as both an alternative, and an addition, to reconstructing the meanings of the scriptures.

BIBLIOGRAPHY

Anderson, Pamela Sue. *A Feminist Philosophy of Religion*. Oxford: Oxford University Press, 1998.

Bass, Bernard M., and Bruce J. Avolio. "Shatter the Glass Ceiling: Women May Make Better Managers." In *Leadership: Classical, Contemporary, and Critical Approaches*, edited by K. Grint, 199–210. New York: Oxford University Press, 1997.

Billing, Yvonne Due, and Mats Alvesson. "Questioning the Notion of Feminine Leadership: A Critical Perspective on the Gender Labelling of Leadership." *Gender, Work, and Organization* 7, no. 3 (2000): 144–57.

Bird, Phyllis. "Images of Women in the Old Testament." In *Religion and Sexism: Images of Women in the Jewish and Christian Traditions*, edited by R. R. Ruether, 41–88. New York: Simon and Schuster, 1974.

Braidotti, Rosi. "Becoming Woman: Or Sexual Difference Revisited." *Theory Culture and Society* 20, no. 3 (2003): 34–53.

Bronner, L. L. *From Eve to Esther: Rabbinic Reconstructions of Biblical Women*. Louisville, KY: Westminster/John Knox, 1994.

Brown, Cheryl Anne. *No Longer Be Silent, First Century Jewish Portraits of Biblical Women*. Louisville, KY: Westminster/John Knox, 1992.

Burrell, Gibson. "No Accounting for Sexuality." *Accounting, Organizations and Society* 12, no. 1 (1986): 89–101.

Butler, Judith. *Bodies That Matter*. London: Routledge, 1993.

Calás, Marta B., and Linda Smircich. "Dangerous Liaisons: The 'Feminine-in-Management' Meets 'Globalization.'" *Business Horizons* (March–April 1993): 73–83.

————. "Re-writing Gender into Organizational Theorizing: Directions from Feminist Perspectives." In *Rethinking Organization: New Directions in Organization Theory and Analysis*, edited by M. Reed and M. D. Hughes, 227–34. London: Sage, 1992.

————. "Voicing Seduction to Silence Leadership." *Organization Studies* 12 (1991): 567–601.

Christ, Carol. "Musings on the Goddess and her Cultured Despisers, Provoked by Naomi Goldenberg." *Feminist Theology* 13 (2005): 143–49.

Clark, Elizabeth, and Herbert Richardson, eds. *Women and Religion*. New York: Harper and Row, 1977.

Collinson, David L, and Jeff Hearn. "Naming Men as Men: Implications for Work, Organization, and Management." *Gender, Work, and Organization* 1, no. 1 (1994): 2–22.

Daly, Mary. "The Looking Glass Society." In *Feminist Theology: A Reader*, edited by A. Loades, 189–93. London: SPCK, 1990.

Doyle, Patricia M. "Women and Religion: Psychological and Cultural Implications." In *Religion and Sexism: Images of Women in the Jewish and Christian Traditions*, edited by R. R. Ruether, 15–40. New York: Simon and Schuster, 1974.

Eagly, Alice H., and Linda L. Carli. "The Female Advantage: An Evaluation of the Evidence." *The Leadership Quarterly* 14, no. 6 (2003): 807–34.

Exum, Cheryl J. "'Mother in Israel': A Familiar Figure Reconsidered." In *Feminist Interpretation of the Bible*, edited by L. M. Russell, 73–85. Oxford: Blackwell, 1985.

Farley, Margaret A. "Feminist Consciousness and the Interpretation of Scripture." In *Feminist Interpretation of the Bible*, edited by L. Russell, 41–54. Oxford: Blackwell, 1985.

Fondas, Nanette. "Feminization Unveiled: Management Qualities in Contemporary Writings." *Academy of Management Review* 22, no. 1 (1997): 257–82.

Goldenberg, Naomi. "The Return of the Goddess: Psychoanalytical Reflections on the Shift from Theology to Thealogy." *Studies in Religion/Sciences religieuses: A Canadian Journal* 16, no. 1 (1987): 37–52.

Grint, Keith, ed. *Leadership: Classical, Contemporary, and Critical Approaches*. New York: Oxford University Press, 1997.

Grosz, Elizabeth. "Sexual Difference and the Problem of Essentialism." In *The Essential Difference*, edited by N. Schor and E. Weed, 82–97. Bloomington: Indiana University Press, 1994.

Hampson, Daphne. "On Power and Gender." *Modern Theology* 4, no. 3 (1988): 235–50.

————. *Theology and Feminism*. Oxford: Blackwell, 1990.

Harrison, Victoria. S. "Modern Women, Traditional, and Abrahamic Religions and Interpreting Sacred Texts." *Feminist Theology* 15, no. 2 (2007): 145–59.

Hearn, Jeff, and Wendy Parkin. *"Sex" at "Work": The Power and Paradox of Organization Sexuality.* London: Prentice Hall/Wheatsheaf, 1995.

Helgeson, Sally. *The Female Advantage.* New York: Doubleday, 1990.

Irigaray, Luce. *An Ethics of Sexual Difference.* Translated by C. Burke and G. C. Gill. Ithaca, NY: Cornell University Press, 1993.

———. "The Bodily Encounter with the Mother." In *The Irigaray Reader*, translated by D. Macey and edited by M. Whitford, 34–52. Oxford: Blackwell, 1991.

———. "Equal to Whom." Translated by R. L. Mazzola. In *The Essential Difference*, edited by N. Schor and E. Weed, 63–81. Bloomington: Indiana University Press, 1994.

———. *Sexes and Genealogies.* Translated by G. C. Gill. New York: Columbia University Press, 1993.

———. *Speculum of the Other Woman.* Translated by G. C. Gill. Ithaca, NY: Cornell University Press, 1985.

———. *This Sex Which Is Not One.* Translated by C. Porter. Ithaca, NY: Cornell University Press, 1985.

Jackson, Stevi, and Sue Scott. "Putting the Body's Feet on the Ground: Towards a Sociological Reconceptualisation of Gendered and Sexual Embodiment." In *Constructing Gendered Bodies*, edited by K. Backett-Milburn and L. McKie, 3–23. Basingstoke: Palgrave, 2001.

King, Ursula. *Women and Spirituality.* Basingstoke: Macmillan, 1995.

Knott, Kim. "Notions of Destiny in Women's Self-Construction." *Religion* 28, no. 4 (October 1998): 405–11.

McLaughlin, Eleanor. "Women, Power and the Pursuit of Holiness in Medieval Christianity." In *Feminist Theology: A Reader*, 99–122. London: SPCK, 1990.

McVey, Kathleen E. "In Praise of Sophia: The Witness of Tradition." In *Women, Gender and Christian Community*, edited by J. D. Douglass and J. F. Kay, 34–45. Louisville, KY: Westminster/John Knox Press, 1997.

Metcalfe, Beverly. D., and Chris Rees. "Gender, Globalization and Organization: New Perspectives on Women's Development." *Equal Opportunities International* (forthcoming, 2009).

Metcalfe, Beverly. D., and Yochanan Altman. "Leadership." In *Organizational Behaviour Reassessed: The Impact of Gender*, edited by E. Wilson, 104–28. London: Sage, 2001.

Miller, Patrick. "Imagining God." In *Women, Gender and Christian Community*, edited by J. D. Douglass and J. F. Kay, 3–12. Louisville, KY: Westminster/John Knox Press, 1997.

O'Connor, J. "The Epistemological Significance of Feminist Research in Religion." In *Religion and Gender*, edited by U. King, 45–64. Oxford: Blackwell, 1995.

———. "Re-reading, Re-conceiving and Reconstructing Traditions: Feminist Research in Religion." *Women's Studies Interdisciplinary Journal* 17 (1989): 101–23.

Oseen, Collette. "Irigaray, Sexual Difference and Theorizing Leaders and Leadership." *Gender, Work, and Organization* 4, no. 3 (1997): 170–84.

Ostriker, Alicia S. *Feminist Revision and the Bible*. Oxford: Blackwell, 1993.

Raphael, Melissa. *Thealogy and Embodiment*. Sheffield: Sheffield Academic Press, 1996.

———. "Truth in Flux: Goddess Feminism as a Late Modern Religion." *Religion* 26, no. 3 (1996): 199–213.

Ruether, Rosemary Radford. *Religion and Sexism: Images of Women in the Jewish and Christian Traditions*. New York: Simon and Schuster, 1974.

———. *Sexism and God-Talk: Toward a Feminist Theology*. Boston: Beacon Press, 1983.

Sakenfield, Kathleen Doob. "Deborah, Jael, and Sisera's Mother: Reading the Scriptures in Cross-cultural Context." In *Women, Gender and Christian Community*, edited by J. D. Douglass and J. F. Kay, 13–22. Louisville, KY: Westminster/John Knox Press, 1997.

———. "Feminist Uses of Biblical Materials." In *Feminist Interpretation of the Bible*, edited by L. Russell, 55–64. Oxford: Blackwell, 1985.

Schor, Naomi. "The Essentialism Which Is Not One: Coming to Grips with Irigaray." In *Engaging with Irigaray*, edited by C. Burke, N. Schor, and M. Whitford, 57–79. New York: Columbia University Press.

Stanton, Elizabeth Cady. *The Woman's Bible*. Boston: Northeastern University Press, 1993.

Stone, Alison. *Luce Irigaray and the Philosophy of Sexual Difference*. Cambridge: Cambridge University Press, 2006.

Trible Phyllis. "Subversive Justice: Tracing the Miriamic Traditions." In *Justice and the Holy*, edited by D. A. Knight and P. J. Paris, 99–109. Atlanta: Scholars, 1989.

Vecchio, Robert. "In Search of Gender Advantage." *Leadership Quarterly* 14, no. 6 (2003): 835–50.

Wajcman, Judy. "Desperately Seeking Differences: Is Management Style Gendered?" *British Journal of Industrial Relations* 34, no. 3 (1996): 333–49.

CHAPTER 7

CUTTING "GOD" DOWN TO SIZE

TRANSCENDENCE AND THE FEMININE

Mike King

For a proper understanding of the spiritual life and the nature of, and possibilities for, women's spirituality, we need a broader language of the spiritual than monotheism can provide. The very term "transcendence" illustrates this because in the Christian tradition it tends to have meaning in binary opposition to "immanence" and refers to characteristics of "God," whereas in Eastern traditions—to the extent that translation can succeed in finding corresponding concepts—it means something closer to the "nondual" or "unitive." The "God"-language of the West has created a limitation of understanding, both within religious and within secular communities, the latter inheriting the equation "religion = God" and therefore remaining ignorant of nonmonotheistic religions. "God" is a construct peculiar to Abrahamic text-oriented monotheism, and it needs to be cut down to size, allowing other religious frameworks space. This means that questions of spirituality and religion need additional, equally powerful, terms to fill the gap. For women's spirituality, the issue is partly that "God" is an inevitably gendered term: monotheism constructs a male "God," served historically by a male priesthood.

Within the tradition of transpersonal psychology and its discourse of spirituality, "transcendence" is now also a term under attack, particularly by Jorge Ferrer. He suggests that the implicit adherence to Perennialism—a term coined by Leibniz, popularized by Aldous Huxley, and meaning a universal spirituality—within the transpersonal tradition, creates a single conception of the goal of the spiritual life: the transcendent (in the Eastern sense of the word). In a typically postmodernist move, he argues that the spiritual life not only has a multitude of starting points—not so controversial—but that it has a multitude of goals: a radical proposition (Ferrer 144). In true post-modernist style, he leaves open what these goals might be, which is to some extent a welcome opening up of possibility. However, this actually leaves little more than a flatland of potential with no landmarks, signs, or, even worse, any powerful language that can stand its ground against the patriarchal language of the "God" traditions. Instead, if "God" is brought down from its dominant conceptual position, not to wander through a relativist flatland as one among millions, it could take its place at the table with just *four* other significant spiritualities. The equal partners proposed here are shamanism, goddess polytheism, warrior polytheism, and the unitive (transcendent).

Luce Irigaray, in her extraordinary little book *Between East and West*, says, "There exists [in India] a cohabitation between at least two epochs of History: the one in which women are goddesses, the other in which men exercise a blind power over them" (65). It is suggested here, instead, the sequence comprises *five* epochs: shamanism, goddess polytheism, warrior polytheism, monotheism, and the unitive. These will be presented as having a historical basis, but beyond that, they are also archetypes of powerfully different spiritual impulses, recapitulated within all people at all times. Like the Jungian archetypes, they are conceived of as universals, but which may come into play more in one individual than another and more in one culture than another. In other words, these five "epochs" of religious manifestation are also five personal spiritual impulses, or five modalities of the spirit.

This articulation of spiritual difference through five historical modalities is not to be read as a development from a lesser, more primitive early modality to a higher, more sophisticated later modality. In other words, it is neither Hegelian, which would imply an inevitable historical vector privileging later periods or peoples, nor is it Wilberian, which would imply a developmental psychology, which is assumed in the work of Ken Wilber. This discussion of the earlier modalities of the spirit is informed by anthropology, ethnology, archaeology, and the ancient literatures, all of which disciplines are subject to new findings, methodologies, or better translations. Simone de Beauvoir, Sigmund Freud, and Carl Jung, to take some examples from the first half of the twentieth century, were profoundly influenced by the anthropology of their day, making many assumptions that would now be discredited by later developments in the discipline. Voltaire, writing in the eighteenth century, was even more constrained by an anthropology at its birth. Similarly, some of the approximate dates given here, or even possibly some of the major transitions alluded to, may well have to be revised in the future. However, the modalities of spirit that we are exploring in this historical fashion are not so dependent on the detail of history, but rather their relevance hinges on whether these modalities are archetypally present in our psyches today. We know that contemporary Western city-dwellers actively take up ancient religious practices (neoshamanism or neopaganism, for example) or adopt Eastern unitive traditions (Yoga, neo-Advaita, or Zen, for example). The flourishing nature of these adoptions illustrates the ability of people to respond at a very deep level to modalities of the spirit that are remote in time or place from their contemporary setting.

The Five Stages of Religion

Here five stages in religion are introduced as an idealized "photofit" composite of world spiritual history, though the complete sequence does not in fact exactly take place anywhere in the world: It is more a psychogeography of the spiritual. These religious stages can be shown diagrammatically:

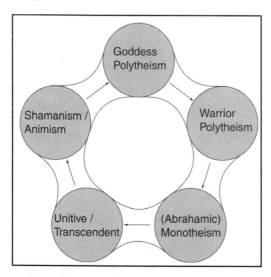

Figure 7.1   Five religious stages.

The diagram has been drawn with curved lines to suggest that the boundaries between the five modalities are fluid, even where, in the case of monotheism, it strenuously resists other modalities of the spirit. Arrows have been drawn to indicate the historic progression, with one exception: the arrow from the unitive/transcendent to the shamanic/animist, which appears to point backward in time, and will be discussed later.

SHAMANISM/ANIMISM

The shamanic/animistic category represents a modality of the spirit that seems to have emerged with humankind itself. No early hominid traces seem to have been found without evidence of shamanistic practices, which include artifacts—such as fetishes and totems—for rites that revolve around Nature and "spirits." The shamanic worldview is predicated on a perception of Nature as imbued with spirit, wherein the elements of Nature, such as rocks, mountains, trees, rivers, animals, and skies, are inhabited by spirits and daily life is also filled with the presence of the spirits of the ancestors. This "spirit world" is both beyond the so-called material world and, at the same time, intimately entwined within it: They are not separable in shamanism. Some scholars believe that there is a meaningful distinction between animism and shamanism in that the latter is served by a functionary or specialist called a shaman, whereas the former is not. For our purposes, this distinction is of little use. This is because both animism and shamanism, as they are generally understood, are grounded in the same spiritual interiority of the spirit world. In an animistic culture, there would surely exist individuals whose gift for entering into the spirit world was more developed than others and who would naturally take on roles of intercession and healing, though perhaps not culturally formalized in the way that shamans are. Conversely, in a shamanic culture it is inconceivable that the rest of the group would not mostly share the worldview and spiritual abilities of the shaman, at least in a nascent form. Hence, we will from here on use the term "shamanic" to cover both animist and shamanic spiritualities, though we are referring more to an inner orientation or sensibility than to outward ritual or practice.

The shaman, who can equally be male or female (as shown in traditions as far apart as in Siberia and South America), is required to mediate between the group and the spirits as the functionary of this religion; conversely, he or she makes the world sacred through the practice of ritual. Shamanism is associated with hunter-gatherer cultures, and though it is understood as the universal ur-religion of mankind (proposed, for example, by Mircea Eliade in his seminal work *Shamanism: Archaic Techniques of Ecstasy*), the word "shaman" itself comes via Russian from the Tungus people of Siberia (or it may have its root in Sanskrit). We are fortunate that shamanism has survived at the margins since the earliest of times, generally driven to unfertile or inhospitable territories by later agricultural societies. Hence, in mountains, deserts, or polar regions, shamanic cultures persist to this day (though increasingly ravaged by their contact with the industrial world) whose practices and beliefs can be studied.

A form of neoshamanism has recently emerged, particularly in the United States, as people with little previous interest in religion take up shamanic practices under modern teachers or guides. The writings of anthropologist and cult author Carlos Castaneda and the work of transpersonal psychologist Stanislav Grof have been significant in this revival. Michael Harner, author of the classical work *The Way of the Shaman*, comments in the tenth-anniversary edition on a "shamanic renaissance": "During the last decade, however, shamanism has returned to human life with startling strength, even to urban strongholds of Western 'civilisation', such as New York and Vienna. . . . There is another public, however, rapidly-growing and now numbering in the thousands in the United States and abroad, that has taken up shamanism and made it part of personal daily life" (xi). Shamanic peoples often display a certain gender fluidity and gender balance, despite the roles of men as predominantly hunters and women as predominantly gatherers. Males of shamanic cultures often look feminine by modern Western standards, while females may not have our contemporary exaggerated femininity. Neither do these men and women have the individualistic or egotistic natures of Western people; perhaps this has led to the widespread but absurd notion that shamanic peoples have a less developed personal consciousness. A better way to understand a defining characteristic of shamanic peoples is as *self-effacing*. Good portrayals in contemporary culture are to be found in the character played by Chief Dan George in Clint Eastwood's film *The Outlaw Josie Wales* (1976), and as Old Lodge Skins in the film *Little Big Man* (1970), or in the character of Dersu Uzula in the film of the same name by Ikuru Kurusawa (1975). Well-known Native American actor Gary Farmer plays "Nobody" in Jim Jarmusch's film *Dead Man* (1995), vividly conveying the humility at the heart of the Native American way of life and what is arrogant in that of the white man.

GODDESS POLYTHEISM

If "shamanism" is a contested term, then anything to do with "goddess" is doubly so. There is in fact a genuine difficulty in the discussion ahead: Shamanism has survived in the margins, has been extensively studied, and so is at least in principle recoverable as an ancient practice. But goddess religions—to the extent that we now posit their existence—were systematically eradicated by later modalities of the spirit *and had nowhere to go.* There is growing evidence from archaeology that Goddess cultures replaced shamanic hunter-gatherer cultures in all parts of the world bar the marginal lands around the period of the late Neolithic and early Bronze Ages (Shlain 35). But the interiority of this modality of the spirit is more problematic and less recoverable than the shamanic because there is no surviving unbroken tradition. Instead, there is a modern revival, led by radical scholars, such as Starhawk, along with women from all walks of life, who seek to imaginatively reconstruct this spirituality. It is the archaeological evidence and the modern revival taken *together* that make the case for Goddess Polytheism as a major modality of the spirit.

In spiritual terms, we can identify two stages in the transition from hunter-gatherer cultures to agrarian ones: first, to "goddess polytheism" and then to "warrior polytheism." Both involve an increasing process of abstraction in the conception of spirits or deities. The hunter-gatherer way of life existed for possibly some three million years, and, as a first approximation at least, we can associate the shamanic modality of spirit with that way of life. The implication is clear: shamanism must be deeply rooted in the human psyche if it were present over such huge timescales. Hunter-gatherer societies in general seem to have been nonsexist and relatively nonviolent, comprising family groups of about eighty to a hundred individuals, all well known to each other. Some seven thousand years ago, two new skills emerged: that of animal husbandry and that of agriculture. Whether as horticulture (small-scale agriculture) or as agriculture proper, the new way of life spread rapidly and pushed the older hunter-gatherer lifestyle to the margins, along with its central spiritual form: shamanism. Baring and Cashford suggest that we can broadly associate goddess polytheism with small-scale horticultural communities of the late Neolithic and early Bronze Age, and warrior polytheism with large-scale agriculture and societies of the later Bronze and Iron Age (416).

The growing scholarship on goddess religions is led by feminist archaeologists and thinkers, whose role as feminists in this is to uncover the layers of patriarchal prejudice that have clouded the disciplines of archaeology, anthropology, and history up to very recently. For example, the huge quantities of goddess figures unearthed in archaeological sites all round the world were routinely dismissed as products of "fertility cults" by male (Christian) academics. Merlin Stone's *When God Was a Woman* is an early but superb account of the endemic and often subtly propagated male prejudice in these matters. Once the same data are looked at from the recognition that goddess religions were not marginal cults, but central to thousands of years of human history, a radically different picture emerges. We can say that the word "cult" is a quick way to dismiss anything non-Christian and the word "fertility" a quick way to dismiss anything nonmasculine; hence, "fertility cult" conveys total contempt in the mind of the male (white) Christian. The work of Marija Gimbutas, Anne Baring and Jules Cashford, and Starhawk (born Miriam Simos) are seminal in this field, while author Leonard Shlain contributes radical proposals about the marginalization of goddess spiritualities because of *writing*.

In the period of goddess polytheism, the discrete, specific, and localized spirits of the shamanic world took their first steps into abstraction as gods and goddesses of early horticultural life. These deities were propitiated perhaps in a different way than in shamanic culture. As less specific spirits and more abstracted deities, the spiritual response to them would have changed, perhaps quite dramatically (Hillman xxi). The shamanic mode of "storytelling" becomes a polytheistic mode of "myth": a transition from an animistic engagement with living spirits to a mythic engagement with psychic entities. It may also be the case that goddess spiritualities were more centered on human-human relationships than human-animal relationships. We have emphasized the *polytheism* in goddess spirituality: This is to counter the Western cultural impetus to merely transpose a male monotheism into a female monotheism, a single "God" into a single "Goddess."

Scholars, such as Leonard Shlain and Marija Gimbutas, now believe that the entire Greek mythology can be understood as arising from the transition from a goddess culture to a patriarchal polytheism, undertaken at the time when oral traditions were first transcribed in the new Semitic alphabet (Shlain 120). Possibly the best illustration of this transition in contemporary culture is to be found in the film *Medea* (1969) loosely adapted by Pier Paolo Pasolini from the play by Euripides, featuring the opera singer Maria Callas in the lead role (her only film appearance). Medea represents for Pasolini the transition from matrilineal, goddess cultures to patrilineal male warrior cultures as she returns with Jason, whose mission it was to steal her golden fleece. Pasolini captures the moment of transition as the Argonauts land in Corinth on a simple raft. Medea cannot understand how the men treat the land of their birth: They do not call to the ancient deities, propitiate the nature spirits of earth and stone; they merely tread on the land as *property*. She is overcome and then rants at them, full of passion and foreboding: "This place will sink because it has no foundations. You do not call god's blessings on your tents. You speak not to god. You do not seek the centre; you do not mark the centre. Look for a tree, a post, a stone."

Once on the soil, which is now to be her new homeland, she runs in despair through the grasses, wailing: "Speak to me Earth, let me hear your voice, I have forgotten your voice. Speak to me Sun. Where must I stand to hear your voice? Speak to me Earth. Speak to me Sun. Are you losing your way, never to return again? Grass, speak to me. Stone, speak to me. Earth, where is your meaning? Where can I find you again?"

To monotheists, steeped in the Old Testament proscription against idolatry, and the wider and endemic scorn within the Old Testament toward the older Nature religions, Medea is merely a pagan among pagans: What is her objection to the paganism of the warriors who take her home? But to those whose spiritual antennae are attuned to the differences between shamanism, goddess polytheism, and warrior polytheism, her anguish has a clear and obvious source: the new, patriarchal polytheism is abandoning Nature and substituting instead more abstract "gods"—those whose interest is only in the narrowly human and the warlike at that. Later in the film, Pasolini makes clear the extent of Medea's spiritual tragedy:

> *Centaur*: Despite all your schemes and interpretations, his influence
> causes you to love Medea.
> *Jason*: Love Medea?
> *Centaur*: Yes. Also you pity her. *You understand her spiritual catas-
> trophe.* A woman of an ancient world, confused in a world which
> ignores her beliefs. She experienced the opposite of a conversion
> and has never recovered.
> *Jason*: What use is this knowledge to me?
> *Centaur*: None. It is a reality.

Pasolini both understands Medea's "spiritual catastrophe"—and it stands for the spiritual catastrophe of all women as they came under the subjugation of patriarchal tradition—and makes it clear that Jason is utterly uninterested. It is a reality of Medea's life, not his.

In this context, then, it is of interest to turn to Irigaray's concept of the "aboriginal feminine," as discussed in *Between East and West*. This is a most useful term, though it needs a little elaboration in the context of the epochal spiritualities proposed here. Irigaray had found in India, at the time of her 1984 trip, signs indicating that an ancient feminine spirituality survived alongside later patriarchal religion, particularly in the south (this is the remnant of the original Dravidian culture driven southward by the invading Aryans of the north). Effectively, India allows us to see today a palimpsest of the historical transition that took place in ancient Greece and so effectively dramatized for us in Pasolini's *Medea*. But what Irigaray practiced in India and brought back with her to the West was Yoga, a spiritual tradition as ancient in epochal terms as Medea but exclusively located within the unitive/transcendent modality of the spirit. Hence, she is quite right to question the apparent genderlessness of Yoga as a discipline and a teaching of transcendence.

WARRIOR POLYTHEISM

As large-scale agriculture developed out of small-scale horticulture, methods of creating surplus came into being through the cultivation, drying, and storage of grain: This became the first form of wealth and wages. Eventually, this led to the emergence of the city-state and created a radically new way of life over the small-scale horticultural community. Complex social and economic patterns emerged that allowed a class of society to live removed from the immediate production of food. At the same time, there had evolved a new sphere of male human activity: warfare. Leonard Shlain believes that the Neolithic and early Bronze Age period from approximately ten thousand to five thousand years ago seems to have been dominated by women, with little militarism or central authority, but the male hunting instinct seems to have been transforming itself during this time into the instinct for war (Shlain 33). Perhaps as crops required defending, not just from wild animals but also from other tribes, defensive and then offensive patterns of aggression developed. With economic surplus and the development of settlements into cities, a military caste came into being, and with it what we are calling "warrior polytheism." Society became stratified in a way that was impossible during the epochs of hunter-gatherer and Goddess societies, leading also to a new priestly caste. The shaman might be called the "priest" or "priestess" of the shamanic way of life, but his or her powers were in healing and in shamanic flight: The new priesthood became guardians instead of great temples and therefore also of wealth and power.

Warrior polytheism continues the proliferation of deities, along with the tendency to anthropomorphism (as opposed to the taking on of animal characteristics within shamanism: zoomorphism), but in the patriarchal pantheon, the female deities were demoted or forgotten in favor of new male ones. (They were literally "written out" of history.) Ancient Greece provides us with a good example of how the new deities were considered to be as quarrelsome as the war ridden human city-states. The key issue here however is the shift from a female-dominated culture and religion to a male-dominated culture and religion: from matriarchy to patriarchy. The flowering of goddess cultures between seven thousand and five thousand years ago was brought to an abrupt end in the Mediterranean world at least, and historians and anthropologists have argued over the causes for more than a century. (In India, as Irigaray saw, there are still vivid traces of the earlier modalities of the spirit.) What brought patriarchy into being is of interest generally, but in terms of religion, the shift was nothing short of a revolution. Shamanic spirituality was equally male and female; Goddess Polytheism was female dominated; but all later religion became male dominated. Shlain considers Engels's theory that the growing concept of property favored patriarchy but refutes it on the basis of many property-based goddess cultures. Shlain suggests instead that patriarchy arose with *writing* and in its most radical form with the linked inventions of the alphabet and monotheism. He bases this on his understanding of the brain (he is a neurosurgeon by profession) and, in particular, on the division of functions between the left and right hemispheres (Shlain 23).

Agriculture led to the stratification of society and to the division between those who worked on the land (and who probably retained their shamanistic practices) and the city-dwellers, who began to live at one remove from nature. The city-dwellers needed more symbolic thinking to deal with the increased social, technical, and political complexities of their lives, and, hence, the process of increased abstraction was necessary. One of the qualities of polytheism is the tendency, possibly inherited from its shamanic roots, to be localized; that is, for gods to belong to regions. Hence, the Romans, in administrating their conquests, acknowledged the local gods and allowed their worship as long as the gods of Rome, particularly the Emperor, were included. (The Jews were a notable exception in the Empire, refusing to cooperate with this.) In fact, the gods in different cultures were rarely so different as to be unrecognizable. Caesar, for example, had

no difficulty in finding the Roman equivalents to the deities he discovered in conquered Gaul. (This is a process referred to by an early
meaning of the word *syncretism*.)

To contemplate what a warrior polytheistic modality of the spirit
might feel like, we can turn to the early Roman, Greek, Mayan, or
Hindu cultures and enter imaginatively into the life of those early
city-states. It is a world of myth making, a mythology that holds
within it a great departure from shamanic storytelling: It is *heroic*
and, in its Greek form, also *Oedipal*. The shaman is amorphous and
self-effacing (also androgyne), whereas the polytheism of the city-
state serves its principal activity: warfare. Of course, when the heroic
emerges onto the world stage, so does the hubristic: success and failure enter the vocabulary in a way unknown to shamanic and goddess
cultures. Tragedy is born with "civilization," articulated in the Greek
myth of Oedipus, as the inevitable competitiveness of the son with
the father. When Freud took this story to be a universal of the human
mind, he was operating only within the Western inheritance of Greek
warrior polytheism. The Far East arrived at its patriarchy in a rather
different way: The Chinese mind would not have made a drama out
of Oedipus's killing of his father and marriage to his mother, both
unintended. "Such things happen in the realm between heaven and
earth," is a more likely response. (Interestingly, Pasolini also chose
to make a film out of the story of Oedipus: Perhaps because Pasolini was a homosexual, he was much interested in the origins of
Western masculinities.)

Although much of the modern mind is born out of the polytheistic context, including its rejection of the shamanic, our Western
cultural heritage of monotheism makes polytheism seem like a distant
form of consciousness for us. Psychologist James Hillman has recognized this and also the psychological need for an essential component
of polytheism: its pluralism. He suggests that the psyche, instead of
striving to some imaginary unity in the image of the single "God,"
should celebrate its multiplicity of impulse in terms of the "gods,"
plural, as a better reflection of the polyvalence of the human mind
(Hillman 30).

MONOTHEISM

When considering Abrahamic monotheism as a modality of spirit,
among other equal epochal forms, it is perhaps useful to point out
the following: It is geographically unique, arising in the Middle East
and nowhere else in the world (it is hence an anomaly on the world

stage of religions); it evolved from warrior polytheism, not goddess polytheism; it is associated with a horrifically violent rejection of earlier epochal forms; it is patriarchal; it is associated with the invention of the (Semitic) alphabet; its "God" is not localized, and it becomes a religion uniquely associated with the written word (giving rise to "language mysticism").

Monotheism retains the idea of "God" as a being, a supreme being, analogous with just one of the previous gods but somehow incorporating the separate characteristics of all of them. Anthropomorphism, that is, the tendency to project human qualities onto the polytheistic gods, is fiercely resisted in Judaic monotheism, with its prohibition on speaking the name of "God," and the denial of attributes to him. However, it is not surprising that a single "God" becomes anthropomorphized in the popular mind, however much this tendency is resisted, and this problem is central to the history of monotheism. Judaic, Christian, and Islamic monotheisms are intolerant of other gods, but in other cultures, a pseudomonotheism has not excluded polytheism. Brahman, for example, the "God" of the Hindus, is worshiped through a plethora of other deities who are understood to represent one or more of his divine aspects. Hence, we cannot say that Hinduism is exclusively monotheistic or exclusively polytheistic. In fact, Westerners have read their Judeo-Christian "God" into Brahman in a quite inappropriate way. Similarly, Jesuit missionaries in China persuaded themselves that the Chinese "heaven" was the equivalent to the Christian "God," though their fellow-missionaries, the Franciscans, thought otherwise and finally convinced the Pope to come down against the Jesuits (Paper 5).

The idea of monotheism seems to have emerged in four possible locations: in fourteenth century BCE Egypt with Akhenaton; in Northern Africa (Barnet); in Persia (modern-day Iran) as Zoroastrianism in the sixth century BCE; and in Israel, as an ongoing process of change that may have been influenced by the Egyptian and Persian examples. Although Egyptian monotheism was rapidly overturned, and Zoroastrianism became a tiny religion on the world stage, it was Judaic monotheism that has had the most impact on the world, through its influence on Christianity and Islam.

THE TRANSCENDENT/UNITIVE

In the final development of the religious life, monotheism becomes a transcendent or unitive religion, represented for example by Buddhism and the concept of *nirvana*. However, there is no simple example of a monotheistic religion developing into a transcendent one; for example, in the case of Christianity and Islam, the mystics who entered into this form of the spiritual life were generally persecuted. Meister Eckhart is an example in Christianity who was condemned by the Inquisition, though he died before any punishment could be inflicted, while Mansur (Al-Hallaj) is an example in Islam who suffered a horrible martyrdom. In both cases, the problem for their mainstream religions was that their understanding of "God" had gone beyond the notion of a separate being: their unitive experiences calling for a language of personal transcendence foreign to monotheism. The position of the mystics in the Judaic tradition is more complex, in that they tended to avoid personal declarations of union, and in any case, any popular anthropomorphism of "God" was balanced by its continual denial in the writings of Judaic scholars (Scholem 63). As a result, the "transcendent" is generally the most difficult component of the spiritual life to describe, particularly in the West. The term "unitive" is equally good but not as familiar. The East has the well-known concept of "enlightenment" (or *nirvana*, *moksha*, or liberation), which describes the goal of the transcendent religionist and a transcendent religion. It is "unitive" in the sense of "not-two" (as in Zen and Advaita formulations) but not conceived as union with "God."

If read in a literal developmental sense, these five stages do not map onto the religious history of the world in any simple way. It is clear that by at least 2,600 BCE all five stages had already emerged onto the religious world scene, though our historical knowledge of this, and earlier periods, is rather sketchy. In both the Mediterranean and Indian cultures of that period, we find evidence that all five strands—shamanism, goddess polytheism, warrior polytheism, monotheism, and the unitive/transcendent—were present and to one degree or another *available*. This means that individuals, depending on their circumstances and mobility, were able to draw on the support for different types of spiritual life. The extraordinary richness of the spiritual life around the Mediterranean at the time of Christ, for example, shows how all five types were present among the different cultures and social strata. This is well documented in *The Jesus Mysteries* by Timothy Freke and Peter Gandy. In India, too, by the time of the Buddha, there was a similar spread of religious practice, and in the ancient Vedas and Upanishads, we find a recognition that is central to the discussion here: Each individual tends to gravitate toward the spiritual life that suits them. More than this, each individual has a spiritual impulse and temperament that aligns itself within these categories and has a *right* to adhere to them without interference. Such a right was never part of the Christian history of the West.

That an individual has a *right* to pursue the spiritual life appropriate to them was of course never enshrined in the ancient world either in law (human rights are a recent development), or very often in opportunity (economic and geographical mobility was limited). Nevertheless, those who devoted themselves to the spiritual life in the ancient world often traveled large distances to seek out the teachings they could not find locally, and a large part of ancient discourse resulted from such travelers bringing back new teachings (Pythagoras being a good example, or Solon in Plato's *Timaeus*). This is of course quite obscured from the secular Western mind so shaped by Christianity. By denigrating all the spiritual traditions previous to Christianity as "pagan," a monolithic and exclusive understanding of early religion held sway. The hostility toward shamanic and goddess spiritualities also came from the Greek inheritance, though, in this case, it is more a question of a prejudice against those people living in the countryside and working the land and against women. The legacy of this prejudice is still highly visible in the United States and the United Kingdom and in the productions of mainstream Western culture.

The transcendent needs a little more explanation at this point. We have implied that it would develop out of monotheism, and in fact, we see many examples of the transcendent impulse in Christian and Sufi mystics. In the transcendent spiritual experience, "God" as "other" gives way to a state of union or identity and, hence, ceases to be thought of as a "being," even as a "supreme being," rather as simply the "being" at the core of the mystic's identity (Eckhart is a good example of this). In Buddhism, there is no concept of "God" to start with, just the extinguishing of the separate sense of self ("not two" in the formulation of some Zen traditions). It is not possible in a brief overview to develop this very difficult idea fully, but we leave it for now with two remaining comments. First, that the Christian mainstream did not easily tolerate the transcendent, any more than it did signs of "paganism." Second, to counter the simplistic notion that there is a linear spiritual trajectory through the five types of spiritual life, we might look at the example of Tibetan Buddhism. It is the result of the integration of a shamanic religion (the Bon tradition of Tibet) and the incoming Buddhist teachings of transcendence. The two live side by side and create a spectrum of spiritual teachings that support a wide range of spiritual temperaments, an example again of spiritual pluralism within a single tradition. We have characterized Christianity as monolithic, but it is not completely homogeneous, rather the permitted range of spiritual expression is narrow compared with Tibetan Buddhism, for example, and even narrower when laid side by side with Hinduism.

The arrows drawn in our diagram from shamanism to goddess polytheism and so on can be read as implying a developmental sequence or even an inevitable sequence. This is not the intention: it just so happens that elements of this sequence can be found everywhere in history. But we have drawn a final arrow from the transcendent back to the shamanic, partly to counter any sense of inevitable historical development and partly to highlight how the shamanic and the transcendent so easily coexist in the East. Tibetan Buddhism is one example, while the coexistence of Zen and Shinto in Japan is another. The arrow linking the unitive or transcendent with shamanism also suggests an *engaged* enlightenment: a Buddha who turns again to the world.

CONCLUSIONS

To recapitulate: while the five religious modalities can be seen to form a historical development, this sequence tends to privilege one form over another. A better use of the distinctions between these forms is to understand them as expressions of five different types of spiritual impulse, as archetypes that are universally present. These impulses may arise in individuals with no regard to history or the prevailing religious form, often leading to a *spiritual dislocation* between individual and culture.

This fivefold schematic allows us to place monotheism in a global and epochal perspective. Although monotheism is a significant modality of the spirit and can be understood as an experiment in spirituality that has created much of value, it has actively denied the other four modalities: In particular, it denies the feminine. However, when the monotheistic "God" is cut down to one-fifth of its claim and takes its seat at the table with the other modalities, it can be a good partner. For the survival of the planet, we need to actively explore those modalities of the spirit that are nonpatriarchal, nonheroic, and that actively elevate the feminine and a profound relationship with the natural world.

We can illustrate these points by considering Irigaray's call, both in her chapter in this volume, and in her book *Between East and West*, to identify a "culture of two subjects"—male and female. She says, "Each subject requires a different manner of becoming divine," perhaps corresponding to the two epochal spiritualities that she detected in India

(Irigaray 65). This idea in itself represents a complete revolution, particularly for the West: It represents a spiritual pluralism denied for millennia. But the scheme presented here cuts the corpus in a different way by suggesting *five* different epochal spiritualities, not in the first instance distinguished through gender difference. Irigaray suggests two, Jorge Ferrer suggests an infinity, and this chapter suggests five. Let us see how this works in an issue raised by Irigaray in the specific context of the Yoga tradition. She found herself acknowledging its apparent openness to women but quickly discovered: "Because of this lack of cultivation of sexual identity, the most irreducible site of reciprocity, reciprocity often seems absent to me in the milieus of yoga" (66). Rather than just understanding Yoga as a patriarchal spirituality, the fivefold scheme presented here quickly locates it in the unitive/ transcendent epochal form. Its core text is the *Yoga Sutras of Patanjali*, which, as Irigaray has picked up on, is disinterested in the question of sexual identity. It also has as its core directive the "cessation of the mind"—a very difficult concept for the West—which can be translated as a "restriction of the fluctuations of consciousness" (Feuerstein 26). For Irigaray, this manifested itself in the instruction from her Indian male Yoga teacher "not to think." Such a teacher is rather unlikely to understand the Western feminist tradition, which leaps on such an exhortation as a patriarchal move to suppress the female. Irigaray muses on this exhortation: "This [Yoga] tradition seems to me to possess a subtlety that demands, on the contrary, a real aptitude for thought" (Irigaray 67). Certainly, the Yoga tradition contains this contradiction, but ultimately, it is a discipline of transcendence that requires cessation of modifications of the mind (or fluctuations of consciousness). These modifications ultimately include all discursive thought and gender. Hence, the Yoga tradition, however modified for the West, cannot meet Irigaray's need for a "manner of becoming divine" for the feminine, particularly because of her emphasis on the *relational*. The unitive/transcendent is precisely an epochal or archetypal spirituality in which the relational ceases. So, in our scheme, Irigaray would need to turn to the other four principal modalities of the spirit to discover where the appropriate relational spirituality might lie. In shamanism, this relationality is mediated through the spirit world, and is ancestor and Nature centered. In goddess polytheism, this relationality is propitionary but locates relationship more within the human world. In warrior polytheism, relations are mostly between men and male gods; divinization is in the context of conquest. And in monotheism, the core relationship is between self and the "wholly other": "God" (Otto 25).

To be restricted to only one modality of spirit by the accident of birth was a specific tragedy of the West. This is now overcome in the multivalency of our postmodern world. Irigaray's search for spiritualities that serve a "culture of two subjects" is one expression of this spiritual pluralism, Ferrer's infinity of goals another. The scheme presented here cuts down the "God" religion of the West to take its place along four other major epochal or archetypal forms: Each represents a major clustering of spiritual wisdom, of means of divinization, of modalities of the spirit. The "accomplished interiority," which Irigaray elsewhere suggests should be the goal of the spiritual life (37), may well even be achieved by a systematic exploration of all five. Perhaps even in a single day, the human spirit needs to move between these different spiritualities, as it does between different relationalities. One does not live in the pocket of one's sexual partner; one does not spend all day with the ancestors, or in Nature; one does not devote all one's energies to conquest or horticulture; one does not even need "God" all day long: a time for the cessation of *all* mentation is also needed. Eckhart showed that most vividly (159).

But such an easy pluralism may be a long way off for a society still struggling to shake off the habits of thought formed by patriarchal monotheism. When the centaur told Jason that Medea had undergone a spiritual catastrophe and the "opposite of a conversion," he is perhaps speaking to a majority of women today: Women are still to some degree traumatized by the indifference of the world of Jason to their spiritual needs. The very different kind of work pursued by Luce Irigaray—emerging from postmodernist thought—and that of Starhawk—often dismissed as "New Age"—both require that the patriarchal "God" sit down at the table and hear the voices of other spiritualities, other relationalities. The establishment of the "aboriginal feminine" or goddess modality of spirit is an essential first step, but a more ambitious goal is to see women reclaim all modalities of the spirit. The shamanic anyway belongs equally to men and women, while warrior polytheism represents a conquestial mode of divinization that women may need to draw on as much as men. (All *great* art, reform, construction, and exploration need a spirituality of courage and risk taking.) Monotheism as a relationship with a "wholly other" is likewise a relational spirituality as potentially cornucopian to the female spirit as the male. Finally, the transcendent modality of the spirit requires that gender as a "modification of the mind" is suspended altogether in ecstatic absorption (or enstatic as Feuerstein prefers it). Why should women (or men, for that matter) be deprived of any of these modalities of the spirit?

BIBLIOGRAPHY

Baring, Anne, and Jules Cashford. *The Myth of the Goddess: Evolution of an Image*. London: Arkana, 1993.

Barnett, Norman. *Black Heroes and the Spiritual Onyame: An Insight into the Cosmological Worlds of Peoples of African Descent*. Croydon: Filament Publishing, 2005.

Castaneda, Carlos. *The Teachings of Don Juan*. Harmondsworth: Penguin, 1970.

Eckhart, Meister. *Selected Treatises and Sermons*. London: Fontana Library, Collins, 1963.

Eliade, Mircea. *Shamanism: Archaic Techniques of Ecstasy*. Bollingen Series 76. Princeton, NJ: Princeton University Press, 2004.

Ferrer, Jorge N. *Revisioning Transpersonal Theory: A Participatory Vision of Human Spirituality*. Albany: State University of New York Press, 2002.

Feuerstein, Georg. *The Yoga Sutras: A New Translation and Commentary*. Rochester, VT: Inner Traditions International, 1989.

Freke, Timothy, and Peter Gandy. *The Jesus Mysteries: Was the "Original Jesus" a Pagan God?* New York: Three Rivers, 1999.

Gimbutas, Marija. *The Language of the Goddess: Unearthing the Hidden Symbols of Western Civilization*. New York: Thames and Hudson, 1989.

Grof, Stanislav. *LSD Psychotherapy*. Alameda: Hunter House, 1994.

Harner, Michael. *The Way of the Shaman*. New York: HarperSanFrancisco, 1990.

Hillman, James. *Revisioning Psychology*. New York: HarperPerennial, 1977.

Irigaray, Luce. *Between East and West: From Singularity to Community*. New York: Columbia University Press, 2002.

Otto, Rudolf. *The Idea of the Holy*. London: Oxford University Press, 1923.

Paper, Jordan. *The Spirits are Drunk: Comparative Approaches to Chinese Religion*. Albany: State University of New York Press, 1995.

Pasolini, Pier Paolo. *Medea* (Maria Callas, Giuseppe Gentile). Euro International Film (EIA) S.p.A., 1969.

Scholem, Gershom. *Major Trends in Jewish Mysticism*. New York: Schocken Books, 1995.

Shlain, Leonard. *The Alphabet versus the Goddess: The Conflict between Words and Images*. London: Penguin/Compass, 1998.

Starhawk. *The Spiral Dance: A Rebirth of the Ancient Religion of the Great Goddess*. New York: HarperSanFrancisco, 1999.

Stone, Merlin. *When God Was a Woman*. Orlando, FL: Harcourt, 1976.

Wilber, Ken. *The Spectrum of Consciousness*. Wheaton, IL: Quest Books (The Theosophical Publishing House), 1993.

Chapter 8

That Which Is God

Daphne Hampson

How had we best conceptualize that dimension of reality that humanity has hitherto called "God"? For those of us concerned with theology, or who have a marked spirituality, this question must be quite fundamental. Given that I am by trade a systematic theologian, it is this that I shall address.

In the first place, it would seem important to acknowledge how tough it has been for women of our generation. To shift one's conception of God, to come to think otherwise than that with which one grew up (and to which others around one continue to hold) takes courage. For one's sense of God is fundamental to one's sense of self. Yet it may also be that women have long aspired to the freedom to conceptualize that which is God differently. For the first time in recorded history, we have our chance. It has become not dangerous to think what one will, nor is the societal tug so strong that we cannot escape it. We should not forget what has been. Until quite recently, a woman who thought as do I would have been ostracized (and could by no means have had a career as a theologian). But a few centuries ago she would have been summarily burned at the stake. One-half of humanity has controlled what it is that we must all perforce think.

Consider this. Religion has supremely been that ideology that has served to keep woman in her place: "man's world, woman's place." Through the co-option of "God," a patriarchal ordering of society in which man is norm and woman "the other" has been made to look

only natural, "God-given." Indeed, we may well think religion to have
played no inconsiderable part in the creation of gender. For through
their religions, men have not simply projected their self-understand-
ing but have also attempted to determine what should be the role and
essence of woman. In India, I am taken to see a huge outdoor mosque.
I am told that, on a certain festival, the "whole community" congre-
gates there. Inquiring further, I elicit the response that no of course
not the women—they stay at home. People laugh that I asked.

The explanatory blurb for the conference "Women and the Divine"
ran "Central to the emancipatory aspirations of feminism is reflection
upon and reinterpretation of notions of the 'divine.'" [1] That is spot
on. Until we have reflected on and reinterpreted that ultimate sense
of things that humanity has variously called "God" or "the divine,"
recasting our conceptual understanding and our language, we cannot
hope to be free. But, as we have already said, to undertake such a shift
is daunting.

We need not of course deny that the "historical" or "positive" religions that we have inherited may have acted as what Kant would have
called a "vehicle" that has served to carry human awareness of that
dimension of reality which is God.[2] (In the eighteenth century, the
word "vehicle" was a technical term for a conducting substance, such
as copper, thought to convey something else, in this case an electro-
magnetic current.) But the particular concretion of that vehicle may
also be thought to have skewed our understanding. Thus God has
been conceived as other than we, the relationship to God hierarchical in nature. The task then is to find new language and imagery,
new paradigms reflecting new understandings, to conceptualize that
of which we would speak. Thereby we shall also come to conceive
otherwise of ourselves.

The concretion is itself crucial. In the last half-century, it has come
to be acknowledged that it is not that, somehow, we possess an awareness of reality, for which we, as it were, subsequently find language.
Rather is it that "language" (in the widest sense of the term as concretion) goes "all the way down." This insight does not foreclose the
possibility of the rightness of the sense we have that we seek for words
as we speak. To put this the other way up, language would seem to
point beyond itself: as T. S. Eliot writes, "Words, after speech, reach
into the silence."[3] But we must surely acknowledge that religiously
it is not that we have some unformed, prelinguistic, awareness on
which we subsequently impose expression. The "shaping" is intrinsic
to that which we grasp. The corollary of this is that our language
and concepts are never incidental to what we would say. Those who

contend that we "just happen" to have called God "He" but it makes no odds—as some say by way of excusing their sexist language—are frankly being naïve. How we speak of God is fundamental to what "God" is to us, to the role the concept performs. To summarize, on the one hand, we need not deny that masculinist religion has acted as a vehicle that has indeed served to carry human recognition of that dimension of reality that is "God." Yet it is also the case that the concrete imagery and form of the religion are not incidental, but rather intrinsic to what "God" has been for us.

In considering the shift required of us, the starting point must necessarily be a consideration as to what it is we experience or what awareness we have, such that we find ourselves compelled to speak of "God." It is strange how often this empirical question comes to be lost or is evaded. If there is nothing that prompts us to use God-language, to express—however differently—that which in the past people have named "God," then we may as well pack up shop. Not forgetting that we are, as we must in order to think, standing within the language we use and the paradigms we employ, we can nevertheless consider what it is that we would formulate and so find an appropriate expression. For if we fail to find concepts that seems to us valid, we shall simply lose all hold on that which, I take it, has been central to many of our lives. Personally, I didn't become a theologian for nothing.

In this task of reconceptualization, we should exercise two criteria: the one epistemological, the other moral. Epistemologically, we should employ concepts or imagery that—to put the criterion negatively—are at least not incommensurate with what we can think actually to be the case. It strikes me that there is little point in employing concretion that is wholly at variance with what we may think credible. If all theological language is metaphorical (there may be wisdom in the theological adage that language and concepts will always be inadequate for God), let us at least exercise judgment as to what might be a true metaphor and what is palpably false. For example, I fail to see how it could be helpful to persist with a creation story in which woman is formed from man. But the exercise of such a criterion is revolutionary in its implications. Thus, in view of contemporary thinking about space and time, it makes little sense to speak of God as in some way "outside" or "before." On epistemological grounds alone (nothing to do with feminism), we are forced to recast what we would say.

Morally, we shall be compelled to find ways of speaking that honor the integrity of all of us. Exercising such a moral criterion is, we should note, not a second and separate issue, unconnected to epistemological considerations. If the very meaning and definition of what we understand by "God" is that God is goodness itself, we must perforce conceptualize God in ways that do not engender sexism. Given the tenacity with which, in the face of all the evidence, otherwise rational people hold onto sexist religious myths, one must wonder as to the role religion plays in shoring up certain social arrangements and masculinist self-understandings from which they apparently cannot conceive of being parted.

Our starting point, then, should be to ask what it is about their experience that leads persons to credit that there is a dimension of reality that they call "God" (or synonyms for God); in any case, that leads them to consider themselves spiritual and not just ethical persons. I find that many of those whom I know well enough to have some conception of what it is they believe, my friends and others whom I admire, do indeed credit this. Theirs is fundamentally an experientially based spirituality. In my experience, thinking in such a way and having such a conviction would seem to be particularly prevalent among women. Such persons do not hold what they do on account of some purported revelation in history. The "male" propensity—if that is what it is—to objectify, creating a dogma or religious myth, seems foreign to them.

Thus, many have reached the conclusion that—whether they call it "prayer" or not—concerted and loving thought directed toward particular others can be effective. Of course it could simply be that thinking of another in this manner so transforms one's attitude toward him or her that one's whole demeanor is such as to make it evidently apparent that one is ready to "hear" that person—and that that itself is transformative. But I should find such an explanation inadequate. I have myself not infrequently (at a time when I was needing help) experienced that someone could hold me in mind so powerfully that I could receive healing. Again, by "centering down" (to employ a Quaker phrase) or coming "to" ourselves, open to "God," things may fall into place, "coincidences" happen, or we see clearly what we should do. Again, one needs to explain the remarkable way in which physical healing can take place. It is these varied phenomena (if one may so call them) that lead people to conclude that, however little we may understand it, there is a dimension to reality beyond that which meets the eye. Minimally, we may conclude that persons can be open to one another at a level other than our everyday selves.

Further, in my experience—and probably that of most of us—we meet the occasional person who impresses us as somehow "translucent" of God. It is as though we are brought into the presence of "more" than that person herself. There is no reason to think other than that this was people's experience of Jesus; the evidence is that it was. It seems to be given to some to live so close to a fuller reality that others are drawn into this orbit. I recall how I have found myself strangely stilled, or brought back to my true self, in such a person's presence. In relation to our present consideration, it is relevant to note that such people are evidently to be found in many different traditions, holding to a whole variety of positive religions (what we have called "vehicles") in conceptualizing that which is. Indeed, in my experience, people who can pray effectively or direct loving thought to another hold to all manner of beliefs. I can think of a spiritual healer who declared himself an atheist. I conclude that there is that which (however shaped by the particular vehicle) is more and other than the vehicle.

The quasi empirical evidence that I have adduced would seem to entail that we should hold a different conception of the self than that which has been common in Western culture. Had we not best conceive of the self as both "centered" and "open," understanding these not as in tension but rather as correlates the one of the other? Unless a person attains to a certain centeredness, she is not able to be truly present to others; while it is as we are receptive of the multiple influences upon us that we come to be a centered, rather than amorphous, self. People who enable mental or physical healing, who at a distance are able to be "present" to others, who are translucent of "God," impress us as integrated but, also and therefore, profoundly open. This is a very different notion of the self than that of the self as atomistic, having "hard" ego boundaries, which has prevailed in masculinist thought.[4]

But does it not follow that the way in which we conceive of that which is God should likewise be other than the masculinist understanding that has hitherto prevailed? God has been held to possess "aseity," to be *a se*—complete in Himself and needing no one else. "He" is transcendent, "other," and all-powerful. What an extraordinary model for that which we should admire! The *evidence* of prayer or healing or the translucent lives of others is suggestive rather of that which moves between people, to which we can be present, as to that with which we are profoundly interconnected. Far from conceiving of the self has having hard ego-boundaries, we should think of ourselves as potentially possessing a permeable ego-boundary; far from being a discrete monad, there is a process of osmosis between self and that which lies immediately beyond self, which is God. This involves a radically other understanding of that which is "God." True, our traditions may have found occasion to speak of God as spirit, but this has rarely been dominant or basic to people's conception.

We may well think that it has been feminist theory, or more widely thinking in which women have engaged, which has developed the paradigms we should employ here. Much feminist thought and practice has conceived of the self as I describe. Oppositional and combative notions have been challenged in favor of relational ones. Feminists have spoken of coming "to" themselves (of having a centered self), while this has gone hand in hand with such practices as an ability to listen at depth to others. The early feminist movement—which formed so many of us—majored on these things. Again, it is notable how many women philosophers (whether or not they call themselves "feminist") have been attracted to virtue ethics with its emphasis on receptivity, on "seeing" or attentiveness. I need only mention Iris Murdoch or Martha Nussbaum. We have to hand conceptual riches that we can employ. Theology can, in consequence, shift. Given their relational understanding of self, women may be well placed to embark on such an endeavor. The experience of meditation, for example, could be valuable here.

Nor is it necessarily the case that there is nothing in the past on which we can draw. Even confining ourselves to Western culture, it is not monolithic. Thus, for example, I find formulations that owe to Friedrich Schleiermacher enlightening. Schleiermacher may have lived at the right time. In early nineteenth century Germany (the age of Romanticism), there was a new focus on the nature of the self and its faculties. Hence Schleiermacher, the theologian, casts the self's relation to that which lies immediately beyond the self, which is God, in a novel way. He speaks of the self as both *Sein*, as being (in my vocabulary, as having integrity and centeredness) but also as having-in-some-way-come-to-be (as *Irgendwiegewordensein*), that is to say, as having a profound relationality to what is more than self. For Schleiermacher also speaks of our being, in our very selves, dependent; and by this I do not think he means heteronomously dependent on an "exterior" other, but rather that the self is connected, grounded, we might say (§3, §4).[5] I know of no other thinker who, commencing from the observation of human capacity for perceptivity and receptivity, has thought more imaginatively of the structure of the human self in its relation to that which is God.

I am suggesting thus that we should think quite otherwise about the nature of the self's relation to God than has commonly been the case. We may think that what has transpired is that our conception of God has been predicated upon a mistaken notion of the self. "God" has been seen as monadic; this concept has then been projected as an anthropomorphic other, transcendent over us. But our experience suggests a very different understanding as to what it is that God may be. We should be considering the way in which, across its boundaries, the self lies open to that which is beyond itself, such that we are intimately connected with "God." We no longer have time for a concept of God as a discrete monad, set over against us in hierarchal fashion, such that God's strength and goodness serves but to show up our weakness and sinfulness. We have moved on.

Past experience suggests that, at this point, I shall be asked why I should wish to name as "God" that of which I speak? The word apparently connotes that transcendent, anthropomorphized entity, which I am claiming is a projection of the male imagination. The answer should be clear from what I have already said. One may reject what I have called the vehicle of past male religion, but there is no reason to deny that, mistaken and distortive though it may have been, through its lens men and women have indeed attempted to speak of a dimension of reality of which they have been aware. If there has always been God, it would seem likely that there have been people in every age and clime who have been sensitive to this; indeed, it would be insolent to suggest anything other. What I am saying is that, drawing on the tradition where this is useful, we should recast our conceptualization of that dimension of reality. The conception may change, but there is a continuity of experience, always and necessarily shaped by the particular concretion in which it has been cast. Inasmuch as we are speaking of the same phenomena, which we are seeking to understand, "God" is the word that we had best employ, however differently we may conceive of God.

I turn to a consideration of why that which has been the dominant conception of God within the Western tradition is, as I should want to contend, both epistemologically inadequate and ethically untenable. It has had dire consequences for women and thus also for humanity as a whole. We should recognize that what is so ethically problematic about the religion is a direct corollary of what makes the Abrahamic religions epistemologically untenable. It follows that women need never argue basing themselves on moral grounds alone, nor suggest that it is simply that the religion does not suit them (as women's plea is sometimes construed). Nor should they permit a relativism, as if these religious concepts have been acceptable in a past age—but we should now move on. Nor the critique that runs that one has replaced a masculinist religion by a "women's" religion. As we now know, the particularist claims of Abrahamic religions can never have been valid.

Further, all that is being called for is a spirituality that (unlike that which we have known) is gender inclusive.

Consider then the nature of the Abrahamic religions. God/JHWH/Allah is considered to be "on high" and humanity "below." This is the case both ontologically (in terms of being or primacy) and ethically: God is everlasting and good; by contrast, humanity will pass away and is sinful. This hierarchical structure is then paralleled by the conception held of man (or the "male"), in relation to woman (or the "female"). Each term moreover is understood in comparison with that which is construed as its polar opposite. The person, or humanity as a whole, understands his/her/itself as he/she/it is reflected back to his/her/itself through the other (as Hegel perspicaciously pointed out). Thus the nature of humanity is understood in contrast with God (and vice versa), whereas woman's self-consciousness is formed in relation to man (and vice versa). Whereas "man," as part of humanity, is placed in the "female" position in relation to the transcendent God (he sees himself as sinful and material or conceives that he should be humble and obedient), in relation to woman he places himself in the upper position, seeing her as material, and he as rightly exercising power over her. Woman always finds herself at the bottom of the heap.

Take the book of Hosea in the Hebrew Bible, a particularly striking example that however simply exemplifies the tradition as a whole. The relationship of the "male" God JHWH to the people of Israel is understood in parallel with Hosea's relation to his wife Gomer. Gomer is conceived as wayward, indeed likened to a prostitute and depicted in lewd terms, whereas she should be obedient to Hosea, as should Israel to JHWH.[6] The problem is built into the Abrahamic religions. When God is posited as good and "male" there is, in consequence, a certain construction of gender in which "male" and "female" have opposite attributes. Thus, the fact that God has commonly been gendered and cast in "masculine" terms has as corollary that man sees woman as that which is contrary to the nature of God. She comes to be construed as earthly, sexual, and fickle, whereas God represents singularity.[7] Note that the people of Israel, or the church as the bride of Christ, are cast as "female" in relation to the "male" divinity. Again, it is interesting that, whereas woman traditionally has been left with the task of feeding, cleaning, and caring for others on a daily basis, when these roles take on sacred connotations, as in baptism and the Eucharist, they must be performed by men.

Such a thought structure—with the implications it always has for "woman"—would appear endemic to the male mind, reflected in his culture and religion. The same disjuncture between spiritual and material is present in the other great source of Western Christian culture, Platonism. The (male) human aspiration must be to rise above that which is material and associated with woman. In the Christian West, the Hebraic and Greek inheritances fused, reinforcing one another in the creation of concepts of gender. But Judaism and Islam, as Semitic and Middle Eastern forms of religion, have been no better. Taboos against women, so that she shall be kept separate from what is holy, which is the preserve of the male, have been yet more marked. Meanwhile, taking on what he designates as the "female" position, man prostrates himself in humility and obedience before the transcendent God. The fact that, in relation to his God, man should cast himself in a position gendered female does nothing to help women; rather, does it serve to reinforce certain hierarchical notions of gender. In ideal form the "female" term may be construed as pure: In Christianity the highest to which humanity can attain is said to be exemplified by the Virgin Mary (as compared with whom, however, all other women fall short). But of what does her exemplarity consist? In her humility and unquestioning obedience to the "male" God. She serves, and is always subordinate to, her (male) Son.

As we have been saying, that which woman shall represent has been designated not by she herself but by man. What notably we find is a "split" conception of woman. On the one hand, she is Virgin, or often Mother (or both); in either case one who is pure, protective of the male, and untouchable. On the other hand, she is associated with the sexual and material, that which is to be shunned, the very opposite of God and a hazard to the spiritual life. What is lacking is any sense of woman as an agent in her own right, having a dignity equal to that of man. Again, these thought forms appear endemic to the male mind. In the West, there is a division between the two: the Virgin, or in Judaism the good wife, on the one hand; Eve, or the sexual woman, on the other. In the East, both good and evil are combined in the one overwhelming figure of Kali; but it is still a split projection of woman. Well may we say, *plus ça change, plus c'est la même chose.*

What quite is going on here at a subconscious level would presumably be difficult to determine, but one may well speculate. Religion would seem to be a screen onto which in his imagination, having free play, the male has projected his fear and desire. What is clear is that human culture, above all human religion, which standing at its pinnacle holds a society together, has been the creation of one-half of humanity: of men. (Jacques Lacan was hardly mistaken in designating the symbolic as male.) We should note that woman is variously represented as that which man needs her to be in relation to himself. She is the virgin of his desire or the mother of his longing. Designating her as evil is presumably bound up with an evasion of his own sexual desire. There are primeval forces at work here. A senior man in the oil industry recently told me of the fear men had of having women on rigs, since if they were menstruating they might bring bad luck! The male difficulty in separating from the mother (as no woman need do) may well be reflected in the attribution of "motherly" qualities to the (male) God. Again, this does nothing to help women: man now attributes all qualities to the (male) image of himself.

We should note how tenacious religion has been, bound into our society and culture. That women should challenge religious understandings has been the ultimate taboo. When she has striven to better her lot within society, not infrequently has this desire for self-actualization been held to stand in contradiction to what is a "natural" and God-ordained ordering of the universe. When she has asked for equality of status within the religious community, she has been told that she could not represent God as can the male, but rather only humanity; or more crudely that she is "unclean." A serious objection to women being ordained was that the woman might act as priest while pregnant. Such an ordering, in which he is norm and woman "other" is held to have God-given status as revealed. To challenge the religious order is still today not in order. While equality is otherwise enshrined in law, religion is still a protected sphere. It is well recognized that removing this God, the keystone of the arch, would unsteady the whole.

How come that, in 2008, it is still prescribed by law that masculinist religion should be taught in British schools? These myths are self-evidently untrue; not even "symbolically true" to our ethical ideal of equality. We should not allow teaching that was racially biased. Yet male religion is taught together with ethics as embodying our highest ideals! What may a young woman take on board, undermining her at a subconscious level? Again, what does a young man absorb if not male priority? It helps not one whit to search out "women" as depicted in the male religions when that characterization derives from a patriarchal culture in which her "place" was designated by man. The discipline of religious studies is somewhat oddly thought to be neutral today because a range of world religions are taught. Does it not rather compound the problem that, in all human cultures in a variety of guises, the pattern is repeated? And why is there no outcry? What challenge would it represent to point to the obvious: that the myths that are male religions are products of a fertile male imagination, designed to reflect his world back to himself and secure a masculinist order in which woman is "other"?

I turn to the question as to why precisely it is that we must think the Abrahamic religions epistemologically untenable and how it follows inevitably from their nature that they are biased against women. All the Abrahamic religions, the religions of the book, confess to a belief in a particularity of revelation. This is simply a corollary of the fact that they have envisaged God as other than humanity, rather than as immediately available, known in and through the world. Such a God must necessarily reveal Himself in history, in the particular history of the Jewish people, in an Incarnation in his Son, or in the revelation given to the prophet. But can there be any such particularity? In view of our present knowledge, such a contention would seem untenable. It is scarcely a valid response to say, "God can do anything." Rather, given that we know our solar system to be part way out in a spiral of a galaxy we call the Milky Way, while galaxies form clusters, must it strain our credibility to think that "He" would send his "Son" to planet earth! Further, for anyone who has eyes to see what these religions have meant for one-half of humanity, the claim to particularity must raise theodicy questions. How could such a God through "His" action create such gender hierarchy as is embedded in these scriptures?

Consider then the claim to particularity; the "scandal of particularity" as it came to be known when, subsequent to the Enlightenment, Christians proclaimed this to be of the essence of their religion. In modernity, we have become clear that nature and history form what we may call an interrelated causal nexus. That is to say, there can be no particularity. Misunderstanding, people will comment that we are all "particular" people, no two alike. Yes, of course, but this is not the sense in which the term particularity is being employed. However various, we are all people. Take nature: whatever exists belongs to a category (though we know the whole to be slowly evolving). If you see a green beetle, you take it for granted that its parents were similarly green beetles. Once there were dinosaurs, but you would not find a one-off dinosaur today. People mistakenly respond: but is there not randomness at the subatomic level? But to say that nature is a causal nexus is not a determinist notion. If there is indeed randomness at the subatomic level, then presumably this has always been the case; it did not suddenly start. Again, history forms such an interrelated causal nexus. It may or may not be that Caesar crossed the Rubicon (and presumably he exercised free choice in doing so). But it is perfectly thinkable that he did this, since such an action conforms to a category of which we have other examples, crossing rivers. Actions are one of a type and interconnected with other actions: getting on a beast of burden to cross a river.[8]

In a world in which we have grasped this it becomes evident that the claims of the Abrahamic religions are untenable. The idea that there could be a "resurrection" is *a priori* ruled out, for it would constitute a unique event, a break in the causal nexus, in addition to being biologically impossible. There is no class of things "resurrections" to which it could belong. Of course, if the claim is simply that, subsequent to his death, his disciples were intensely aware of the "presence" of Jesus, that may be the case. There are plenty of other such examples; notably in Tibetan Buddhism there are cases of seers experienced as almost "physically" present. (Indeed one may well think that it is an experience of this kind to which the Christian literature witnesses.) Such an experience is then one of a type and not unique. Though it may be beyond our understanding, we are clearly not speaking of a literal resurrection. The Christian claim however has to be that in Christ there was a peculiar and unique revelation of God. Christians stake a claim to particularity.

Again, given that there is no particularity, it cannot be said of one human being that he is an Incarnation of God in a sense in which this is true of none other. Again, of one body of literature, that it is somehow revealed, rather than simply a record of human experience of that which is God. Again, of one people that they are the "chosen" race. Or of one religious institution that it has God-given authority. We see that, on account of the type of religion which they are, faiths predicated on belief in a God conceived of as transcendent who reveals Himself in history, Judaism, Christianity, and Islam are riddled with such claims. If an adherent of these religions would wish to drop claims to particularity to chime in with modernity (which these religions can scarcely do while remaining what they are), then there is nothing to distinguish such a person from those of us who acknowledge that there is a dimension to the totality, everywhere and at all times available, which we would call "God." Indeed, the sexism becomes the less excusable when the adherents of these religions continue to proclaim such myths while no longer actually believing that they could be true.

That there can be no particularity does not of course entail ruling out that it may well be that, in some ages and among some people, there is to be found a peculiarly profound realization of that dimension of reality that is God. Nor are we prevented from finding past expression of people's religious awareness an inspiration. Nor need

we deny that our own experience of God has a shaping that owes
to a tradition. Again, there is no particular problem in thinking that
Jesus had healing powers about him. The evidence is overwhelmingly
that this was the case (though this may have been comprehended and
expressed in terms other than those that we should employ today).
But then there are plenty of examples of spiritual healing in our own
world. Miracles, however, in the sense of interruptions or interven-
tions, are not possible. Water cannot change into wine, for wine has
carbon atoms and water does not. We need more clarity of thought.

From the mistaken nature of the claim to particularity, which adherents of Abrahamic religions make, I move on to the ethical question as
to why its implications are horrendous. If it is held that there has been
a revelation of God in history, then reference must constantly be made
to that particular history. The literature that tells of this supposed revelation in turn comes to have a peculiar status, forming a benchmark
for what we should think. Obviously, not all adherents of these religions are fundamentalist; nevertheless, they must constantly refer to
the past. In considering everything from the ordination of women to
pacifism, Christians of all persuasions adduce biblical evidence. If these
foundational events were not to be recited in synagogue, church, and
mosque, the religions acknowledged in their rites would not be what
they are. Now this reference is, necessarily, to a past, patriarchal, Near
Eastern society. Thus, the customs and habits, the take on women
and the relation pertaining between the sexes of that past, are constantly propelled into the present. Indeed, these scriptures are enunci-
ated within a sacred setting. They must form the human imagination,
acting not least at a subconscious level. Moreover, male imagery is
employed for God. This cannot but be powerful.

Yet further. Such religions are, necessarily, heteronomous. By heteronomy is meant that something other than oneself becomes the law
to one: Greek *heteros* = other, *nomos* = law. As we have said, the claim
to revelation is a claim to particularity, which in turn involves a reference to a past point in history that becomes in some sense normative.
Persons look to something other than their own experience, or that
of the human community to which they belong, as the criterion as to
what is the case, or that to which, ethically, humanity should hold.
Indeed, the very notion of God as other and separate from humankind is heteronomous, for "He" is Lord (this belongs to the definition
of such a God). Fundamental to feminism however is the assertion of
autonomy, self-rule: Greek *auto* = self.[9] Enlightened modernity rightly
claimed such autonomy to be the measure of human maturity. The
heteronomous nature of religions of revelation may well be something

to which feminists are peculiarly sensitive, for it represents the denial of all that to which they most vehemently adhere.

I would thus contend that there is no way in which these religions can adapt, either epistemologically or ethically, to that which we think either true or good today. Moreover, they are intrinsically sexist. We could muse further as to why religion took on the shape it did in the ancient world; we have already noted its ideological usefulness in justifying a particular ordering of society. If, as people did, one thinks the universe minute, the world at its center—and Jerusalem the center of the world—it is not incredible that God should have humanity (particularly humans in the small part of the world of which you know) in His particular care. If one thinks of space and time as humankind did previously, it is comprehensible that God should have been conceived of as "outside" and "before."

Today, however, we think according to a wholly different paradigm. It is a gross misunderstanding to think that the universe has an "edge" or that the Big Bang was a moment "in time." Rather is it that (while the mathematics is untranslatable into normal imagery) we set up certain coordinates, in relation to which other realities are measured. The totality is like a sphere—as one theoretical physicist put it to me; the "top" is no more an "edge" than any other point. Measurements are simply a certain distance from the point chosen. Such an understanding, if we could grasp it, must cause us to wholly reconceive our theological presuppositions. We need to re-form our religious imagination. It would seem that whatever metaphors we employ, we must conceive of God not as "other" or "separate" but as one dimension (I imply no mathematical connotation) of that which is. Incidentally, such a spirituality implies no heteronomy.

Theology should come to be like all other disciplines. No other discipline makes a claim to a particularity of revelation. Whether we think of science or music, humanity draws on past conceptions insofar as these are still relevant and thinks anew insofar as the past must be discarded. True, there are traditions within which we think and create. Theology can draw on its past insofar as that still seems relevant or true. But, as in all other disciplines, the criterion must lie with us. Such theology will allow us to think anew for our day and age. We should foster religious conceptions and employ metaphors that are commensurate with that which we now know about the nature of the world. Integrity is crucial here. Given our ethical presuppositions, we shall require language and imagery that is gender inclusive.

It would seem that much that many women are expressing today, their conception of spirituality, is prescient for the direction in which we must needs move. It is hardly surprising that women should find themselves in this position; it is we who have been excluded from what has been and have no stake in it. Moreover—dare I say this—it seems to me that another and relational way of thinking comes naturally to women. We have different sensibilities, employ different paradigms. Indeed, one could well read women's involvement in past religion as a straining at the leash to be allowed to conceive of things otherwise: consider Julian of Norwich's metaphors. We must surely employ the paradigms of wholeness, not those that imply opposition or separation. Now these are they that appear true to what we now know.

Now, returning to where we commenced. It is shattering to dismantle one's childhood understanding of God, the more so when that conception has been fundamental to our culture since forever. But it may be necessary. If that conception comes to be epistemologically unthinkable and ethically unacceptable, we must move on. Some declare that they stay within traditional religion for what else is there? They fear that, losing what they have known, they will lose all. May it not be that exactly the opposite is the case? Namely, that unless we can imaginatively conceptualize anew, the idea of God will lose all meaningfulness. For, as we have said, the concretion we employ is built into what reality is for us. If it is indeed the case that there is a dimension to reality that we have named God, we shall surely not be defeated in finding conceptual imagery that, true to our experience, is both epistemologically tenable in view of what we know and at one with our ethical ideals.

NOTES

1. "Women and the Divine" Conference, Liverpool Hope University and Liverpool University, Liverpool, United Kingdom, June 2005.

2. Immanuel Kant's *Religion within the Limits of Reason Alone*, trans. T. Green and H. Hudson (1793; New York: Harper & Row Publishers, 1960) has surely been seminal for all future consideration of religion here. Kant thinks religion a myth that has served as a vehicle for human moral precepts.

3. T. S. Eliot, "Burnt Norton, V," *Four Quartets* (1935; London: Faber and Faber, 1986), 17.

4. Such a different concept of the self, contrasting it with the masculinist conception, is widespread in feminist thought. The term "hard" (and, by contrast, "permeable" ego boundaries) owes, in the first place, to Nancy Chodorow's *The Reproduction of Mothering* (Berkeley: University of California Press, 1978) and was subsequently taken up by Carol Gilligan in *In a Different Voice* (Cambridge, MA: Harvard University Press, 1982). I discuss such the feminist concept of the self that I am here advocating, in my *After Christianity* (1996; London: SCM Press,

2nd ed., 2002; Philadelphia: Trinity Press International, 1997), chap. 3, "Feminist Ethics."

5.   See Friedrich Schleiermacher, *The Christian Faith*, trans. H. R. Mackintosh and ed. J. S. Stewart (1821–22; rev. ed. 1830; Edinburgh: T&T Clark, 1999).

6.   See Drorah Setel, "Prophets and Pornography: Female Sexual Imagery in Hosea," in *Feminist Interpretations of the Bible*, ed. Letty Russell (Philadelphia: Westminster Press; Oxford: Basil Blackwell, 1985), 86–95.

7.   There has of course been considerable analysis of these thought forms. Notable is Julia Kristeva's fine reading of the Genesis myth. In the religion of monotheism JHWH/Adam represent the singularity of the law, which stands over against multiplicity and sexuality (the very obverse of God) represented by woman and the snake. See Julia Kristeva, *About Chinese Women*, trans. Seán Hand, in *The Kristeva Reader*, ed. Toril Moi (1974; Oxford: Basil Blackwell, 1986), chap. 2, "The War Between the Sexes."

8.   For further elaboration, see my "Christian Particularity," chap. 1 in *After Christianity*.

9.   The term "autonomy" by no means has the implication of separation: that it should have acquired this within patriarchy is in itself significant.

BIBLIOGRAPHY

Chodorow, Nancy. *The Reproduction of Mothering*. Berkeley: University of California Press, 1978.

Eliot, T. S. "Burnt Norton, V," *Four Quartets*. 1935. London: Faber and Faber, 1986.

Gilligan Carol. *In a Different Voice*. Cambridge, MA: Harvard University Press, 1982.

Hampson, Daphne. *After Christianity*. 1996. London: SCM, 2002. Philadelphia, PA: Trinity Press International, 1997.

Kant, Immanuel. *Religion within the Limits of Reason Alone*. Translated by Theodore Green and Hoyt Hudson. 1793. New York: Harper & Row Publishers, 1960.

Kristeva, Julia. *About Chinese Women*, translated by Seán Hand, in *The Kristeva Reader*, edited by Toril Moi, chap. 2. 1974. Oxford: Basil Blackwell, 1986.

Schleiermacher, Friedrich. *The Christian Faith*. Translated by H. R. Mackintosh and edited by J. S. Stewart. 1821–22. Rev. ed., 1830. Edinburgh: T&T Clark, 1999.

Setel, Drorah. "Prophets and Pornography: Female Sexual Imagery in Hosea." In *Feminist Interpretations of the Bible*, edited by Letty Russell, 86–95. Philadelphia: Westminster Press; Oxford: Basil Blackwell, 1985.

CHAPTER 9

ISLAMIC SPIRITUALITY AND THE FEMININE DIMENSION

Haifaa Jawad

As a social, economic, and political system, Islam is not monolithic. Hence, the religion in these contexts tends to be susceptible to different interpretations and different readings; some could be dogmatic and authoritarian, others could be liberal, and still others could be spiritual, depending on the social, political, and economic settings. But also one has to take into consideration the personal backgrounds of the individual readers. For instance, a Muhadith (someone who is specialist in Hadith literature) could read Islam in a more conservative way, and a Faqih (someone who is specialist in Islamic jurispudence) could understand it in a more legalistic form, while a Sufi saint could comprehend and present it in a more spiritual and mystical way. This is a fact that needs to be borne in mind, especially when considering the position of women in Islam and their relationship to the Divine. Historically, the conservative patriarchal readings of the position of women in Islam have been the dominant ones, while other readings, especially the spiritual/mystical have been left in the shadow. This is mainly due to the historical rivalries between the legalists and the Sufis and the eventual triumphal of the legalists over the Sufis.

This trend was underpinned by the overall decline of the Muslim world that reached its peak during the colonial period as a reaction to Western intrusions. For various reasons, the West, especially Western politicians and travelers, played an important role in projecting and perpetuating distorted images of Muslim women. Hardly any attempt was made to draw attention to the mystical readings of Islam.[1] These images continue to prevail until the present time. Hence, one can easily see that in the West, it is widely believed that Islam is inimical to women, and sweeping assertions—such as that Muslim women are oppressed, confined, and subordinated—are very often affirmed but not carefully questioned. These statements assume that Muslim women have no significant social, political, or religious roles. Within the context of religious life, the emphasis is that Muslim women have no conspicuous role among religious leaders and have rarely participated in the development of Islam on the religious side. Western opinion has assumed that Muslim women were and still are unable to gain religious positions; some even go further by asserting that Islam does not permit women to have a spiritual life: "The path of holiness in Islam was seldom trodden by women and we find but few women on the same. It is too difficult for them, so at least think the men. These everywhere take the front place: all glory, all advantage, all authority, is for men. They have made everything contribute to their advantage and pre-eminence; they have appropriated everything, monopolised everything, holiness and even Paradise, for themselves" (Smith 134–35).

True, there are abuses in certain parts of the Muslim world, and true, there are no visible religious roles for Muslim women, especially in contemporary times; but these are not related to Islam per se, rather they are due to the disfiguration of the religion of Islam and the reductionism inherent in the attempt to apologize and politicize the message of Islam, thus depriving it of its living spirituality, which is at its core. For when the spiritual appreciation of the religion is weak, its message becomes susceptible to ideological distortions that can always lead to or justify such abuses. The spiritual dimension of the faith, therefore, must be brought to the fore to rectify the situation and avoid abuses: "Without an appreciation [the] spiritual, ethical, and intellectual dimensions, the religion of Islam will appear as a series of external forms—legal, ritual, dogmatic—deprived of that inner power which undergirds and sustains the moderate and normative traditions of Islamic culture, and provides formal Islam with its spiritual infrastructure, its life-giving sap. It is this normative, traditional Islam, buttressed by spiritual values, that constitutes the most important and effective bulwark against all forms of (abuses and) extremism masquerading as Islam" (Shah-Kazemi, *The Other in the Light of the One* x–xi). This chapter will attempt and present another reading of Islam, namely, the spiritual/mystical one. In this context, the emphasis will be primarily on the Sufi paradigm.

Islam has a rich spiritual way of life, which is, contrary to common opinion, open to both men and women. The Quran, which is the source par excellence of all Islamic spirituality, makes this clear: "For Muslim men and women, for believing men and women; for devout men and women; for men and women who are patient; for men and women who humble themselves; for men and women who give charity; for men and women who fast; for men and women who guard their chastity; for men and women who remember Allah much—for them all has God prepared forgiveness and a great reward" (Quran 33:35). Many verses in the Quran and various sayings of Muhammad demonstrate Islam's recognition of a woman's spiritual aspirations as an individual human being.

In Islam, the prospects of spiritual growth and development are fully opened to the female sex. Muslim woman can tread the spiritual path and gain access to all the possibilities of the Islamic tradition and become, like man, the vicegerent of God on earth. Islamic history is replete with distinguished women who "adorned themselves with spiritual virtues and equipped themselves with various branches of Islamic knowledge and learnings and engaged themselves in spiritual activities" (Chishti 217). Historically speaking, Islamic spirituality or the informal spiritual dimension of the tradition has favored and venerated feminine spirituality. It is important to highlight the main features of Islamic female spirituality and observe its various manifestations over the ages, for in the context of the Islamic tradition, there exists a type of spirituality with distinctly feminine attributes.

UNDERSTANDING SPIRITUALITY IN ISLAM

In Islam, the term "spirituality" means *ruhaniyyah* (spirit) or *ma'nawiyya* (meaning), and both are derived from the language of the Quran. They refer to that which is related to the world of spirit, is in proximity to the Divine, has inwardness, and is identified with the real. Spirituality also means the presence of *barakah*, or grace, within the life of a person who dedicates his/herself to God. Furthermore, it evokes the sense of moral perfection and beauty of the soul in those who have spiritual life (Nasr, *Islamic Spirituality* xvii).

Islamic spirituality is nothing more than the awareness of the One, of Allah (*taqwa* in Arabic), and a life lived according to His will: "To live by the Will of God Who is One and to obey His Laws is the alpha of the spiritual life. Its omega is to surrender one's will completely to

Him and to sacrifice one's existence before the One Who alone can be said ultimately to be" (Nasr, *Islamic Spirituality* xvi). The main aim of Islamic spirituality is to gain Divine attributes via emulating and observing those virtues, which were possessed in their perfection by Muhammad. The spiritual life in Islam is therefore based primarily on reverential fear of God, obedience to His will, sincere love of Him, and knowledge of Him. To love God and to realize Him is, from the Islamic perspective, to attain the highest rank of spirituality and to gain sanctity and become a friend of God, or *wali Allah*, as it is used in the Quranic Arabic. This kind of spirituality has kept Muslim society, spiritually speaking, alive over the ages and is open to both men and women. It has also produced many women (and men) with saintly natures who attained the goal of human life and brought balance and equilibrium to other fellow Muslim men and women (Nasr, *Islamic Spirituality* xviii).

Female Islamic spirituality has been manifest in various forms and dimensions: socially, politically, and religiously. To explore these dimensions, I shall examine living historical figures as examples of female spirituality in Islam. The importance of these figures lies not only in their historical contexts—these women played an important role in shaping the image of the ideal pious Muslim woman to be respected and venerated for her spiritual endeavors—but also in the way these figures serve as an inspiration and a model to be emulated by contemporary Muslim women: especially important at a time when there is widespread antispiritualism, desacralization of knowledge, diminishment of feminine spiritual values, and distortion of feminine dignity. I will concentrate on the Sufi approach to feminine spirituality because it provides concrete paths for female spiritual realization. My approach will combine theological and textual analysis in a wholly original manner, rooted in a mystical and metaphysical conception of religion. The subject is especially timely, giving current interest in female spirituality in the West, along with considerable misconceptions and misunderstanding about the teaching of Islam concerning women.

Sufi Spirituality and the Feminine Dimension

The spiritual values of Islam that Sufism espoused, even when they were not always made explicit, found broad acceptance by Muslims and non-Muslims. Whereas the attraction of Sufi spirituality is widely studied, less is known about the appeal of the Sufi notion of the feminine. Here I shall concentrate on the Sufi theological paradigm rather than Sufi practices, which might, in some cases, be more authoritarian than the paradigm. But before elaborating this issue, it is necessary to give a brief summary of the importance of Sufism to the overall faith of Islam.

The Sufi perspective on Islam has informed the overall Islamic principles and contributed to the process by which Islam is made, not just into an interesting approach to life but also into an acceptable way of life. This phenomenon is important given the increasingly grim picture of Islam that prevails in our times: For Sufism is Islamic spirituality, even if Islamic spirituality is not confined to the phenomena of Sufism. The spiritual values of the religion of Islam are brought into sharp focus by the Sufis and are implemented practically by them in various ways. But the Sufis do not claim that these values and the doctrines and practices emerging therefrom are anything other than those of quintessential Islam. Their "esotericism" is but the complement to the exotericism of the formal religion, and both are rooted in the sources of the Islamic revelation—the Quran and the *Sunnah* of the Prophet. To understand the inner, spiritual values of the revelation, one can turn to the Sufis, who have incorporated these values organically into a dynamic way of life. Insofar as most Sufis integrate these inner values with outer *Shari`a* practice, they have strengthened religion as a whole; it has not been the case that Sufis promoted inner values at the expense of the outer forms of Islam.

> Sufism . . . became the framework within which all popular piety flowed together; its saints, dead and living, became the guarantors of the gentle and co-operative sides of social life. Guilds commonly came to have Sufi affiliations. Men's clubs claimed the patronage of Sufi saints. And the tombs of local saints became shrines which almost all factions united in revering. It is probable that without the subtle leaven of the Sufi orders, giving to Islam an inward personal thrust and to the Muslim community a sense of participation in a common spiritual venture quite apart from anyone's outward power, the mechanical arrangements of the Shari`a would not have maintained the loyalty essential to their effectiveness. (Hodgson 125)

Sufism, as Martin Lings says, "is necessary because it is to Islam what the heart is to the body. Like the bodily heart it must be secluded and protected and must remain firm-fixed in the centre; but at the same time it cannot refuse to feed the arteries with life" (Lings 106).[2]

Historically, Sufism has played a major role in spreading Islam and recruiting non-Muslims to the faith. It has been stated that the spread of Islam beyond the frontiers of the Muslim states and therefore the Islamization of such areas as Anatolia, Bosnia, Kashmir, Indonesia, India, and West Africa should be attributed in large part to the efforts of Sufi saints. This is the conclusion reached by Thomas Arnold, in his classic and still unsurpassed study of the spread of Islam, *The Preaching of Islam*. Arnold shows that far from being "spread by the sword," as the common stereotype would have us believe, Islam was in fact spread by peaceful means: by the preaching of the Sufis, on the one hand, and by the impact of traders, on the other hand. From the thirteenth century onward, often the two in fact went hand in hand, as traders were themselves often members of a Sufi order. The appeal of the Sufis continues to this day, especially among those who are longing for spiritual fulfillment. Nasr describes it as "the flower of the tree of Islam . . . or the jewel in the crown of the Islamic tradition" (*Islam and the Plight of the Modern Man* 49).

The emphasis of Sufism on a universal supra-intellectual but very real *tawheed* (or science of God's unity), its focus on inner practices as a force for the transformation of individuals, its insistence on the detachment of the individual from the world rather than abandonment of it, its care for the welfare of the community, and its aim to bring about justice through injecting moral and ethical values into human lives, has made it one of the most attractive forces of the religion of Islam (Dutton 163).

In addition, its ability to fill the spiritual vacuum created by such ideologies as secularism, socialism, and modernism has made it particularly attractive to a considerable number of people in the West. Currently, there are many Sufi groups in Europe and America that are able to attract converts to Islam (Haddad and Lummis 22, 171). Moreover, there are centers that are dedicated to the study of Sufism in the West, chief among them being the Muhyiddin ibn Arabi center in Oxford. The number of people who have adopted Sufism and then Islam both in Europe and the United States is considerable; they include "ordinary" people who sought inner peace, such as now middle-aged people who lived through the "hippie" periods in the 1960s and 1970s; those who were disillusioned with the Western material way of life and decided to embrace Islam to fulfill their spiritual needs. Also, a significant number of Western intellectuals found consolation in the wisdom of Sufism. These include the late French philosopher René Guénon, whose teachings on Sufism have become a model for Europeans who are interested in the spiritual dimension of Islam[3] such as the English mystic Martin Lings, the Swiss intellectuals Schuon and Burckhardt,[4] and the American scholar James Morris. The same can be said with regard to Nuh Keller of the Shadhiliyya order and his New Zealand wife, Umm Sahal, and Tim Winter of Cambridge University, although the latter do not belong to the traditional or perennial school of thought.

Those people who showed interest in Sufism were challenged by what one might call "the spiritual intellectuality" of the inner dimension of the religion. Having read literature on Sufi spirituality written both by practicing Muslims/Sufis and Western academics, they became aware of the link between the inner, universal spirit of the faith and its outer, particular form. Whereas in the 1960s, Sufism was part of the "hippie" movement and divorced from its Islamic roots, in the 1990s, it was becoming known increasingly, and more accurately, as the form taken by Islamic mysticism. Many intellectuals came to see such values as secular cleverness, wealth, relativism, and pragmatism in the light of Sufi ideals of wisdom, sacrifice, sense of the absolute, and idealism. These characteristics ultimately lent a sense of balance and completeness, primarily through the power of integration proper to Sufism. Integration means tawheed, the verbal noun stemming from the verb Wahhada, literally, "to make one." Whereas theologically this means declaring or affirming God's oneness, in Sufism it comes to mean realizing oneness—the oneness of God, and the oneness of being, and thus the necessity of "being one," or being "integrated" as a personality, to properly affirm and realize the oneness of God. Thus, tawheed is fully realized when God is worshiped by the "whole" human being: to be "whole" is to be "holy" (the words being etymologically related). This state of integration stands at the very antipodes of the dissipation and agitation that so many feel is generated by modern life, for: "To be dissipated and compartmentalized, to be lost in the never-ending play of mental images and concepts, or psychic tensions and forces, is to be removed from that state of wholeness which our inner state demands from us" (Nasr, *Sufi Essays* 43–44). Sufism strives toward the attainment of the state of purity and wholeness "not through negation of intelligence, as is often the case in the kind of piety fostered by certain modern religious movements, but through the integration of each element of one's being into its own proper centre" (44). As such spiritual practice is crucial for the integration of the person because it brings back together the dispersed elements in a human being and ensures that the outward-going tendency is controlled and reversed, and thus a person can live inwardly: emotions, reactions, and tendencies aiming primarily on the centre rather the rim (Nasr, *Islam and the Plight of the Modern Man* 3). For, "at the centre resides the One, the Pure and ineffable Being which is the source of all beatitude and goodness, whereas at the periphery is non-existence, which only appears to be real because of man's illusory perception and lack of discrimination" (Nasr, *Sufi Essays* 49).

To achieve such transformation in the human mind, body, and spirit, normative Sufism does not go outside the framework of the law but seeks to base its practices on the injunctions of the Shari`a. Sufism integrates the outward (*zahir*) and the inward (*batin*) aspects of the faith and integrates male and female on the basis of the integration within God of jalal (Majesty) and jamal (Beauty), ultimately resulting in a totality on the metaphysical plane, which implies complementarity at the human level within and between man and woman. This is very much a part of the traditional Islamic conception of the nature of things. Therefore, when men lack beauty (jamal) of the soul, on the one hand, they tend to oppress those weaker than themselves through lack of compassion, thus also disobeying God through lack of wisdom and submission. When women lack strength (jalal) of the soul, on the other hand, they are unable to assert their true strength, whereas Sufi women have always been able to bring forth their reserves of strength and remain impassibly independent. Sufi women throughout the ages have been an inspiration to other women and have taken on male disciples.[5] This affirms the necessity of the feminine/spiritual dimension as a balancing factor; for when men (and women) lose the balance between the two sides of their nature, then *ihsan*—that is, virtue or beauty of soul—loses its meaning. Where there is no perception of, or conformity to, beauty—*ihsan* in the deepest sense—there is no virtue, and where men (and women) have no virtue, society collapses into the kind of chauvinism and abuse that characterize male-female relations in so many parts of the Muslim world nowadays.

Besides the spiritual values of Sufism, there is also a Sufi gender paradigm that offers a particular notion of feminine equality and dignity. To understand this concept, it is important to consider the Sufi approach to the feminine principle within Islam. The capacity of Sufism to incorporate and encourage feminine activities within its sphere in both spiritual and social terms attests to the importance attributed by the Sufis to the feminine element in the Divine Nature itself. I shall examine each of these elements in turn.

SUFISM AND THE ACCEPTANCE
OF FEMININE ACTIVITIES

Sufism continues to favor the development of feminine activities more than any other branch of Islam, in keeping with the Quranic emphasis on the spiritual equality between the sexes: "And whoso doeth good works, whether male or female, and is a believer, such will enter paradise, and will not be wronged the dint of a date-stone" (Quran 4:124; see also the earlier quotation of Quran 33:35).

There can also be detected an almost constant reminder of the ability of women to fulfill their spiritual needs; the respect of the Prophet for women in general, his ideal relationships with his wives, his kindness and care for his daughters "excluded that feeling of dejection so often found in medieval Christian monasticism" (Schimmel, *Mystical Dimensions of Islam* 426). Although one can find what could be seen as antifeminine sayings in the tradition and among some early Sufis, "the Muslims scarcely reached the apogee of hatred displayed by medieval Christian writers in their condemnation of the feminine element" (Schimmel 429). For example, Eve was never regarded as the cause of the fall of Adam, nor was it ever considered that women did not have souls. On the contrary, the prophet declared, "God has made dear to me from your world women and fragrance, and the joy of my eyes is in prayer" (Schimmel, *My Soul Is a Woman* 21).

Such principles from the Quran and the prophetic example gave rise in Sufism to a particularly rich tradition of female spirituality. Hence, large numbers of women followed (and continue to follow to the present day) the spiritual path and in due time excelled in their virtues and piety. Chief among them was Rabia al-Adawiyya, considered to be the first woman saint in Islam (after the Prophet's wife, Khadija, and her daughter, Fatima). She is credited with introducing the concept of unconditional love of God into Sufism, thus transforming "sombre asceticism into genuine love mysticism" (Schimmel, *My Soul Is a Woman* 34). The following anecdote illustrates the notion of unconditional love: "[One day Rabia] ran through Basra with a bucket of water in one hand and a burning torch in the other, and when asked about the reason behind her actions, she replied: 'I want to pour water into hell and set paradise on fire, so that these two veils disappear and nobody shall any longer worship God out of a fear of hell or a hope of heaven, but solely for the sake of His eternal beauty'" (34–35). Her devotion, and asceticism, and her contribution to the development of Islamic mysticism earned her the respect and affection of all the Sufi masters of her time (Attar 39–51).

Rabia was not the only such woman of her times; there were several other women at the forefront of the Sufi tradition who developed and articulated the Sufi way of life. Among them are Maryam of Basra, Rabia of Syria, and Fatima of Nishapur, to name but a few; they attended Sufi meetings, consorted freely with Sufi masters, sponsored Sufi activities, and organized circles in the pursuit of the mystical path. Some of them who were advanced in learning and mystical knowledge guided their husbands in religious and practical matters and contributed to the spiritual formation of future Sufi masters, educating great mystical thinkers such as Ibn Arabi, who was taught for two years by the great Sufi saint Fatima of Cordova. His early encounter with her and other female mystics greatly influenced his positive attitude toward the feminine role in Sufism.

In general, these women played an important role in shaping the image of the ideal pious Muslim woman to be respected and venerated for her spiritual endeavors. These feminine activities continue to take place in modern times and can be found in some parts of the Muslim world, where Sufi women still teach and train souls who are longing for spiritual enlightenment, maintaining the continuity between the early example of Rabia and her fellow Sufi women following the spiritual path.[6] The example of Rabia, and other pious Muslim women like her, serves as an inspiration and a model to be emulated in women's personal lives, especially at a time when there is widespread antispiritualism,[7] the desacralization of knowledge, the diminishment of feminine spiritual values, and the distortion of feminine dignity. For an ailing society, inner renewal and purification is the first step toward a more general cure for society as a whole. In this context, the following quotation is important: "The more I pondered, the greater emptiness I felt within. I was slowly beginning to reach a stage where my dissatisfaction with my status as a woman in this society, was really a reflection of my greater dissatisfaction with society itself. Everything seemed to be degenerating backwards, despite the claims . . . of success and prosperity. I wanted to find that thing which was going to fill the vacuum in my life."[8]

SUFISM AND FEMININE SOCIAL VALUES

The emphasis by the Sufis on feminine values pertaining to the family while at the same time maintaining a dignity and strength as a worshiper before God has a special appeal for women who choose to fulfill an orientation toward the family and community. This is at a time when feminine social values are diminishing and no longer esteemed, in fact when there are constant efforts to undermine them in society. Ideals and concepts pertaining to womanhood and the family are no longer regarded as sacred but, on the contrary, as stigmatizing and stereotyping. These processes have resulted in confusion, leading to a void in the life of millions of women who want to live a life fulfilled by the capacity to nurture and strengthened by the independence of faith, which are pejoratively assumed as "traditional norms." Sufism with its strong affirmation of the sacred role of womanhood in society presents an attractive alternative to fill the vacuum for those women who desire to live their lives as mothers, wives, or daughters in a spiritual way. For example, Sufis (and Muslims in general) highly respect mothers; the exhortation in the Quran and by the Prophet to be respectful to mothers testifies to the honor bestowed on the maternal role, especially in its spiritual aspect. "There are several well-known hadiths that either state or imply that motherhood spent in accordance with the *Shari`a* is one of the expressions of the spiritual role of a female" (Chishti 204). One of the most detailed hadith that brings to life the spiritual reality of the travails of motherhood was related by Anas who had heard from Sallama the nurse of the Prophet's son Ibrahim:

> O Messenger of God, you have brought good tidings of all the good things to men, but not to women." He said: "Did your women friends put you up to asking me this question?" "Yes, they did," she replied, and he said: "Does it not please any one of you that if she is pregnant by her husband, she receives the reward of one who fasts and prays for the sake of God?" And when the labour pains come no one in the heavens or the earth knows what is concealed in her womb to delight her? And when she delivers, not a mouthful of milk flows from her and not a suck does she give, but that she receives, for every mouthful and every suck the reward of one good deed. And if she is kept awake at night, she receives the reward of one who frees seventy slaves for the sake of God. (Schleifer 49)

The Quran and the *Sunnah* demand that mothers be venerated and cared for, especially in old age; the famous hadith of the Prophet "heaven lies at the feet of mothers" provides much cause for reflection in the life of the pious Muslim who then endeavors to ensure that mothers are always respected, treated kindly, and gracefully obeyed. The very fact that the word for womb in Arabic, *rahm*, derives from the word *rahma* (mercy), which itself stems from the divine attributes of Ar-Rahman (the Compassionate) and Ar-Rahim (the Merciful), signifies the tremendously rich and deep understanding in Islam of the creation process as deriving from the very unfolding of compassion and mercy, so that each and every dimension of motherhood precipitates and participates in that unfolding. For Sufis, this symbol, and in fact spiritual reality, of the maternal facilitation of Divine Mercy was irresistible: as exemplified in one of the many Hadith Qudsi (the very words of God spoken on the tongue of the Prophet), such as that reported by Ghazzali: "If My servant falls sick, I care for him as a loving mother tends her son." Also, the great mystic Rumi is reported to have said: "[Since] a mother's tenderness derives from God, it's a sacred duty and a worthy task to serve her" (Schimmel, *My Soul Is a Woman* 89). For the believers who benefit from the Sufi exegesis of the metaphysical understanding of the creation process, it is no wonder that they hold their mothers in awe and do their best to be good to them so that the blessings of God descend upon them, for pious spiritual mothers possess *baraka* (the quality of the sacred) by virtue of their proximity to God.

The role of spiritual mothers starts originally with Maryam (Mary) the mother of Jesus and the only woman after whom a chapter in the Quran is named. She is considered the "Chosen amongst all women," and highly revered (among Muslims) for her piety, purity, and submission. In this context, the following hadith is of great importance: "Aisha [the wife of Muhammad] asked Fatima [the daughter of Muhammad]: Did I see [you truly] when you leaned over the Messenger of God and cried; then you leaned over him and you laughed? She said: He informed me that he would die from his illness, so I cried; then he informed me that I would precede the other members of his family in being reunited with him, and he said, You are the chief lady [*sayyida*] of paradise, with the exception of Mary the daughter of Imran" (Schleifer 63).

Among the women in the history of Islam, the first wife of the prophet Muhammad, Khadija, was the first to enter Islam and she, while supporting her husband in his mission as messenger of God, also looked after her children and ensured that peace and tranquility prevailed in her home, thus becoming the "embodiment of devotion and noble qualities" for Muslims, especially Muslim women (Smith xxx). Her daughter Fatima, mother of Hasan and Hossein, is regarded as the fountainhead of female spirituality in Islam; her extreme piety and devotion to her family elevated her to a high station. Together with her mother, they both "stand at the beginning of Islamic piety and occupy a very distinguished rank" (Smith xxx). Aisha, the youngest wife of the Prophet, is also highly honored and respected; she served her husband as devoted wife and guided Muslims with her

Divine knowledge; her close relationship with the Prophet made her an authentic source of knowledge about his personal life and so ranks her among the most reliable sources in the tradition of hadith science (Smith xxx). Other wives of the Prophet followed suit in their holiness and piety. They all set examples for Muslim women by expressing their spirituality through their roles as mothers, wives, or daughters.

Thus, from the Islamic spiritual and, therefore, Sufi perspective, the role of women within the family is highly valued and considered to be sacred as they are viewed as no less than the unfolding of God's Mercy. Feminine qualities and the homage paid to womanhood and their social and family roles become vital for women who desire to live in and through God. However, because Mercy is understood to have derived from the feminine attributes of God's Nature, the example of women who bore no children but dedicated their lives to God was also a source of reverence and inspiration, as we shall discuss next.

SUFISM AND THE FEMININE ELEMENT IN SPIRITUAL LIFE

Conscious of the positive aspects of womanhood, the Sufis more than others highlighted beautifully the role of women in spiritual life and thereby ensured that Sufism is permeated throughout with feminine traits. Within this context, the purely spiritual role of the female is fully accepted and elevated to a high degree. They bestowed upon women (in equality with men) the title of saint and accepted a woman (Rabia) to be a leading figure in the early development of Islamic mysticism (Smith 2–3). Ibn Arabi, in particular, played a major role in explaining the importance of the feminine element as a component of the Divine Reality (Schimmel, *My Soul is a Woman* 105; *Mystical Dimensions of Islam* 431). His belief that the Divine Reality ultimately contains and transcends the polarity of the masculine and the feminine continues to exert influence on Sufis until the present day. He declared that "there is no spiritual quality pertaining to men without women having access to it also" and "men and women have their part in all degrees [of sanctity] including that of the function of [spiritual] pole [a designation attributed to the most formative and inspiring figure of any particular phase in the life of the religion]" (Chodkiewicz 126). For Ibn Arabi, woman reveals the mystery of the compassionate God and the feminine aspect is the form in which God can best be contemplated. He stresses: "God can not be seen apart from matter, and He is seen more perfectly in the human *materia* than in any other, and more perfectly in woman than in man" (quoted in Schimmel,

Mystical Dimensions of Islam 431). In doing so, he elevates the image
of the feminine to a high degree and paves the way for other Sufis to
follow suit. For example, in the eighteenth century, Wali Muhammad
Akbarabadi, the commentator on Rumi, declared: "Know that God
can not be contemplated independently of a concrete being and that
He is more perfectly seen in a human being than in any other, and
more perfectly in woman'than in man" (Austin 12).

Thus, from the spiritual perspective, women embody and express
aspects of the Ultimate Reality, which comprises the masculine and
the feminine principles as prefigured in the ninety-nine names of God.
These names are traditionally classified according to Majesty (*Jalal*—
the archetype of masculinity) and beauty (*Jamal*—the archetype of
femininity). God is conceived, for example, both as the "wrathful"—
an eminently masculine trait—and as the "merciful"—identifiable as a
feminine quality. Moreover, if God is referred to as a He, "the essence
of God is referred to as a She" (Shah-Kazemi, "Women in Islam"
2). In their approach to Divine Reality, the Sufis have always *stressed*
the feminine dimension of that Reality. As Murata explains, while the
legalistic authorities emphasize the incomparability and distance of
God, the Sufis insist on the similarity and nearness of God. Hence,
for the dogmatic theologians, God is wrathful, distant, dominating,
and powerful. His rules must be obeyed otherwise there is only punishment and hellfire. In other words, God's attributes "are those of
a strict and authoritarian father" (Murata 8–9). In contrast, the Sufis
see God as gentle, kind, and near. They believe "that mercy, love, and
gentleness are the overriding reality of the existence and that these
will win out in the end." For them, "God is not primarily a stern
and forbidding father, but a warm and loving mother" (Murata 9).
As such, they argue that the God of the theologians is a God Whom
nobody would ever love, essentially because He is too distant and
difficult to comprehend, while the God of the spiritual authorities is
a God Who is compassionate and loveable because His prime concern is the care of His creatures; as a result His creatures love Him in
reciprocal terms. This loving caring God can easily be understood and
approached (Murata 9).

In conclusion, the dogmatic theologians, while accepting the
feminine characteristics of the Divine Reality, lay strong emphasis on
the masculine dimension of that reality, reducing in the process the
feminine aspect to a second place. In contrast, the Sufis affirm the
supremacy of the feminine dimension, primarily because the famous

hadith of the prophet "God's mercy precedes His wrath"—(implying that God's feminine characteristics take priority over his masculine qualities)—permeate their understanding and their approach to the ultimate reality (Murata 9).

These spiritual ideals, which relate to femininity, are not only derived from mystical interpretations but comprise the very fabric of the authentic Islamic tradition; they are enshrined in the Arabic language that powers Islamic theology and are reflected in the intellectual and social manifestation of the overall Islamic heritage. These ideals "permeated the ethos of traditional Islam. They may not have been articulated or even respected by all, but they were nonetheless implicit in the cultural ideals that defined gender relationships in societies that remained true to integral Islam. Ideals which continue to influence those who are trying to live according to the inner spirit of the tradition and not just outward prescriptions. This spirit leads to women being venerated and not incarcerated, held in awe and not treated with contempt" (Shah-Kazemi, "Women in Islam" 2).

NOTES

1. One exception in this context is Annemarie Schimmel.
2. See also J. Nurbakhsh, *Sufism I: Meaning, Knowledge, and Unity* (New York: Khaniqahi Nimatullahi Publications, 1981); R. Nicholson, *The Mystics of Islam* (London: Routledge and Kegan Paul, 1997); and G. Eaton, *Islam and the Destiny of Man* (Cambridge: Islamic Text Society, 1994).
3. See L. Le Pape, "Communication Strategies and Public Commitments: The example of a Sufi Order in Europe," in *Muslim Networks and Transnational Communities in and across Europe*, ed. Stefano Allievi and Jørgen S. Nielsen (Leiden: Brill, 2003), 232–34.
4. See A. Köse, *Conversion to Islam: A Study of Native British Converts* (London: Kegan Paul, 1996) 20, 142–43.
5. For more information, see M. Smith, *Rabia the Mystic and Her Fellow-Saints in Islam* (Cambridge: Cambridge University Press, 1984); J. Nurbakhsh, *Sufi Women* (New York: Khanaqahi-Nimatullahi Publications, 1983); and W. El-Sakkakini, *First among Sufis: The Life and Thought of Rabia al-Adawiyya, the Woman Saint of Basra* (London: Octagon Press, 1982).
6. See Annemarie Schimmel, *Mystical Dimensions of Islam* (Chapel Hill: University of North Carolina Press, 1975), 426–27, 430–35; S. H. Nasr, "The Male and Female in the Islamic Perspective," *Comparative Religion* 14(1, 2): 67–75.

7.   See P. Sherrard, *The Rape of Man and Nature: An Enquiry into the Origin and Consequences of Modern Science* (Ipswich: Golgonooza Press, 1987).

8.   See "Islam: the Modern Religion," http://www.themodernreligion .com/women/w_whyconvert.htm (author anonymous).

BIBLIOGRAPHY

Attar, Farid Al Din. *Muslim Saints and Mystics.* Translated by A. J. Arberry. London: Arkana, 1990.

Arnold, T. W. *The Preaching of Islam: A History of the Propagation of the Muslim Faith.* London: Archibald and Constable, 1935.

Austin, Ralph. "The Feminine Dimensions in Ibn Arabi's Thought." *Muhyiddin ibn Arabi Society Journal* 2 (1984): 5–14.

Chishti, Khawar Khan. "Female Spirituality in Islam." In *Islamic Spirituality, Foundations,* edited by S. H. Nasr, 199–219. London: SCM Press, 1989.

Chodkiewicz, Michel. *The Seal of the Saints.* Paris: Gallimard, 1986.

Dutton, Yasin. "Conversion to Islam: The Quranic Paradigm." In *Religious Conversion. Contemporary Practices and Controversies,* edited by C. Lamb and M. Bryant, 151–65. London: Cassell, 1999.

Eaton, Gai. *Islam and the Destiny of Man.* Cambridge: Islamic Text Society, 1994.

El-Sakkakini, Widad. *First among Sufis: The Life and Thought of Rabia al-Adawiyya, the Woman Saint of Basra.* Translated by Nabil Safwat. London: Octagon Press, 1982.

Haddad, Yvonne Yasbeck., and Adair T. Lummis. *Islamic Values in the United States.* Oxford: Oxford University Press, 1987.

Hodgson, Marshall G. H. *The Venture of Islam: Conscience and History in a World Civilization.* Vol. 2, *The Expansion of Islam in the Middle Periods.* Chicago: University of Chicago Press, 1974.

Köse, Ali. *Conversion to Islam: A Study of Native British Converts.* London: Kegan Paul, 1996.

Lapidus, Ira Marvin. *A History of Islamic Societies.* Cambridge: Cambridge University Press, 1988.

Le Pape, Loïc. "Communication Strategies and Public Commitments: The example of a Sufi Order in Europe." In *Muslim Networks and Transnational Communities in and across Europe,* edited by Stefano Allievi and Jørgen S. Nielsen, 225–42. Leiden: Brill, 2003.

Lings, Martin. *What Is Sufism?* London: George Allen and Unwin, 1975.

Murata, Sachiko. *The Tao of Islam.* New York: State University of New York Press, 1992.

Nasr, Seyyed Hossein. *Islam and the Plight of Modern Man.* London: Longman, 1975.

———. ed. *Islamic Spirituality, Foundations.* London: SCM Press, 1989.

————. *The Male and Female in the Islamic Perspective*. In *Studies in Comparative Religion*, edited by William Stoddard. Middlesex: Perennial Books, 1980.

————. *Sufi Essays*. London: George Allen and Unwin, 1972.

Nicholson, Reynold A. *The Mystics of Islam*. London: Routledge and Kegan Paul, 1997.

Nurbakhsh, Javad. *Sufism, Meaning, Knowledge, and Unity*. New York: Khaniqahi Nimatullahi Publications, 1981.

————. *Sufi Women*. New York: Khanaqahi-Nimatullahi Publications, 1983.

Schimmel, Annemarie. *My Soul Is a Woman: The Feminine in Islam*. New York: Continent, 1997.

————. *Mystical Dimensions of Islam*. Chapel Hill: University of North Carolina Press, 1975.

Schleifer, Aliah. *Mary the Blessed Virgin in Islam*. Louisville, KY: Fons Vitae, 1997.

Shah-Kazemi, Reza. *The Other in the Light of the One: The Universality of the Quran and Interfaith Dialogue*. Cambridge: Islamic Texts Society, 2006.

Shah-Kazemi, Reza. "Women in Islam: A Reminder to the Taliban." Dialogue. London: Al-Khoei Foundation, 1996.

Sherrard, Philip. *The Rape of Man and Nature: An Enquiry into the Origin and Consequences of Modern Science*. Ipswich: Golgonooza Press, 1987.

Smith, Margaret. *Rabia the Mystic and Her Fellow-Saints in Islam*. Cambridge: Cambridge University Press, 1984.

CHAPTER 10

SHEKHINAH'S KISS*

TRACING THE INTER-FACE BETWEEN MOTHERHOOD AND GOD IN THE HOLOCAUST

Melissa Raphael

During the Holocaust, Jewish mothers and their children were treated by the Nazis not as noncombatants but as enemies posing a direct racial threat to the Reich. This chapter will use the recent research into gender and the Holocaust and oral histories of mothers and daughters who survived the Holocaust to show how women experienced and resisted their status as "enemies" of the Reich. More to the theological point, this chapter will explore how the suffering of these mothers, and their resistance to their own and their children's suffering, signals toward *another* model of covenantal relation between God and Israel. In this new model, God's promise to Israel in Leviticus 26, "I will be ever in your midst; I will be your God, and you shall be My people," need no longer be figured in terms of loyalty and obedience to the commandment of an overbearing Lord.

---

* Sections of this chapter are taken from parts of my book *The Female Face of God in Auschwitz*. I have updated references to the literature on women and the Holocaust and have added further prefatory material and a concluding response to Irigaray's article included in this volume. Some of this chapter was published in an earlier version in *Temenos* (2006).

This chapter will develop the notion of the Motherhood of God in Auschwitz from my book *The Female Face of God in Auschwitz* (2003) and propose that an alternative feminist model of female love, power, and providence *does* resist evil; that, in particular, the power of motherhood is not merely a sentimental bourgeois idea beloved of first-wave religious feminism, but that it tells us something important about the nature of divine love and about female love's resilience, resourcefulness, and resistance. For *in extremis* the maternal resistance of mothers and quasi-mothers helped women and children to survive the Nazi assault spiritually and occasionally physically as well.

To be faithful to the actual and particular suffering of *all* persons during the Holocaust and to the covenantal presence of God in the midst of that suffering, the post-Holocaust project must reflect on the gendered variety of Jewish experience. It cannot proceed, as it has usually done, as if the suffering of mothers and children has offered a graphic illustration of Nazi barbarism but not insight into God. In fact, the theology presented in this chapter may be feminist, but its method is fairly traditional: Judaism is traditionally reluctant to merely theorize God, rather the presence of God is detected and articulated in the given historical situation.

The extreme and often unprecedented conditions of the Holocaust should not be generalized in theory and then applied to the environments most of us inhabit, for these do not normally, minute by minute, test our bodies and spirits to the breaking point. It is therefore interesting to compare my reading of women's Holocaust memoirs with the claims made by Luce Irigaray in this volume, which do make a certain bid, if not to universality then, at least, to generality. It is perhaps unfair to subject Irigaray's chapter to a Jewish historical and theological interpretation, which she has not herself invited nor been given the opportunity to answer. Nonetheless, my concluding comments, based on Irigaray's chapter, do not presume to theologize on her behalf, nor do they make any claim to exhaustive scholarly knowledge of Irigaray's literary corpus. Rather, the conclusion to this chapter reads her given text from a Jewish feminist, post-Holocaust perspective to see whether Irigaray's spirituality of self-affection, of the closed lips, can address or console the suffering other. Since suffering is always specific to a historic subject, I want to see whether Irigaray's chapter, which appears to address all women regardless of their social and historical situation, is at all relevant to the historic suffering of Jewish women in the Holocaust and the theological position of the women who remember them.

MOTHERHOOD DURING THE HOLOCAUST

To begin, then, at the historical beginning of that situation: as Nechama Tec has pointed out, ironically—because of their consistently subordinate roles—mothers may have been more adaptable to traumatic changes than were fathers. In the early days of the Nazi occupation when men were publicly humiliated with beatings and other tortures and robbed of their livelihoods, they tended to succumb to depression and "gave up." Even though very few would be ultimately successful in their efforts, wives then had to use their flexibility and resourcefulness to organize the family into a unit that could survive or at least continue to eat (Tec 10, 26, 349). Theirs was an especially demanding situation in that they had, in such cases, lost the traditional means of emotional and financial support from the man who had been the head of the family.

Of course, after the deportations to death and concentration camps had begun, women's circumstances, already dire, deteriorated sharply. When relatively young mothers had teenage daughters and no other young children, they sometimes managed to stay together in the women's camp in Auschwitz-Birkenau, assembled for forced labor over a period of about three months (the length of time it was expected that they would take to die). As well as the elderly and infirm, mothers with young children were the most vulnerable of all those entering Auschwitz. By the summer of 1944, Hungarian Jewish babies and children were being torn from their mothers outside the crematoria and sent separately to the gas or burned alive in a fire pit near the crematoria.

I am not suggesting that motherhood as such could withstand the Nazi genocide by some kind of supernatural or moral force. The forcible deportation of children under the age of ten from the Lodz ghetto on September 10, 1942, to the death camp at Chelmo was ample evidence of the impotence of most mothers to save either themselves or their children. However, once the relative impotence of mothers (and fathers) has been acknowledged, a post-Holocaust feminist theology should not continue to ignore the experience of those children's mothers and the theological possibilities of maternalist language and values. Maternal experience and the ethical difference that produces has been an important focus of second-wave feminist scholarship. It is this, and (among a number of other studies) Susan Sered's analysis of Jewish women's traditional concerns with love, death, and familial relationships, that contextualizes my situating the experiences and tropes of motherhood at the center of the feminist theological inquiry in ways that will challenge, modify, and finally alter the character and substance of the post-Holocaust project (Sered, *Women as Ritual Experts;* "Mother Love, Child Death, and Religious Innovation"). In particular, I am convinced that a feminist theological reading of women's narration of broken (and sometimes preserved or restored) familial relationships during the Holocaust shifts our conception of God's presence among European Jewry between 1933 and 1945.

Theological and other theorizations of the Holocaust are rightly preoccupied with brokenness, fragmentation, rupture, and disappearance. Yet women survivor testimonies often construe and redeem loss through their sense of unbroken relational continuities with their mothers and foremothers. The narratives of more memoirs and testimonies than can be cited here are almost entirely constituted by the story of the turbulent passage of the mother and daughter (or sister and sister) relationship, which, whether actual or adoptive, either survived or ended in the holocaustal period. Giuliana Tedeschi, for example, particularly mourned the loss of a small bunch of dried violets that her daughter had picked for her grandmother in the Italian spring of 1944 and which had been taken from Tedeschi with her other belongings on arrival in Auschwitz (57). Here the female line was symbolized in the giving of flowers, by one generation of women to another. The dry, dead, crushed, and, finally, vanished flowers evoke the withering death and disappearance of countless maternal lines. But after the Holocaust, Charlotte Delbo (a member of the French resistance who had been sent to Auschwitz) could see a new baby as having been born on behalf of all those mothers who had died: "You remember this peasant woman, lying in the snow, dead with her newborn frozen between her thighs. My son was also that newborn. . . . My son is their son, he belongs to all of them. He is the child they will not have had" (261–62). Similarly, women survivors continue to draw strength even from their memories of their mothers. In the many women's memoirs of the Holocaust published in recent years (one thinks of those of, say, Trudi Berger, Sara Tuvel Bernstein, Rena Kornriech Gelissen, Kitty Hart, Clara Isaacman, and Schoschana Rabinovici), it is the author's relation with her mother (whether living or dead) that gives meaning, purpose, and substance to her survival and thence to the narration of her experience.[1] Sisters, especially in the absence of a mother, similarly anchor meaning and hope. Kornreich's memoir, for example, is shaped by the promise she made to her mother to protect her sister Danka, who, the physically weaker of the two, also helps Kornreich herself to survive Auschwitz.

It is as if within the story of Israel's relationship with the male father/king God is another (untold) story: the story of the female bond of protective love between the mother-God and the daughters of Israel *in extremis*. If love is stronger than death (Song of Songs 8: 6), then so is maternal presence—a phenomenalizing of divine and human love that can be read from the memoirs. There is also, in my view, an iconography of maternal love and sisterhood in some of the photographic record, caught, as it were, for the future, and in spite of itself.[2] These female Jewish bodies carry the historical process as an ark or tabernacle inside which is wrapped the story or Torah Jews have told about the relationship between themselves and God, and which unfolds and rolls on and out through time in the carrying and opening of the body to new life. And just as the Torah scrolls must be cherished, dressed, crowned with silver, and cradled in our arms, so too must be each woman's (derelict) body in Auschwitz on which desecrated scroll is inscribed another (not the last) chapter of the story of the love between God and her daughter Israel. I shall turn now to some of these body-stories within stories as *midrashim* on the love of God for Israel, the utmost sign of which was God's presence as (a) Mother in Auschwitz and other sites of holocaustal mass death.

All of the brief survivor narratives that can be found on Judy Weissenberg Cohen's Web site on the subject of women and the Holocaust demonstrate that maternal or quasi-maternal relations with other women were of ultimate concern. For example, alone in Bergen-Belsen, the sixteen-year-old Weissenberg Cohen herself asked the Feig sisters to adopt her as their *Lagerschwester*. They did so and proceeded to share all that they had. For Cohen, these women assumed some of the functions of a mother: "It was very important to know that someone cared whether you woke up in the morning."[3] Elisabeth de Jong's account of surviving Auschwitz's human experimentation Block 10 also focuses on how the female doctor there would "gently wash and dress our wounds and try to console us" and how she herself struggled to keep her sister Lilian alive. Judith Rubenstein's two entries speak of little more than two women: the tragic manner in which her mother sacrificed her own life in Auschwitz to save that of Judith, and of the kindness and compassion of Ethel, a *Blockälteste* who "attempted to ease the pain" and also saved her life. Irene Csillig, a Hungarian dressmaker, tells her story in such a way that all other experience is omitted from her narration except that of the preservation of her relationship with her mother and sister. After Liberation, having survived a period in Auschwitz—her mother died in Stutthof—Csillig went on a fruitless journey to their hometown to find objects—a wedding ring and a petit-point embroidered cushion—that would remind her of her mother, or more, represent her mother to her. Although these were not returned to her, like those of other women survivors, her account is at least partially resolved by its closing reassurance to the reader (common to the genre) that she has married and has had children and grandchildren.[4] The maternal line, a covenant of trust between mothers and daughters, can go on into the future; grieving, consoling maternal love could take on the redemptive function and attribute of divine love.

In Judith Jaegarmann's testimony, divine presence is knowable in the traditions of maternal love associated with Shekhinah—the traditionally female figure that hypostasizes the divine presence in both traditional and feminist Judaism and in whose wings Israel finds refuge. In 1943, at the age of thirteen and from an Orthodox family, she was deported from Theresienstadt to Auschwitz. There, her mother, described as a "guardian angel," continued to give her the courage to live. She offered motherly comfort to all the girls who were alone: "All the girls tried to stay near to her and felt sheltered by her." In the women's camp in Birkenau, Jaegarmann's mother tore her own blanket apart and made bands to protect her daughter's legs from the frostbite wrought by winter temperatures of –20° centigrade. On one occasion, transported out of Auschwitz to another work camp, Jaegarmann lost consciousness while laboring in the snow. As in the moment of birth, she opened her eyes to a circle of female faces above her: "Suddenly I felt as if someone wakes [sic] me and I saw the faces of many women over me. I overheard them saying 'the little one almost froze to death.' They let me lie down for a little while longer and then many girls started massaging and rubbing me, so that I started to feel my body, hands and feet again."[5]

Women survivors' memoirs show that motherhood—whether as a socioethical posture or as a biological relationship—is not always an asymmetrical relation of care. During the Holocaust, care for children could give women themselves a sense of meaning, purpose, and hope. When an orphaned, four-year-old Jewish girl arrived at the house in Antwerp where Clara Isaacman and her mother were hiding, her mother's depressed, withdrawn face "lit up when she held the child on her lap, singing to her and combing her curls" (Issacman 103). Often, the sustenance of children by mothers was reciprocated by children. Ghetto children sometimes worked for their mother's survival by finding food for them and tending them when they were sick (fathers and older brothers having been commonly separated from their families at an earlier stage of the genocide). Children could themselves become "mothers" where their own mothers had numerous children to care for. Isabella Leitner mourns her baby sister Potyo, who was probably thrown alive into the fire pits of Auschwitz on May 31, 1944, as if she had been her own baby: "She was 'my' baby." Leitner had bathed and changed her diapers as if she were Potyo's mother. Speaking as her mother might have done had she survived, Leitner writes: "She would be a middle-aged woman now, and I still can't deal with having lost her" (21).

Motherhood itself began to lose its usual relational contours as sisters took on the providential functions of mothers to one another, and mothers took on those of quasi-divine presence. Even in the days after liberation, Isabella Leitner's sister Rachel remained what she calls the "mother hen," sewing a cut-up blanket into a coat to keep her sister warm. Speaking for her sisters as well, Leitner writes to Rachel: "The endless care. The endless concern. Our complete confidence that we could rely on you. We always blessed you. Did you know that?" (81). Women's friendships could also entail mothering. Mothers mothered mothers in Auschwitz. Lying in her bunk and in great distress, Giuliana Tedeschi's friend Zilly held Tedeschi's hand in her own "small, warm, hand." Zilly pulled the blanket around Tedeschi's shoulders and in a "calm, motherly voice" whispered in her ear, "Good night dear—I have a daughter your age!" Sleep then "crept slowly into [her] being along with the trust that hand communicated, like blood flowing along the veins" (9–10). Or, again, Charlotte Delbo used to hold her friend Germaine's hand in Auschwitz to help her get to sleep. Germaine later says, "Do you recall how you used to say, in Auschwitz, 'Let me hold your hand so I'll fall asleep. You have my mother's hands.' Do you remember saying that, Charlotte?" (310). Once voiced in the promise of Ruth to her mother-in-law Naomi that she will go where Naomi goes, where Naomi dies she shall die; that nothing but death shall part her from Naomi (Ruth 1:16–17), it may be that maternal presence in its multiple forms and surrogates offers a different means to trust in God than those tradition has accustomed us to.

Of course, it can be difficult for Anglophone Jewish women over the age of forty not to read Jewish motherhood through the stereotypes of their own times, especially that of Jewish-American caricature (the most excessive being that of Sophie in Philip Roth's puerile 1967 *Portnoy's Complaint*). Even after the Holocaust had consumed so many of them, the Ashkenazic *Yiddishe mama* was something of a comic turn. An ambivalent object of both derision and sentimental yearning, she was a smothering, overprotective, overfeeding emasculator of sons; a woman who was aging into the fussing, needy "old" woman for which Yiddish has numerous derogatory terms: *yidneh*, *yenta*, and *yachne*. The contemporary Ashkenazi Jewish mother is no longer caricatured as the (now somewhat dated) *Yiddishe mama* but—if she is prosperous enough—a materialistic, flashy, overdressed, selfish Jewish Princess or (in the United States) Californian Jewish Valley Girl who is a lot less interested in children than in her designer wardrobe.

The "Jewish Princess" caricature is worthy of study in itself,[6] but infinitely more theologically interesting, however, is the *mama* of the eastern European *shtetl*, who, if taken seriously as a resourceful woman who often earned the wages to feed and clothe her family, can become a symbol of strength and responsibility: a very good image of divine providence. Etty Hillesum describes one such mother in the desperate conditions of the Westerbork transit camp. The woman's husband and two elder sons had been deported. Herself starving, the mother had seven children left to care for, as she made ready for her own deportation from Holland to Auschwitz. Hillesum writes: "She bustles about . . . she's busy, she has a kind word for everyone who goes by. A plain dumpy ghetto woman with greasy black hair and little short legs. She has a shabby, short-sleeved dress on, which I can imagine her wearing when she used to stand behind the washtub, back in Jodenbreestraat. And now she is off to Poland in the same old dress, a three day's journey with seven children. 'That's right, seven children, and they need a proper mother, believe me!'" (132)

During the Holocaust, motherhood was, in Katharina von Kellenbach's view, as much a form of resistance as armed revolt. Those seeking to understand Jewry's struggle for spiritual and material survival should not overlook women's reproductive labor. In hope and faith, couples partook in a tradition of resistance to genocidal persecution dating back to the time of Moses: They chose to have children at the least auspicious of moments, and when most couples were aware that the mother could face caring for the child destitute and facing her persecutors alone (19–32).

The Holocaust imposed a complex set of maternal and quasi-maternal responsibilities. We have already seen that maternal obligations often had to be reciprocated by children prematurely matured by danger and need. Mothers had responsibilities not only to their children but also to their elderly parents. This traditional duty of daughterly care further endangered women's lives; had it not been that women felt that they could not leave their parents to an unknown fate, many could have escaped before emigration became impossible.

Lucie Adelsberger, for example, refused to leave her elderly mother in Germany. Although she was offered a visa for the United States for herself, she could not obtain one for her mother and chose to remain with her as the gates of life closed before them (12).

This is not to lapse into cliché: Mothers are often bored, irritated, and angered by their children. Not all mothers and children are immunized by love, some do not like one another, and some children are frightened of their mothers. The notion of maternal power is strongly associated with nineteenth-century social and religious rhetoricians who compensated women's sociopolitical powerlessness by ascribing a largely toothless domestic moral authority to mothers. During the Holocaust, however, motherhood became both an ever more necessary fiction, a way of suspending disbelief, and, sometimes, a real material force. Clara Isaacman's memories of hiding from the Nazis in occupied Belgium illustrate my point. During their two-and-a-half years in hiding, Isaacman's mother would hold and comfort her, speaking confidently and with conviction of their future. It was only when the war was over that Isaacman wondered whether her mother had ever really believed her own reassurances (37). Isaacman recalls how the expression of love had become ritualized; it had become almost a performance of sympathetic magic. Mothers would hold their children before the latter went out on dangerous errands, willing that, if nothing else, their love would protect them (60). Sometimes the "strong wishing" worked and children might often not have survived were it not for the love and proximity of their parents (97). Even when, in the great majority of cases, children did not survive, their end could be eased by a fiction that maternal or quasi-maternal presence would be their redemption.[7] And it was not only mothers whose presence could induce (or fiction) a calming sense of trust that all would soon be well, even in the palpable presence of death. To take but two examples: The physical presence of charismatic male Hasidic rabbis in the ghettos and camps also gave quasi-magical reassurance to their male followers (Schindler 74–79). Or, in the Warsaw ghetto, orphans in the male doctor Janusz Korczac's care felt that, "Whatever would happen, they were to know that it would not matter as long as he, the doctor, would be with them. All he asked was that they remain together . . . And so the children set out on their journey [to the death camp, Treblinka] . . . Nothing mattered, as long as the doctor was with them" (Zeitlin 56–57).

TOWARD A MATERNALIST THEOLOGY

When God calls to Abraham, Jacob, and Moses they answer, "*hinneni*": "I am here" or "here I am" (Genesis 22: 1, 31: 11, 46: 2; Exodus 3: 4). For Levinas, this "I am here" is the meaning of love (*Otherwise than Being* 113, 147). In this regard, a maternalist theology is not quite the departure from twentieth-century Jewish thought that one might expect it to be. Rosenzweig, Buber, and Levinas, all in different ways, developed an ethic of interdependence and vulnerability that they themselves recognized as "feminine." Indeed, Levinas regarded the feminine and the maternal as the very condition of the ethical and rejected Heidegger's ontological prioritizing of death in favor of an ethic of actual responsibility in life for the other ("Judaism and the Feminine Element" 30–38). It is also arguable that this sense of the "femininity" of a God in exile can in fact be traced to the very beginning of the post–Second Temple period when, after the failure of Jewish military strength, the rabbis "created a Judaism that could survive without political power" and an image of God whose power was deferred but whose present imitation was located in prayer and the "service of the heart" (Lubarsky 310).

Yet twentieth-century Jewish theology's deeply humane relational inclination stopped short of considering how presence could become a condition of the theological in, and after, Auschwitz. The absence or hiding of the divine and the human(e) was instead to become the dominant theme of post-Holocaust Jewish theology. By contrast, from a feminist perspective, in Auschwitz, maternal attention to suffering was not reducible to the mere ineffectual gestures of kindness, but, in this situation, where all gestures against Nazism were more or less materially ineffectual, it phenomenalized the maternal quality of divine love. To be a mother of babies or young children was, and is, to be entirely vulnerable to harm at the same time as it is to be presentative of a mighty love, which, as refuge, takes and holds its object within and against itself. This is the love of a Mother-God, known to tradition as (the) *Shekhinah*, and recently voiced by Penina Adelman's liturgical words: "I give praise to you, *HaMakom*, the Place of Power. *Shekhinah*, in the darkness of Your Womb we find comfort and protection. *Rakhameima*, Mother of Compassion, in the Darkness of Your Hidden Place we find the Source and the Power" (165).

Where the metaphor of a Mother-God represents not merely an aspect of God but a function of God that reconfigures the entire concept of God, then the figure of the mother, bereaved and bereft of her children or remaining with her daughters in Auschwitz, assumes a particular theological poignancy. For most Jewish feminists, "The Holy One is *Gaol-tanu*, *Ima-ha-olam*, our Redeemer, Mother of the World. She is *Ha raham-aima*, Compassionate Giver of Life. She is *Makor hahaiim*, Source of Life. She is our neighbourly spirit, the Shekhinah" (Broner 12). In Jewish feminist liturgy, drawing on the maternal imagery found in the Hebrew Bible (Psalm 22; Israel 46):

> Blessed is She who in the beginning, gave birth . . .
> Blessed is She whose womb covers the earth.
> Blessed is She whose womb protects all creatures. (Janowitz 176)

Contemporary Jewish feminist liturgy widely expresses the faith that, "The Lord is warmth / She will cradle me. The Wings of the Lord will cover me. Her breath will soothe me" (Wenig, quoted in Blumenthal 79). There are, in short, important intertextual connections to be made between scriptural words, these contemporary words, and women's words about Auschwitz where the meaning and purpose of Jewish motherhood was to be destroyed and where pregnancy—the motherhood of an unborn child—could not be declared. Much Jewish feminism has insisted that the motherhood of God is the undeclared, untold story still unborn from the body of Israel, and it seems necessary to bring these narratives of maternal disappearance together and to reflect upon them without confusing their historical reasons.

Narratives of maternal presence and disappearance thread their way through women's Holocaust memoirs, whether they write as mothers of hidden children, of children struggling to survive, of dead children, or whether they write as daughters with, or longing for, their mothers. As I read it, this narrative corpus is both a historical and theological commentary on presence and absence, appearance and disappearance. In these stories and fragments of stories, the face of *Shekhinah* shines dimly, almost imperceptibly, through the smoke clouds of Auschwitz. Hers was a countenance figured by the *tremendum* of divine maternal wrath at the despoliation of her love, Israel, and the *fascinans* of her longing, seeking and calling to what was disappearing—literally going up in smoke—before her. God weeps with Rachel for her children who are gone (Jeremiah 31: 15). The maternal presence of God is not a redemptive one insofar as it could not carry Jews out from a place of atrocity and dereliction to a place of safety. In Auschwitz, death was omnipresent and omnivorous; to be (still) alive was necessarily, and by decree, to be dying (Langer 1–15).

Yet Jewish dying cannot be defined by the perpetrators. In rabbinic and mystical tradition, the kiss of the *Shekhinah* is the kiss of death, where God bends over the dying and gently extinguishes the spark of life in a consummation of love that is at once erotic and maternal.[8] But that kiss was also a redemptive one insofar as divine love, and the human love that performed divine love, at once retrieved its object from hatred and death and bid her farewell from life. The kiss was a gesture of, and to, a depth of grief, which, like pure joy, is a moment of revelation. Suffering is not *itself* redemptive, but the visual spectacle of maternal grief *qua* witness and judgment on the destruction of creation is both a recapitulation and prolepsis of God's wrathful grief;[9] a grief whose *tremendum* betokens the cosmic reversal that turns death to life: the resurrection that is and has always been a classical tenet of Jewish faith.

SITUATING TRANSCENDENCE

It is immediately evident that there are significant connections between Irigaray's chapter and my own. That much is to be expected since, like many other feminist scholars whose careers took shape in the early 1990s, I have followed Irigaray in her attempt to elucidate a different female subject position that does not defer to male subjectivity; that makes use of a strategic essentialism, and which reclaims or reverses the terms, practices, and categories that patriarchal society have used to oppress women. Irigaray's focus on the mother-daughter bond and her insistence on the need for a love that does not appropriate or subjugate the irreducible difference of the other has echoed through numerous religious feminist studies of motherhood. Like Irigaray and other feminist commentators, I have examined the mother-daughter relation. My study of that relation, situated in Auschwitz, examines how maternal love both empowered women and made them vulnerable. That is, I have examined how, during the Holocaust, whose purpose was to end the possibility of Jewish motherhood, women were, as Irigaray puts it in her own context, "made fragile by the intervention of the other in her: in love, in motherhood" (Chapter 1 in this volume, 14). My own study of maternal love in Auschwitz has shown that maternal, and quasi-maternal love, between women camp-inmates generated the meaning and will to live and die for the other, but the exercise of love also left women emotionally and physically drained, and when the other died, meaning and hope could die with her, often accelerating the death of the woman left behind.

Irigaray's well-known contention that, as she puts it in Chapter 1, "lack of respect for the identity or subjectivity of each one is the most important fault since this amounts to a kind of murder: a spiritual murder, the most serious murder" (in this volume, 15), is also pertinent to a post-Holocaust feminist theology. The murder of women in Auschwitz, and the systematic destruction of their self- and other-affection, was paradigmatic of the genocidal murder that is usually characterized by a lethal combination of ethnic hatred and misogyny (Fein 43–63). The women's camp at Auschwitz-Birkenau was not only established for physical killing but also for the desecration and erasure of identity of women as Jews and as women.

Despite such commonalities, including also a shared sense of the presence of the divine in the relation with the other and a coincidentally shared trope of closed lips, I did not find adequate resources for a theology of suffering in the spiritual posture Irigaray proposes. Indeed, I found the closed lips in Irigaray's chapter to be an inscrutable and inherently nonmaternal image, with unsettling affinities to the patriarchal theology of the Holocaust that relies so heavily on the trope of *hester panim*, a Hebrew term translatable as "the averted face" (of God). Post-Holocaust theologians have commonly argued that God was compelled to turn his face—to abandon us in silence to the consequences of his absence—since to intervene and stop the catastrophe would have been a violation of the definitively human (that is, male) freedom to do evil; to make the wrong choice. God's ontological separation from the human predicament is preserved by closing his mouth against any expression of wrath or grief (Raphael, "The Price of (Masculine) Freedom and Becoming" 136–50).

In my chapter, the closed lips of the silent and unseeing patriarchal God are contrasted with the opened divine lips of the *Shekhinah*—the female, immanent dimension of the God who accompanies the Jewish people in their exile; who is in exile from God-self. Whereas the *Shekhinah*'s kiss imagines God-She bending over and touching the lips of the dying with her own lips, breathing in their life in love and grief, the closed lips evoked by Irigaray as a means of female becoming are akin to the patriarchal closed lips of God. Irigaray's closed lips are sealed in an act of ontological self-preservation so that the one divine self is not reduced to the other; so that the other will be "safeguarded" against becoming disintegrated into one. The patriarchal God's closed lips do, in fact, speak, but it is the nonspeech of a refusal to speak. God's closed lips say, "I will not answer your cry for help; I will not speak to your predicament; I will not ease your burden with words of comfort, I will make no promise to you, I will not cry out in judgment or lament." Irigaray laments that "we lack a culture of relating with the other" (Chapter 1 in this volume, 22). But it seems to me that her spirituality and, indeed, her account of the possibility of divinity, is ultimately and necessarily self-enclosed or sealed. So that the self can be autonomous, which is seen as a mark of its divinity, the mouth may, but will not always, open to gasp in shocked, compassionate pain or to smile in friendship and reassurance.

There is, of course, plenty of common sense in a philosophy that asserts that relationship is created by the encounter of two separate willing subjects, not a fusion into one. Yet it seems to me that *in the presence or remembrance of the suffering other*, Irigaray's "self-affection in the feminine," the gesture of closing the lips so that the subject can gather herself into herself, "preserving a free space between the two" (17), can become indistinguishable from an abandonment or dereliction of love. In Auschwitz, to respect the other who has been in all senses stripped naked was to touch her, to speak to her, to welcome her into the open circle of the *Lagerschwestern* or camp sisters who took care of one another in friendship or quasi-familial love. Here, "self-affection in the feminine" was possible, if only as a reminder of a former state of being. But if the term "self-affection in the feminine" can mean anything at all in a death camp, it seems, from the memoirs, to have been effected not through a private act of will, but through the loving care of other women. This movement of the one toward the other established precisely the only "free space" in Auschwitz. The care of one for the other was an act of substitution or restoration of the humanity stripped from women inmates by the camp's regime of dehumanization. The survivors' memoirs seem to suggest that to merely close the lips against the drowning tide of excrement, tears, and noise was not enough; nor was self-love.

Perhaps by way of a correction to the relational philosophy that dominated late twentieth-century Jewish and Christian thought, Irigaray wants the cultivation of intimacy to transcend the external touch of a physical hand, lest that reduce the other to what she calls a "simple body" (how or when is the body ever simple?). Yet, in a number of women's Holocaust memoirs, it becomes clear that in Auschwitz and other death and concentration camps, it was precisely the external touch of a physical hand that was sought. To have another take your hand or encircle your shoulder could be a moment of respite or even grace that remembered a once lovable body and, theologically speaking, betokened its eschatological restoration or *tikkun* from starving, beaten abjection to its first and final wholeness.

Irigaray sees "the virginity of woman" as a condition of autonomy. The lips—both those of the mouth and the labia—touch one another "without any external intervention or tool" (Chapter 1 in this volume, 17). Yet like many other feminists, I regard the quest for autonomy as a symptom and function of patriarchal alienation, whose terms were at once established and protested in one of the primal questions of the Hebrew Bible, when God asks Cain, "Where is thy brother Abel?" and Cain replies, "I do not know. Am I my brother's keeper?" (Genesis 4: 9). And it is in reading women's Holocaust memoirs that one is compelled to ask how maintaining Irigaray's tight-lipped, virginal, "irreducible," and "insuperable" transcendental difference between "the other and herself" could permit the "recovery of the self" from the extreme phallocratic alienation from both self and other induced by a death camp and which has more or less absolute power to break the seal of personal dignity. How, in any situation, can Irigaray's spirituality of the closed lips do more than to remind us of the merely self-evident fact that I am me, (a), not her, (b)? For a Jew, this is theologically uninteresting. Being a covenantal people, Israel, assembled before God, entails the ontological permeability of the self to the present and historical collective other. While traditional Judaism would not deny that each Jew is an individual who is free to obey or disregard God's commandment, it has little sympathy with the modern quest for the fulfillment or becoming of the private self. Jews, like most other religious subjects, do not wish to merely, as Irigaray puts it, take "care of their own part of earth and of sky" (Chapter 1 in this volume, 22).

Even without reference to the Holocaust, it may be that Irigaray's spirituality of the closed lips is outside the range of Jewish women's values or experiences, especially that of religious or observant Jewish women. In some senses, it hardly matters whether Irigaray's spirituality, inflected by Marian Catholic traditions, is relevant to the situation of being Jewish or to the specific conditions of Jewish historical catastrophes; few people are Jewish, and Jewish ways do not need to be their ways. But, in other senses, it does matter: Irigaray's chapter, despite being framed in the essentially Christian terms of the "everyday cross, our internal and invisible everyday cross" (Chapter 1 in this volume, 22), seems to be proposing an essentialist reduction of Jewish or other religio-conceptual difference to feminine sameness. Yet, this is neither possible nor desirable for Jewish women. Her spirituality is, in many respects, simply alien to Jewish tradition and Jewish women's experience.

Although, for example, Irigaray's chapter proposes virginity as a way of coming back to the self within a patriarchal dispensation, there is no concept of vocational celibacy for Jewish men or women, in either a literal or spiritual sense. More centrally, the whole project of what Irigaray calls "becoming divine"—of "how to turn our original material and dependent existence into an autonomous and spiritual existence through a change of our energy" is, if I might speak for other Jews, alien to Jewish spirituality in a way that few other spiritual projects are truly alien. While God's presence might be invited into the world in a number of ways (chiefly through the practices of *kedu-shah* or holiness), no one can become, or aspire to become, divine since the primary Jewish commitment is to the monotheism that underwrites Judaism's struggle against false gods. Jewish feminism largely shares the traditionally Jewish monotheistic commitment, even when it invokes feminine divine names, since it regards patriarchy's assertion of its divine ordination and likeness to an exclusively masculine God as idolatry's paradigm instance. Where Irigaray's chapter indicates "some stages for the journey toward our becoming more divine: faithfulness to self-affection; sharing with the other in respect for their/our difference(s); crossroads between horizontal and vertical transcendences" (24), my chapter argues that for a woman to become human or, in the case of a woman in Auschwitz, to have her humanity restored to her by the practical humanity of another, is redemption enough.

As a Jew, I am more interested in *Jewish* feminine (or, better, female) becoming than "feminine becoming" per se. That is not because Jewishness is a universalizable quality of becoming or because it has more merit than any other sort of becoming. But for a Jew, becoming is about becoming in a real place and time within a real historical continuum that patterns her becoming and lends it a tran-shistorical meaning. This entails sharply critical negotiation with, but not subsumption into, a tradition in which Jewish women are not speaking subjects. Irigaray's chapter adverts to the perennial feminist problem of "how to escape the feminine status of our past tradition in order to affirm and promote a culture of our own as women, a culture appropriate not only to our body but above all to the relational world that is ours from birth" (16). Yet Jewish feminists—whether liberal or Orthodox—would not seek an essential feminine culture stripped of its Jewishness. For many Jews, especially but not exclusively religious Jews, Jewishness is ontologically primary. For myself, being Jewish is, I think, prior to my "being-woman." Certainly, most Jews would agree that Jewishness is not contingent on existential choice or religious confession alone. It is not an assumed identity or a performance, but nor is it racial type or quality of "blood." It is irreducibly and inalienably who we are, not something we will become. Moreover, liberal and Orthodox Jewish feminists have found that Jewish tradition can be reworked and interpreted in contexts that celebrate female culture; it already contains a history of foremothers who have with less or greater success adapted traditional beliefs and practices to their immediate spiritual needs and familial circumstances.

Finally, Irigaray's article strikes me as representative of the contemplative spirituality of the privileged (among whom I would, of course, include myself). After Auschwitz, and in remembrance of the traumatic journey that constituted deportation to Auschwitz, Irigaray's metaphors of journey and cultivation are perhaps too leisured. This chapter examines not women's becoming, but women caught in a system that precisely set all human becoming in reverse, where the only becoming was from flesh to ash. The spiritual tropes of journey and cultivation, travel and gardening, are difficult to apply to in situations of socioeconomic or psychological pressure, let alone genocide. Irigaray writes: "If I am worrying too much about something or someone, this means that I have lost harmony in self-affecting and have probably taken too mental a path. To turn back to my self-affection, I could try to stay peacefully in a quiet place, keeping my lips touching one another, until I find the capability of being well and remaining silent. Walking alone in nature is also a means of turning back to oneself" (Chapter 1 in this volume, 21). Perhaps the recurrent criticism of Irigaray as having privileged women's psychological difference over their political and material difference is not entirely wide of the mark. Reading her article in conjunction with women's Holocaust memoirs shows her to have elided historical difference—here that of Jewish women during the Holocaust—into a universal subject position for women whose prescription turns out to be far more socially, religiously, politically, and historically particular than it intends to be.

NOTES

1.   Further instances of women's Holocaust memoirs as narratives of relational sustenance are too numerous to list here. But see, for example, Trudi Berger and Jeffrey Green, *A Daughter's Gift of Love: A Holocaust Memoir* (Philadelphia: Jewish Publication Society, 1992); Rena Kornriech Gelissen, with Heather Dune MacAdam, *Rena's Promise: A Story of Sisters in Auschwitz* (Boston: Beacon Press, 1996); Kitty Hart, *Return to Auschwitz* (London: Granada Publishing, 1983); Schoschana

Rabinovici, *Thanks to My Mother*, trans. from German into English by James Skofield, and from Hebrew into German by Mirjam Pressler (London: Puffin, 2000); Brana Gurewitsch and Leon Weinberger, eds., *Mothers, Sisters, Resisters: Oral Histories of Women Who Survived the Holocaust* (Tuscaloosa: University of Alabama Press, 1999); Roger Ritvo and Diane Plotkin, *Sisters in Sorrow: Voices of Care in the Holocaust* (Austin: Texas University Press, 1998). There is also a significant body of testimony on the centrality of the mother-daughter, sister-sister relationship that is not recorded in single-author Holocaust memoirs. For example, see Rochelle G. Saidel, *The Jewish Women of Ravensbrück Concentration Camp* (London: University of Wisconsin Press, 2004).

2. See, for example, photographs taken by the perpetrators of the Lepajya massacre in Latvia. One, taken by SS Oberscharfüher Strott, shows Jewish women and their daughters standing huddled together awaiting execution in the freezing Baltic wind on December 15, 1941. Some of the women in these photographs have been identified. In a photograph of the women of the Epstein family, the ten-year-old Sorella Epstein takes shelter behind her mother Rosa's legs; the women support one another with linked arms, the heads are inclined toward one another. A theological ethic is not, however, easily derived from such pictures as photographs of the Holocaust were usually shot through the voyeuristic, objectifying eyes of the perpetrators—the German soldiers stationed in the camps and ghettos that were closed to the outside world. Photographs were also sometimes staged for propaganda purposes. See Andrea Liss on the risks of using documentary photographs of the Holocaust to make artistic and political points, in which theological arguments of the sort proposed here might be included.

3. http://www.interlog.com/~mighty/'personal reflections' (accessed November 19, 1999). Now available at http://www.theverylongview.com/WATH/personal/judy.htm.

4. http://www.interlog.com/~mighty/'personal reflections' (accessed November 19, 1999). Now available at http://www.theverylongview.com/WATH/personal/dejong.htm, http://www.theverylongview.com/WATH/personal/judith.htm, http://www.theverylongview.com/WATH/personal/judith2.htm, http://www.theverylongview.com/WATH/personal/irene.htm.

5. http://www.interlog.com/~mighty/'personal reflections' (accessed November 22, 1999). Now available at http://www.theverylongview.com/WATH/personal/jaeger.htm.

6. See Joyce Antler on Jewish women as not only the objects of stereotyping but also as those who shape their own representation; *Talking Back: Images of Jewish Women in American Popular Culture* (Waltham, MA: Brandeis University Press, 1997).

7. Note André Schwartz-Bart's fictional account of this phenomenon in his novel *The Last of the Just*, trans. Stephen Becker (London: Secker & Warburg, 1962).
8. See Numbers 33: 38; Deuteronomy 34: 5. In the Bible, Moses, Aaron, and Miriam die by the mouth of the Lord. Maimonides developed this trope to describe the attainment of spiritual perfection at the end of *Guide of the Perplexed.*
9. For a Jewish theology of the visual spectacle of Jewish history, see Melissa Raphael, "The Mystery of the Slashed Nose and the Empty Box: Towards a Theology of Jewish Art," Journal of Modern Jewish Studies 1 (2006): 1–19.

BIBLIOGRAPHY

Adelman, Penina V. "A Drink from Miriam's Cup: Invention of Tradition among Jewish Women." *Journal of Feminist Studies in Religion* 2 (1994): 151–66.

Adelsberger, Lucie. *Auschwitz: A Doctor's Story.* Translated by Susan Ray. London: Robson Books, 1996.

Antler, Joyce, ed. *Talking Back: Images of Jewish Women in American Popular Culture.* Waltham, MA: Brandeis University Press, 1997.

Berger, Trudi, and Jeffrey M. Green. *A Daughter's Gift of Love: A Holocaust Memoir.* Philadelphia: Jewish Publication Society, 1992.

Blumenthal, David. *Facing the Abusing God: A Theology of Protest.* Louisville, KY: John Knox Press, 1993.

Broner, Esther M. *The Women's Haggadah.* With Naomi Nimrod. New York: HarperSanFrancisco, 1993.

Delbo, Charlotte. *Auschwitz and After.* Translated by R. C. Lamont. New Haven, CT: Yale University Press, 1995.

Fein, Helen. "Genocide and Gender: The Uses of Women and Group Destiny." *Journal of Genocide Research* 1 (1999): 43–63.

Gelissen, Rena Kornriech. *Rena's Promise: A Story of Sisters in Auschwitz.* With Heather Dune MacAdam. Boston: Beacon Press, 1996.

Gurewitsch, Brana, and Leon J. Weinberger, eds. *Mothers, Sisters, Resisters: Oral Histories of Women Who Survived the Holocaust.* Tuscaloosa: University of Alabama Press, 1999.

Hart, Kitty. *Return to Auschwitz.* London: Granada Publishing, 1983.

Hillesum, Etty. *Letters from Westerbork.* Translated by Arnold J. Pomerans. London: Grafton Books, 1988.

Isaacman, Clara. *Clara's Story.* As told to Joan Adess Grossman. Philadelphia: Jewish Publication Society of America, 1984.

Janowitz, Naomi, and Maggie Wenig. "Sabbath Prayers for Women." In *Womanspirit Rising: A Feminist Reader in Religion*, edited by Carol P. Christ and Judith Plaskow, 174–78. New York: HarperSanFrancisco.

Kellenbach, Katharina von. "Reproduction and Resistance during the Holocaust." In *Women and the Holocaust: Narrative and Representation*, edited by Esther Fuchs, 19–32. Studies in the Shoah. Vol. 22. Lanham, MD: University Press of America, 1999.

Langer, Lawrence L. *Using and Abusing the Holocaust*. Bloomington: Indiana University Press, 2006.

Leitner, Isabella. *Fragments of Isabella: A Memoir of Auschwitz*. New York: Thomas Y. Crowell, 1978.

Levinas, Emmanuel. "Judaism and the Feminine Element." Translated by Edith Wyschogrod. *Judaism* 18 (1969): 30–38.

———. *Otherwise than Being, or Beyond Essence*. Translated by Alphonso Lingis. The Hague: Martinus Nijhoff, 1981.

Liss, Andrea. *Trespassing through Shadows: Memory, Photography and the Holocaust*. Minneapolis: University of Minnesota Press, 1998.

Lubarsky, Sandra. "Reconstructing Divine Power: Post-Holocaust Jewish Theology, Feminism, and Process Philosophy." In *Women and Gender in Jewish Philosophy*, edited by Hava Tirosh-Samuelson, 289–313. Bloomington: Indiana University Press, 2004.

Rabinovici, Schoschana. *Thanks to My Mother*. Translated from German into English by James Skofield, and from Hebrew into German by Mirjam Pressler. London: Puffin, 2000.

Raphael, Melissa. *The Female Face of God in Auschwitz: A Jewish Feminist Theology of the Holocaust*. London: Routledge, 2003.

———. "The Kiss of the Shekhinah: Narratives of Human and Divine Motherhood in the Holocaust." *Temenos: Nordic Journal of Comparative Religion* 42 (2006): 93–110.

———. "The Mystery of the Slashed Nose and the Empty Box: Towards a Theology of Jewish Art." *Journal of Modern Jewish Studies* 1 (2006): 1–19.

———. "The Price of (Masculine) Freedom and Becoming: A Feminist Response to Eliezer Berkovits's Post-Holocaust Free Will Defence of God's Non-Intervention in Auschwitz." In *Feminist Philosophy of Religion: Critical Perspectives*, edited by Pamela Sue Anderson and Beverley Clack, 136–50. London: Routledge, 2004.

Ritvo, Roger A., and Diane M. Plotkin. *Sisters in Sorrow: Voices of Care in the Holocaust*. Austin: Texas University Press, 1998.

Roth, Philip. *Portnoy's Complaint*. Harmondsworth, Middlesex: Penguin, 1986.

Saidel, Rochelle G. *The Jewish Women of Ravensbrück Concentration Camp*. Madison: University of Wisconsin Press, 2004.

Schindler, Pesach. *Hasidic Responses to the Holocaust in the Light of Hasidic Thought*. Hoboken, NJ: Ktav Publishing, 1990.

Schwartz-Bart, André. *The Last of the Just*. Translated by Stephen Becker. London: Secker & Warburg. 1962.

Sered, Susan Starr. "Mother Love, Child Death, and Religious Innovation: A Feminist Perspective." *Journal of Feminist Studies in Religion* 12 (1996): 5–23.

————. *Women as Ritual Experts: The Religious Lives of Elderly Jewish Women Living in Jerusalem.* New York: Oxford University Press, 1992.

Tec, Nechama. *Resilience and Courage: Women, Men, and the Holocaust.* New Haven, CT: Yale University Press, 2003.

Tedeschi, Giuliana. *There Is a Place on Earth: A Woman in Birkenau.* Translated by Tim Parks. London: Minerva, 1994.

Zeitlin, Aaron. *The Last Walk of Janusz Korczak.* Translated by Hadassah Rosensaft and Gertrude Hirschler. In *Ghetto Diary*, edited by Jerzy Bachrach and Barbara Krzywicka and translated by Janusz Korczak. New York: Holocaust Library, 1978.

CHAPTER 11

A VERY PARTICULAR BODY

ASSESSING THE DOCTRINE OF INCARNATION FOR AFFIRMING THE SACRAMENTALITY OF FEMALE EMBODIMENT

Hannah Bacon

INTRODUCTION

It is no secret that the Christian tradition has been renowned for its somewhat ambivalent attitude toward embodiment and the female body in particular. Many reformist feminist theologians have responded to this difficult pattern by highlighting those motifs within the Christian tradition that seemingly subvert patriarchal and phallocentric readings of female embodiment. Of particular interest within this chapter is the way in which the notion of Incarnation has been adopted as a means of affirming the female body as good. The principle of the Word becoming flesh, it has been argued, especially by those developing feminist sacramental theologies, confirms the sacramentality of the body. However, such a focus on Incarnation is not without its problems. Most obviously, such an emphasis seems to affirm the sacramentality of the *male* body at the expense of the female body on the grounds that the divine becomes manifest in one particular person; namely, the *man* Jesus. In light of these kind of concerns, there has understandably been, and continues to be, a tendency within much contemporary feminist scholarship to avoid a classically "orthodox" reading of Incarnation. Feminists such as Sallie McFague and Rosemary Radford Ruether, for example, have developed less particularized and more cosmic Christologies, which do not tie Christ or Incarnation to the particular body of the historical Jesus.

It is the view of this chapter, however, that such a move away from particularity when considering the meaning of Incarnation fails to pay sufficient attention to the radical nature of this doctrine. Indeed, it is the task of this discussion to articulate one way in which we might promote a "generous orthodoxy," which retains the particularity of Incarnation in such a way that need not undermine the sacramentality of the female body. This is a "generous" orthodoxy,[1] however, insofar as the goal is not simply to reiterate the Nicene-Chalcedonian Christological formula but also to consider how an emphasis on *particularity* might expose and challenge readings of Incarnation that serve to support phallocentric constructions of the female body. Importantly, the aim is not simply to address how the notion of Incarnation might affirm female bodies but also how this notion might challenge and destabilize the very phallocentric economy by which women's bodies are currently defined. A dialogue with Irigaray will therefore be key to this agenda.

OVERVIEW

Throughout history the Christian imagination has conceptualized the body in somewhat ambivalent terms. Although it is possible to cite harmful attitudes expressed by the likes of Augustine, Tertullian, Aquinas, and others, it is also possible to cite examples from the Christian tradition where the body has been valorized and respected. Paul, for example, often seen as Christianity's prime culprit when it comes to the denigration of the body, particularly the female body, presents a wholly embodied theology. It is the decaying, sinful body that is redeemed; it is through the body of Christ that we are saved; it is into the body of the Church that we are incorporated; it is through Christ's body in the Eucharist that the Christian community is sustained; and believers await with anticipation the resurrection of the body (Robinson in Isherwood and Stuart 62). The medieval period, although often remembered for the witch hunts and self-imposed fasting of many religious women, also provided a voice of resistance to the antibody tendencies within the Christian tradition. Female mystics, by speaking of their direct, embodied, and often erotic encounters with the divine, indicated a bodily knowledge of Christ that provided them with a sense of authority quite outstanding for the time.

Despite this, however, it is fair to say that Christianity has contributed to a certain distrust of the body, particularly the female body. Influences from Hellenistic Greco-Roman culture meant that much classical theology interpreted women and men within a dualistic framework, pitching man *over* woman and consequently fueling patriarchal associations. Whereas man was associated with spirit, intellect, and reason, woman was linked with the less desirable features of corruption, materiality, bodiliness, and emotion. Of course, it followed that if reason was to dictate to the body and its "passions," then man was to control and contain woman so that he was not tempted away from God. Unfortunately, such a dualistic framework has continued to persist within Christian consciousness throughout the centuries, making it difficult to celebrate the female body as wholly good.

In an attempt to engage with this difficulty, this chapter wishes to glean something useable from the Christian tradition as a means of securing and theologically affirming the goodness of the female body. Like much sacramental and body theology, this chapter insists that the notion of Incarnation confirms the body as sacramental. However, rather than simply viewing Incarnation as a general theological "principle" or "metaphor,"[2] it is claimed that it is only by first establishing Jesus as the historical Incarnation of God that the "principle" of Incarnation can subsequently be established. It therefore aims to engage with the so-called scandal of particularity and to explore how this scandal might support rather than undermine the sacramentality of the female body. However, before we proceed with this task, let us first clarify how the term "body" is being used.

THE BODY AS "SITUATION"

I am not working with an essentialist understanding of the female body. Indeed, I do not want to suggest that all women have the same body or that because women share particular physical features (breasts, vagina, etc.) they are all the same in terms of abilities, personality, or characteristics. Certainly, in light of Judith Butler's insights on the performativity of gender, it seems we must insist with her that there is no body that preexists discourse (Butler 140). The body is not purely a "given" but is socially and culturally produced (Graham 107). In other words, the biological body cannot be separated from its locatedness within culture. In this sense, I deliberately use the term "embodiment" in this chapter since this draws particular attention to the fact that the world is experienced and known *only* through bodies. It also identifies that bodies are "positioned" and therefore lived differently by different people. A stress on embodiment then essentially recognizes that that there can be no universal, suprahistorical reading of the female body just as there can be no universal, suprahistorical reading of the male body. All bodies are differently positioned, which negates any attempts to generalize on the basis of sexual difference.

In light of these insights, I have found de Beauvoir's articulation of woman as "situation" (54–65) helpful for theorizing the body. For her, the body constitutes our grasp on the world, comprising a lived reality that undermines the separation of biological facts from social context (Beauvoir 66). Like men, women define themselves through the actions they take and by the way they live, but there are certain "biological facts" that cannot be escaped. Pregnancy, menstruation, reproduction, and childbirth, for example, may each, respectively, affect a woman's ability to act and thus constitute part of a woman's situation, although not the only part (Beauvoir 54–65).

In endorsing this view, however, it is important that the body is not viewed as some-"thing" to be transcended and overcome in the pursuit of freedom and independence.[3] Indeed, this is a central difficulty with de Beauvoir's argument. Such an understanding perpetuates the male body as the archetypal human "free" body, doing little to establish the inherent goodness of the female body. The body is not an "other" object that can be colonized or overcome by the mind. Indeed, this is a phallocentric reading of the body that only serves to perpetuate the mind/body dualism evident within much Western philosophy. As a phallocentric account of the female body, it also implies that women can determine their own self-becoming through the actions they take and thus pays no attention to the way in which phallocentrism itself serves to construct and sanction female embodiment through the imaginary existence of the male gaze.

Irigaray offers a helpful contribution at this point. Influenced by both Derrida and Lacan, she identifies the order of meaning, symbol, and law as phallocentric. Within this symbolic, the erect penis—the phallus—becomes the chief signifier for meaning. Importantly, for Lacan, however, it is the cultural power of the penis and what the erect penis represents that defines the current symbolic order. Because the symbolic order is defined by the power of the phallus, then it is necessarily phallocentric. Irigaray thus argues that within this phallocentric order there can only ever be room for one subject, the male. He possesses the phallus because he has the penis; the woman, however, can only ever take the place of the phallus for him. For Irigaray,

this means that woman is unable to signify. Since the symbolic constitutes the order of the same, of the one, of the phallus, it only includes
woman inasmuch as she is *not* man. Hence, the language and logic of
the symbolic order are phallocentric, determined by the phallus, serv-
ing to reinforce and to stabilize his position as norm.

According to Irigaray, this means that women fail to speak as
women (and therefore as sexed subjects) within the phallocentric
order because the only language available to them is that which is
isomorphic with the male body (Irigaray, *This Sex Which Is Not One*
148–49, 265). Phallocentric language is owned and controlled by the
phallus and serves the purpose of his self-affection and autoeroticism.
Woman's body therefore serves as mirror (or speculum) through
which the male reflects himself and reinforces his own subjectivity
and status as the phallus. She only exists insofar as the male exists
and is only valued insofar as he values himself (Irigaray, *An Ethics of
Sexual Difference* 63). Consequently, Irigaray argues that inasmuch as
woman fails to be "the same" as man, she is defined as lack, complementary, less, or equal to him. Indeed, she argues that the male is nos-
talgic about the loss of his original home in the woman/maternal and
so establishes his own self-love (and therefore subjectivity) by a return
to and through the maternal feminine (see Bacon 226). As such, the
female body constitutes a place from which the male cannot separate
himself. Because the woman is used to establish his subjectivity, her
body is always possessed, owned, or appropriated for the man's own
ends.[4] Her body is thus constructed and defined through the male
gaze (Irigaray, *An Ethics of Sexual Difference* 308–15). As a phallocentric construct, female embodiment is therefore situated within a
binary logic, which cannot help but define her in terms of what the
male is not.

This is an important critique since it essentially recognizes the phallocentric construction of female embodiment and the situatedness
of female embodiment within phallocentric discourse. It recognizes
that this symbolic positioning is part of a woman's "situation" and
that there is more at stake than what de Beauvoir sought to express.
Although it is debatable how far Irigaray's articulation of sexual difference and female subjectivity fall into the "trap" of essentialism (this
will be discussed briefly later), she is nevertheless useful for us here
given that she draws attention to the way in which this positioning
prevents women from speaking and thus from existing as subjects.

The key question facing us now, in light of this brief dialogue with
de Beauvoir and Irigaray, is how might such a phallocentric reading
of female embodiment be overturned through an understanding of

Incarnation, which takes the historical particularity of Jesus seriously? Indeed, we have to ask, can the doctrine of Incarnation challenge and overturn phallocentric accounts of embodiment or must it necessarily fall prey to such accounts? To address these questions, we must first outline what is meant by Incarnation and more importantly, how an emphasis on particularity might cohere with feminist concerns.

INCARNATION: PRIORITIZING THE HISTORICAL PARTICULARITY OF JESUS'S EMBODIMENT

A traditional reading of the Incarnation cannot help but take Jesus's particular embodiment seriously. According to Christian orthodoxy as developed through the early church councils, the eternal and unfathomable God is made manifest in a body, specifically in the body of Jesus of Nazareth. The Nicene-Constantinopolitan creed of 381 identifies Jesus as the Son of God, as the one "Who for us men [*sic*] and for our salvation came down from heaven, and was Incarnate of the Holy Spirit and the Virgin Mary, and was made man" (in Bettenson 26). It is therefore not surprising that such a reading of Incarnation has been used to support a positive reading of the body. It has been argued by many, for example, that the Incarnation of Jesus signifies the sacramental nature of embodiment per se. If sacrament is understood as an outward sign of an inward grace, then Jesus constitutes the visible sign of God's grace with us. In this sense, sacrament rests on the principle and action of Incarnation: namely, the birth, life, teaching, death, resurrection, and exaltation of Jesus (David 25). Because the Word becomes flesh and tabernacles amongst us (John 1: 14), the goodness of embodiment is seemingly affirmed—indeed, not only affirmed but also identified as being revelatory of God.

Edward Schillebeeckx famously refers to Jesus Christ as the "primordial sacrament" (Schillebeeckx, quoted in Schreiter 43), the original sacrament of God. For him, sacrament is a concrete and visible bestowal of God's salvation. Jesus is then seen as sacrament because he is the concrete manifestation of communion between God and humankind (Bowden 43); his human acts are a visible sign and cause of grace. Jesus is thus the primordial sacrament because he is the one through whom God's salvation is made effective (Schillebeeckx, quoted in Schreiter 205). The sacraments of the church then are essentially a means through which humankind encounter the risen Jesus; they are both concrete signs and visible evidence of God's love and as such, bridge the gap between the earthly Jesus (who is no longer living amongst us) and humankind today. The sacraments make Jesus physically present and thereby enable a personal encounter with him. As Schillebeeckx puts it, "the church's sacraments are . . . our quasi-bodily encounters with the transfigured man Jesus" (Schillebeeckx, quoted in Bowden 44).

Of course, Schillebeeckx is not the only scholar to have voiced this connection between the Incarnation and the principle of *sacramentum*. Within the feminist arena, Susan A. Ross has suggested that sacramentality is rooted in the person of Jesus Christ (Ross 35), in his life, works, death, and resurrection. In Christ, the principle of sacramentality is made a historical reality so that the self-giving of God in Jesus becomes the root of all the sacraments (Ross 38). Ross thus refers to the sacramental principle stating that this underpins all the sacraments, being rooted itself in the Incarnate Christ (32). Fundamental to this principle, according to her, is a reverence for the created order and for embodiment. Indeed, the principle asserts that everything is capable of embodying and communicating the divine (Ross 34). She says, "On the most fundamental level, the sacramental principle means that creation is sacred: all of life—human, animal, vegetable, mineral—is potentially revelatory of the divine and is to be treated as such" (Ross 34).

Of course, such views seem beneficial at first. Understanding Jesus as the primordial sacrament or as the root of the sacramental principle, seemingly affirms embodiment as good and materiality as revelatory of God. However, the claim that God is uniquely made manifest within a *male* body seems to carry damaging theological significance for the status and place of women, implying that the male is somehow more fitting for divine revelation. Such a focus on the particularity of one male body surely only affirms the sacramentality of *male* bodies and may therefore do more harm than good when it comes to affirming the sacramentality of female embodiment. In addition, the insistence that Christ is the unique and particular revelation of God may be seen as scientifically and intellectually weak. If we are to maintain a traditional reading of Incarnation, which insists on the historical and particular Incarnation of God, we must engage these difficulties and make clear the usefulness of such a traditional understanding for exploding the phallocentric construction of female embodiment.

Let us then first engage with the issue of Jesus's maleness. This is, of course, a well-documented problem within the feminist arena. Mary Daly, for example, states that "the idea of a unique male savior may be seen as one more legitimation of male superiority . . . The image itself is one-sided as far as sexual identity is concerned, and it is

precisely on the wrong side, since it fails to counter sexism and functions to glorify maleness" (72)

Thus, according to Daly, if Jesus is to be maintained as the particular and unique manifestation of God in the world, a link comes to
be forged between divinity and maleness to the extent that the male
becomes idolized. Daly therefore renames Christology "Christolatry,"
rejecting any claims that Jesus might offer or achieve salvation for
women (96).[5] Daphne Hampson echoes similar concerns, demanding
that God's choice to reveal God's self in a patriarchal time through the
male Jesus seems to indicate that God somehow favors male humanity, viewing it as more fitting for divine revelation (Hampson 51).
Indeed, for her, patriarchy and maleness both come to be sacralized
and divinized in such a way that it becomes impossible to glean anything liberating from this.

However, such a reading of Incarnation, in my opinion, fails to
fully understand the ramifications of Jesus's particularity for female
embodiment. If the body of Jesus is indeed read as "situation," as
previously outlined, then his maleness need not be given priority.
Jesus was not simply male; his "situation" comprised other aspects,
including his age, his Jewishness, his Galilean roots, his social class,
and so on. There is therefore no need to insist that any of these aspects
of his embodiment should be tied to the being of God. Instead, what
this indicates is that Jesus's maleness is best understood as a historical option rather than an ontological necessity (Johnson 107) for it
constitutes part of his historical "situation" but not the only part.
Given this, difference between Jesus (as male) and women can be
seen as no greater than difference between Jesus (as male) and other
men. All embodiments are particular, so Jesus's maleness need not be
given priority.

Particularity is indeed a necessary part of becoming human, but
this does not mean that only those who share Jesus's particularities are
redeemed. Indeed, if this is so, then Ruether's classic question of "can a
male saviour save women" (116) confronts us once more. Certainly, if
we are to agree with Gregory of Nazianzus that only that which Christ
assumes is saved, then this arguably raises far-reaching difficulties for
all bodies other than that of Christ's. Are we to insist, for example,
that because of Jesus's particular embodiment, he can only affirm and
save Galileans, Jews, the able bodied, and so on? If this seems strange,
outlandish, and disturbing, then it is surely equally strange, outlandish, and disturbing to insist that Jesus's maleness prevents those with
female bodies from sharing in his salvific work. In light of this, we
may therefore say that it is particularity itself that is affirmed by the

Incarnation: more specifically, the particularity of being a body-in-the-world. Understood this way, the Incarnation of God in the male Jesus need not serve to marginalize female embodiment or undermine it. Instead, female bodies in all their difference and diversity might be affirmed on the grounds of their own particularity.

However, insisting on the particularity of Jesus as *the* Word made flesh presents arguably a more profound problem than this for feminists. If Jesus constitutes the unique, once-and-for-all revelation of God in history, then this clearly implies that only his particular body manifests the divine since only he is the Christ. Indeed, Daphne Hampson comments that in order to be Christian one must necessarily make a claim about Jesus's uniqueness; the Christian, she says, "must say of Jesus of Nazareth, that there was a revelation of God through him in a way in which this is not true of you or me" (8). For Hampson, however, to uphold the uniqueness and particularity of Jesus in this way is nonsensical because it demands a break in the causal nexus of nature and history and this, she argues, is deeply illogical (8). That Jesus constitutes the once-and-for-all revelation of God is unfeasible within a contemporary scientific worldview and without such a claim of uniqueness, Christianity loses its Christology and as such, fails to be Christian (Hampson 50).

Mary Daly offers similar concerns, arguing that it is nonsensical to think that God would become manifest in only one individual. Instead, she says, "the creative presence of the Verb can be revealed at every historical moment, in every person and culture" (Daly 71).[6] Indeed, the "scandal of particularity," as it has come to be known, has caused many feminist theologians to refer to the "cosmic" Christ as opposed to the particular revelation of God in Jesus. The hope is that such a symbolic representation may avoid the patriarchal overtones of more "traditional" readings of Christ as the unique Incarnation of God. Rosemary Radford Ruether, for example, argues that Christ continues to be revealed in the world today through men and women alike. For Ruether, Jesus the man does not constitute the last word on revelation, so "Christ" is presented as an inclusive symbol, which is ascribed cosmic significance, reaching beyond, while at the same time including the historical person of Jesus (116–38). For Sallie McFague, the world itself constitutes the "Cosmic Christ," embodying the presence of God in concrete form (179, 183).[7] In her publications *Models of God* and *The Body of God*, McFague argues that the exclusivity, uniqueness, and particularity of Jesus are deeply problematic because they encourage an apathetic attitude toward the world. Jesus saves and so all we need to do is sit back and let salvation run its course. For her, then, God is incarnated by all who demonstrate care toward the world (McFague 135–36).

Such a focus on the "cosmic Christ," however, may prove essentially dissatisfying for those feminists (like myself) who wish to retain a sense of Jesus's historical and particular significance. Indeed, it seems to me that there is a danger in overlooking the historical particularity of the embodiment of Jesus in that this may provide little reason for not overlooking the historical particularity of female embodiment and, as such, the historical particularity and concreteness of women's experiences and the multidimensionality of oppression. If the historical particularity of women is important, and we are to affirm the reading of the body as "situation" previously identified (i.e., to pay attention to women's social, historical, cultural, and discursive locations), then it seems problematic, at least in theory, to dismiss the significance of the embodied particularity of this man Jesus. Indeed, we must note that the historical embodiment of the man Jesus has been, and continues to be, viewed with great significance by some women. Jacquelyn Grant, for example, notes that the historical Jesus constitutes an invaluable resource within the Womanist tradition. Because Jesus suffers and experiences persecution as God Incarnate, this is considered a source of empowerment and dignity for black women who suffer and identify with his persecution (Grant 304). Thus, rather than shifting attention to the cosmic Christ as a means of conveniently dismissing difference between the male historical Jesus and women as insignificant or irrelevant, it seems to me that we must instead consider a way in which we might *begin* our Christological thinking with the historical, particular body of Jesus but in such a way that does not deny the uniqueness of Jesus or reduce Christ to maleness.

Central to this agenda, I suggest, is an understanding of Incarnation that presents the particularity of the historical Jesus as the grounds on which the "principle" of Incarnation might be established. In other words, I want to suggest that there is an order in which our theology of Incarnation must proceed: It must begin with the actual lived reality of the life of Jesus and then proceed to place this in the wider context of the Trinity and understandings of the *logos*. This is not an ontological ordering in the sense of insisting that the historical Jesus predates or preexists the eternal Word, the second person of the Holy Trinity; however, it is an ontological ordering insofar as it suggests that the Incarnation of God in the historical Jesus provides the ontological grounds on which the principle of Incarnation might be established. Importantly, however, this is not to reduce Incarnation to the historical revelation of God in Jesus as such an historical manifestation of God takes place also within the eternal being of the Triune God. Such a view then places the historical particularity of Incarnation within the context of the eternal life of the Trinity and, on this basis, establishes the sacramental and incarnational value of all bodies.

Indeed, if the principle of sacrament is rooted in the self-giving of God in the person of Jesus (i.e., rooted in the Incarnation), then the principle of Incarnation is also rooted in the self-giving of God in Jesus. To lay hold of the principle without acknowledging its roots in the historical Jesus, it seems, is to abstract Christ from history (much like the dichotomy between the so-called historical Jesus and the Christ of faith). To understand Incarnation as I present it then means to understand Jesus as revealing God fully. More than this, however, it means to understand Jesus as revealing God as the kind of God who is known through material things and through bodies. It is this historical manifestation of God that reveals that embodiment has always been integral to the divine and thus to the eternal *logos*. In this sense, the historical Incarnation of Jesus reveals Incarnation as part of God's very being. Incarnation, we might say, reveals the creative love shared within the Trinitarian community itself—what John Zizioulas refers to as God's ecstatic love (Zizioulas 91); that kind of love that cannot help but create outside of itself. To this extent, creation itself can be seen as a reflection of the Incarnate Christ, as the outworking of God's ecstatic love, and as testament to the fact that matter has always been integral to the eternal life of God. With Ruether then, we can rightly say that Christ continues to be revealed in the world today through men and women alike; that Incarnation is ongoing and dynamic rather than static and limited to one man.

However, given that Jesus establishes the principle of Incarnation, Incarnation means something different for Jesus than it does for the world or any other individual. Jesus establishes the revelatory nature of material things and reveals the fullness of God; the universe and its inhabitants, however, only provide glimpses through virtue of being created by the Triune God. It is because Jesus is the "primordial sacrament" that our bodies may be seen as sacramental. It is because Jesus is God Incarnate that the principle of Incarnation can be established in the cosmos. Bodies thus share in the Incarnate body of Christ by virtue of their particularized embodiment. To say God is Incarnate within the world or within bodies then is to recognize that Incarnation is first of all grounded in the historical Incarnation of God in Jesus.

In this sense, the body of Christ can be seen as an "extendable" body (Ward 167), not limited by historical or geographical location. The historical situation of Jesus, although constituting the starting point of Incarnation, is not where Incarnation (or redemption) ends. Incarnation is opened out to include all bodies, including the body of the world. This is particularly evident when we consider the Church as the body of Christ. Understood within this context, the Church as the community of God provides a prime example of the continuity and inclusivity of Christ, revealing the transgendered nature of Christ and, therefore, of God. Essentially, it testifies that God is not reducible to maleness but is inclusive and welcoming of all embodiments. Within this setting, the body of Christ is revealed as a communal body—a body that seeks to reflect the perichoretic relations of the Triune life (D'Costa 35). Gavin D'Costa thus contends that the variety of gendered people who make up the Church actually "fills out" Christ, thereby signaling a refusal to allow closure on the Incarnation (196). He states that such a view "pushes us to see that Christ is not a limited event, but a body coming into glory, a body that is a crucified body, and a body in which male and female are co-constituted" (34–35). Hence, the Church as the continued or extended embodiment of Jesus in the world reveals the inclusivity of Christ and identifies all gendered people of the church as co-redeemers (32–35).

INCARNATION AS AFFIRMING THE SACRAMENTALITY OF FEMALE EMBODIMENT

Assessing the implications of such a reading of Incarnation for the affirmation of female embodiment presents exciting although difficult challenges. If Jesus as God Incarnate is the sacrament of God and as such establishes both the principle of Incarnation and the principle of sacrament, then all bodies-in-the-world can be viewed as extensions of the body of Christ and, as such, sites of sacramental encounter with the divine. Because it is Jesus's particular and local embodiment that is considered central to the Incarnation, all persons are able to identify with him through virtue of their own particular and localized embodiments. Embodiment itself thus becomes sacramental. Indeed, maintaining the particularity of embodiment as the defining feature of Incarnation means that particular female (and male) embodiments can be affirmed without assuming that all women embody the same historical situation. If embodiment itself is sacramental, then the diverse array of female embodiments can each be affirmed as sacramental.

This clearly challenges the anti-body tradition detectable within the Christian tradition, proclaiming instead that the body is inherently good. Indeed, what the Incarnation profoundly asserts is that matter is good, and to paraphrase McFague, that God is not anti-body nor the body anti-God (McFague, *The Body of God* 179, 183). In the same vein, associations of the female body with sin and corruption are similarly undermined and exposed as fiction. To be sure, Incarnation announces that it is not by transcending the body that one comes to encounter God but by being a body in the world. It is embodiment itself that is understood as a place of sacred encounter with the divine. Viewing the body as sacrament, however, claims that God is known through the world, through bodies and as such, through female bodies as well as male bodies. This is the heart of the sacramental principle.

Understanding the body as sacrament, however, also demands that the body be seen as subject rather than object, thereby undermining any attempts to appropriate or colonize the female body. Leonardo Boff, for example, claims that sacrament signals a shift from looking at an object from the "outside" to looking at an object from the "inside." Whereas the former approaches the material as some "thing" to be used and abused for one's own ends, the latter recognizes that materiality is a site of dynamic encounter with God (Boff 5). This encounter, for Boff, is not limited to the official seven sacraments of the Catholic Church and must be allowed to transcend these. Indeed, he says, "Daily life is full of sacraments. In the archaeology of everyday life the sacraments thrive" (Boff 11). Because the eternal Word, that is Christ, is always present within human history, *all* things come from Christ and therefore lead to Christ (Boff 70). Thus, according to Boff, the distinction between the sacred and the secular is here challenged: Everything is Christ's, hence any object has the potential to be sacramental.

However, despite the usefulness of this view, the implication is, nevertheless, that material things *become* sacramental through virtue of them taking on symbolic significance; that material things are transformed from objects into subjects when they communicate something of the divine to us. This, however, implies that matter is only extrinsically sacred rather than intrinsically so. Clearly, this is problematic when applied to female (and male) embodiment as female (and male) bodies are only here shown to be potentially sacramental rather than inherently so. If, however, we return to the argument presented so far—that God has identified with materiality eternally through the historical Incarnation of Jesus—then the particularity of embodiment must be seen as intrinsically sacramental. To be sure, such a view provides a strong voice of resistance to the abuse, appropriation, and exploitation of women's bodies.

Of course, such a view places female embodiment firmly within the *imago dei*. In fact, it does not simply assert that women are theomorphic (that is, in the likeness of God) but more specifically, that women are Christomorphic (in the likeness of Christ)—a claim that, as we have already seen, feminist theology has grappled with through virtue of Jesus's maleness. Women are in the image of Christ because they, like the man Jesus, each embody a particular historical situation. Thus, through virtue of their particular embodiment, men and women can both represent Christ, each in different ways but each to the same degree.

INCARNATION AS CHALLENGE TO THE PHALLOCENTRIC CONSTRUCTION OF FEMALE EMBODIMENT

Up to this point, we have seen how an understanding of Incarnation that takes the historical particularity of Jesus as its starting point might affirm female embodiment as sacramental. What still remains to be seen, however, is how such an understanding might undermine the phallocentric logic that continues to construct the female body as lack in relation to the male phallus. Indeed, it seems that there remains a fundamental problem with the agenda set out in this chapter so far in that such a reading of Incarnation, however seemingly helpful for affirming female embodiment as sacramental, fails to challenge the phallocentric construction of female embodiment. To this extent, it may be perceived as achieving nothing meaningful for women's subjectivity, for if this central defining symbolic structure is not challenged then there is little point in attempting to affirm female embodiment in this way.

How then might such an understanding of Incarnation serve to challenge phallocentric accounts of female embodiment? My suggestions here are threefold. First, I want to argue that by proposing an understanding of Incarnation that is rooted in particularity rather than Jesus's maleness, the normative and central role of the phallus is hereby challenged. If it is the particularity of the Word becoming flesh that is the defining feature of Incarnation, then this principle can (as Irigaray contends) encourage women to construct bridges between their particular "flesh" and their particular "words" so that they may speak as sexed subjects and thus claim subjectivity. Second, if we are to insist, in light of this, that the body of Christ is an extendable body that cannot be reduced to the oneness of the male phallus, then it seems that his body is unspeakable within the current symbolic order. The body of Christ cannot be forced into the position of speculum through which the oneness of the male phallus is reinforced because his body cannot be reduced to oneness. Third, I want to suggest that the notion of Incarnation developed in this chapter can challenge the male gaze that only ever identifies women as objects of male desire. If the body of Christ is an irreducible yet particular body, then this means that differences between individual women and individual men (in terms of geographical, social, cultural, political, and economic location), and between men and women, can be affirmed by the particularity of Incarnation without such differences being reduced to sameness. If difference is recognized and affirmed within the notion of Incarnation, then difference can be theorized in subjective rather than objective terms.

Let us therefore turn to my first point. If the historical Incarnation of God in Jesus constitutes the ontological grounds on which the principle of Incarnation is established, then it can be argued that the particular Incarnation of God in Jesus establishes the principle and indeed the importance of speaking the body. However, two questions immediately confront us: first, what exactly do we mean when we refer to this notion of speaking the body? Second, how can women's bodies be affirmed by the particular Incarnation of God in Jesus given that the Word becomes *male* flesh? Indeed, we must ask, is this not just another phallocentric account, which threatens to reinforce the female body's location as object/speculum within the logic of the same?

In response to the first question, I turn to Irigaray's notion of *parler femme*. According to Irigaray, to situate women within discourse is to understand that women and the female body have no positive significance within the realm of meaning. To say "woman" is to say "nothing," hence women are denied subjectivity within the symbolic order. Indeed, as we have already seen for Irigaray, the phallocentric order is an order in which the man owns and possess everything as a means of securing his own stability as the One. Here there is only room for oneness and sameness, hence difference can only ever be theorized negatively. Such ownership, she claims, becomes particularly significant in the case of language.

In the symbolic, language is the means by which subjectivity is achieved. It is because language is phallocentric and therefore owned and controlled by the phallus for the purpose of the male's self-affection and autoeroticism[8] that women fail to be subjects and, therefore, fail to exist. Language serves the agenda of sameness, establishing the subjectivity and exclusivity of the phallus, and consequently can only ever signify the reality of the male body. Irigaray therefore argues that because the female body is not signified and escapes language, women are alienated to the extent that they are cut off from their self-affection and exiled from themselves (Irigaray, *This Sex* 133). Because there is only room for one within phallocentric language, there is only room for one sex, hence Irigaray argues that women have no language of their own. Instead, they use male language to speak about themselves and as such can never "speak" as "women." Thus, whereas there is an isomorphic relationship between male sexuality and language, Irigaray argues that there is a discontinuity between female sexuality and language (Grosz 111). To speak as a woman either means to speak as a man or to not speak at all; either way, it can never mean what it implies. Hence, Irigaray comments, "I am a woman. I am a being sexualized as feminine. I am sexualized female. The motivation of my work lies in the impossibility of articulating such a statement" (*This Sex Which Is Not One* 149).

According to Irigaray, this is "impossible" for three reasons: first, because "to be" a woman does not make sense since "being" is always already occupied by the male sex; second, because "I" necessarily excludes being a woman-subject—the only "I's" are ever male; and third, "I am sexualized" can only ever mean sexualized male as this is the only sex available to us (*This Sex Which Is Not One* 148–49). Irigaray's central contention then is that the reality of the female sex cannot be expressed in discourse because as soon as woman speaks, she fails to speak as a woman (*This Sex Which Is Not One* 265). In short, she argues that women have no language of their own because they have no sex of their own.

In response to women's absence and silence within the symbolic, Irigaray suggests that women must find ways to speak their sex—a notion summarized by the phrase *parler femme*. According to Irigaray, *femme* refers to the position of the female subject within discourse and to this extent, fails to exist at the moment. She says, "woman has not yet taken (a) place" (Irigaray, *Speculum of the Other Woman* 227), that "woman, for her part, remains unrealized potentiality—unrealized, at least, for/by herself" (*Speculum of the Other Woman* 165), thus highlighting the need for a woman-speaking-subject in order to bring about a place for women within discourse. As such, *parler femme* constitutes a vision of a feminine space that is truly "different," allowing women to be themselves and to speak (for) themselves rather than to speak as men or through men. It is a vision of a different sexual economy in which the binary system of A/not-A is broken down and destabilized, making a "place" for women as sexually different (see *An Ethic of Sexual Differences* 40ff.; *Speculum of the Other Woman* 226). This is a place in which the female sex corresponds with female language; where to speak will no longer equate to a contradiction of her existence as woman. As Morny Joy rightly points out, "it is here that body and expression can combine in a unique fashion that is markedly feminine" (13–14). This means speaking from a different position to the one presently available to women, speaking from a position of autonomy and subjectivity rather than lack. Hence, this will necessarily affect the shape of language and meaning within the symbolic order.

Indeed, Irigaray presents the central metaphor of the two lips speaking together in order to communicate the multiple and unsignifiable nature of women's words. She argues that speaking the multiplicity of the female body actually stands to disrupt and destabilize the phallocentric economy where language reflects the oneness and sameness of the male sex. The two lips, she argues, are in continuous contact and therefore identify that her body cannot be reduced to oneness. This, according to Irigaray, defeats the logic of the same making "woman" unsignifiable within the present order. For her, woman is not one; she is made up of two, which cannot be divisible into ones. Indeed, she states, "*woman has sex organs more or less everywhere.* She finds pleasure almost anywhere" (Irigaray, *This Sex Which Is Not One* 28; emphasis original). Her pleasure is unable to be located in one single place (Irigaray, *This Sex Which Is Not One* 28). Because she has two lips, she always already contains the other within herself. She touches herself all the time without the need of an instrument and so does not need to look outside herself (like the phallus does) for affirmation.

So what does this mean for women in terms of speaking the female sex? Essentially, Irigaray argues that such a reading of female morphology serves to subvert phallocentric discourse surrounding female embodiment, for if woman is not one but is many, then her language is similarly characterized by multiplicity and diversity and stands to undermine the phallocentric economy of oneness. Indeed, she, like others, cite hysteria as a subversive example that serves to undermine the oneness of phallocentric language and logic. Certainly, citing *parler femme* in the multiplicity of the female sex reveals that women cannot occupy the static position of not-A ascribed to them by the phallus. The female cannot be a stable lens through which the male reflects himself because the female sex reveals that she is always on the move, reflecting an image of multiplicity in which the man inevitably loses his bearings and is thrown off center.[9] Thus, if the female sex is used as speculum in the phallocentric order, then mimicking this logic stands to deconstruct the oneness, singularity, and sameness of the male sex and of phallocentric language.

The question for us, then, is how can women's bodies be affirmed by the particular Incarnation of God in Jesus, given that the Word becomes *male* flesh? How might an understanding of Incarnation that identifies particularity as its defining feature help explode the phallocentric logic and affirm women in their attempts to speak their bodies as Irigaray sets out by her notion of *parler femme*?

At one level, we may say that the particular Incarnation of God in Jesus establishes a precedent for women to speak their bodies. If Jesus establishes the ontological basis on which the principle of Incarnation is established, then the historical event of the Word becoming flesh may establish a theological imperative for speaking the body, for bringing the "flesh" to speech. Indeed, it seems that if Incarnation is primarily about the Word becoming flesh, then this does indeed signal the importance of being able to speak as a body and therefore as a sexed subject. In this sense, Incarnation might provide a helpful and potentially liberating "logic" in contradistinction to the phallocentric denial of the female sex. Rooted in the particularity of the historical Jesus, this logic stands to destabilize the very basis on which the non-being of women is constructed.

Indeed, Irigaray argues that the principle of Incarnation points toward the coming together of *word* and *body* and as such establishes the importance of speaking sexual difference; of creating what she refers to as a "bridge between this language [of my own] and my body" (*Luce Irigaray* 145). She writes: "Putting myself in search of *my* word, *my* words, seems to be the first fidelity to a theology of Incarnation . . . Women have to discover their word(s), be faithful to it and, interweaving it with their bodies, make it a living and spiritual flesh" (Irigaray, *Luce Irigaray* 151).

The problem with traditional Incarnational theology, however, according to her, is that it makes reference to an exclusively *male* word. Indeed, this is a central difficulty with the understanding of Incarnation proposed here in that it grounds the principle of speaking as a body in the *male* body of Jesus. The female body, Irigaray argues, must find meaning in relation to this male Jesus (*Luce Irigaray* 150), and this effectively disenables any "bridge" between the female body and the female word (the language of women). The female body is thus subjected to a masculine word and as such cannot find a voice of her own (Irigaray, *Luce Irigaray* 149). Clearly, this threatens the liberating potential of the Incarnational motif. Certainly, for Irigaray,

Incarnation as imaged traditionally through the person of Jesus Christ (as is upheld here) is essentially unhelpful because there can be no continuity between a male word and a female body. In fact, this simply reinforces the phallocentric logic of the same where women are forced once more to use the language of the phallus and are thus prevented from becoming speaking subjects in their own right. Instead, she argues that women need to recognize themselves as divine—a principle she links with the concept of self-love[10]—in order to reconnect their bodies with their words.

However, need this be the only solution to this predicament? Must a traditional reading of Incarnation necessarily separate women's bodies from their words? I would suggest not. If we maintain that the Incarnation should not be simply reduced to maleness because it is particularity itself that constitutes its defining feature, then we must also insist, in opposition to Irigaray, that the divine Word need not be exclusively limited and reduced to a masculine Word. Thus, if rooting the principle of Incarnation in the particular Incarnation of God in Jesus does not have to lead to an understanding of Incarnation that is rooted in maleness, then the phallus, it seems, is decentralized. If the body of Christ is "extendable" as has already been suggested, then the Word of God must be similarly "open" rather than closed or fixed. Indeed, it is only in this way that there is continuity between the body of Christ (a particular but inclusive body) and the Word of God. This serves to undermine the phallocentric logic of the same insofar as God's Word is both one and many at the same time; embodied in the historical person of Jesus of Nazareth but opened out to include us also. The Word of God thus does not return as a singular word.

Turning now to my second suggestion, the body of the Incarnate Christ is a particular but irreducible body and thus may serve as a destabilizing force within the symbolic arena. If the phallocentric economy is an economy typified by oneness and sameness, where only the male sex is signified as subject because his sex is isomorphic with phallocentric language and logic, then the Incarnation confronts this logic and undermines the very grounds on which it is established. Here, the body of Jesus is presented as an unsignifiable body. His body is unspeakable within the present symbolic order because it is not reducible to oneness (whether that is to maleness, Jewishness, or even divinity). Jesus's body is indeed a site of contestation: It is a male body but also a transgendered body (on account of the inclusivity of the body of Christ), a temporal, suffering body but also a timeless, resurrected, glorified body; a divine body but also a human body. His body thus cannot reflect a stable image of oneness back at itself. The body of Jesus is always more than one and thus undermines a phallocentric reading of subjectivity.

In distinction from Irigaray then, this understanding insists that the body of Christ need not be viewed and used as a mirror or speculum through which to reflect the nonidentity of women. Although Jesus's maleness stands to potentially support the phallocentric claim that only male bodies are symbolically significant, the irreducibility and inclusivity of Incarnation replaces a logic of oneness with a logic of difference. Certainly, the Incarnation announces the existence of *bodies* (plural) rather than the *male* body (singular) because it places the focus on Jesus's particularity as a body in the world rather than on his "humanity" or "maleness." Such a stress on particularity serves to affirm the particularity of all bodies, thereby undermining the logic of the same that only recognizes (and values) the existence of the male body.

Finally, turning to my third suggestion, it seems that if we seriously engage with the notion of Incarnation as it has been presented here, this cannot help but challenge the male gaze that only ever identifies women as objects (as lack, complementary or the same) in relation to a male subject. Indeed, the logic of Incarnation and sacrament provides a symbolic context in which women can be recognized as *women* (subjects) rather than as instruments (objects) used by the male to enable his own return. In this sense, the logic of Incarnation supports female becoming by promoting the development of *parler femme* (female language that brings the female body to speech). If the divine Word is continuous with female bodies (as well as male bodies), then women are hereby encouraged and empowered to build bridges between their words and their bodies and to speak thus as sexed subjects.

However, there may be some unresolved problems with these suggestions. We may ask, for example, if women are affirmed as subjects on the grounds of their own embodied particularity, then in what sense is difference really maintained between subjects? Does difference now collapse into sameness? Of course, if we maintain, as I have suggested, that all identify with Christ through virtue of their own particular embodiments, and that no one body (male or female) can claim to be more *like* Christ than any other given that all "situations" differ, then we may ask in what sense is difference between subjects really affirmed? We may also wonder why it is admirable or even acceptable to place so much emphasis on the female body given that such an emphasis on the male body has been opposed when considering Incarnation. Where does the justification for this lie?

In answer to the first problem, it seems that protecting difference must be of the utmost importance. Indeed, Irigaray is clear that subjectivity cannot exist except through the fulfilling of sexual difference. If there is no difference, there can be no love (Irigaray, *An Ethics* 186). However, asserting that all "situations" are different need not constitute another account of sameness. It is not to say that all situations are equally different (as some bodies may hold more in common than others); it is, however, to say that such difference should not be seen as being grounded in biological essence. Thus, it should not be maintained that the male situation of Jesus necessarily identifies more with those who share his sex than with those who do not. Such an essentialist reading of sexual difference is rejected here on the grounds that it pays no attention to the historical, social, cultural and discursive positioning of the body proposed in this chapter.

In answer to the second problem—why focus on the female body as a method for working toward female subjectivity when such a focus on sex has been criticized in our discussion of Incarnation—we may again turn to the female body's structural positioning within phallocentric discourse. To assert that women must speak their sex is not, in my opinion, to make an essentialist statement; it is however to recognize that women have been denied subjectivity on the basis of their sex/bodies and that the female sex/ body may consequently be used as a strategic tool for destabilizing phallocentric logic. If we are to admit that the female body is a constructed morphological body and thus a body that is constructed through discourse, then *parler femme* is also constructed because it finds its roots in the morphological as opposed to the anatomical/ biological body. It is not that female biology determines *how* women speak but that the two are *constructed* in close proximity of one another. Irigaray thus outlines this in terms of nearness whereby one cannot be reduced to the other but is nevertheless related: a relationship between a constructed body and a constructed language.[11] Such a focus on the female body then is strategic and is not to insist on an essentialist reading of female biology.

CONCLUSIONS

What then can we draw from this discussion? Certainly, this chapter has tried to argue that the notion of Incarnation can affirm female embodiment as sacramental without privileging male embodiment at the expense of the female. It has argued that if particularity is understood as the defining feature of Incarnation, then all women (and all men) can identify with Jesus on the basis of their particular embodiments. Given that no one body shares the same features as Jesus's particular "situation," it is not feasible to claim that men identify more with Jesus on the basis of their sex. It has also been argued that the particular Incarnation of God in Jesus establishes the "principle" of Incarnation; that it is because the Word becomes flesh in history that others, men and women included, might Incarnate God and share as co-redeemers in his salvific work. In this sense, the body of Christ is an extendable body, one that does not end with the historical Jesus but that incorporates the multigendered Church also.

This said, however, there is a more pressing critique that has been dealt with here. Even if we are to recognize that the Incarnation can theoretically affirm female embodiment in all its difference and diversity, we have to admit that the female body's location within phallocentric discourse means that such affirmation may do little to affirm the female body outside the current phallocentric order. The question was therefore asked as to how such an understanding of Incarnation that takes particularity as its defining feature might affirm female embodiment outside the confines of phallocentrism.

In response to this question, it was argued that such an understanding of Incarnation may provide an alternative symbolic framework in which the female body might find affirmation. Rather than being constructed in relation to the male body as lack, too much or too less, the female body is here affirmed as speaking subject on the grounds that the particular Incarnation of God in Jesus establishes the principle of Word becoming flesh and thus models this process. It does not, however, mean that women are reliant on a male Word in order to speak, since this is to repeat the logic of phallocentrism. Instead, the maleness of Jesus as Word is read once more within the context of his extendable body—a body rooted in particularity but opened out to include endless difference. Indeed, the body of Christ, it is argued, is an irreducible body that cannot reflect a stable image of oneness back at itself and which subverts (rather than supports) the logic of the same. As such, it is claimed that an understanding of Incarnation that takes its starting point in the particularity of Jesus need not reinforce a phallocentric reading of female embodiment. On the contrary, this may affirm the importance of women connecting their words to their bodies so that they may speak as sexed subjects.

Notes

1. Taken from Hans Frei, this phrase is used here to identify orthodoxy as an emerging, incomplete process that is never closed in on itself, always receptive to the voice of the other.

2. John Hick provides one notable example of this approach. In his text, *The Metaphor of God Incarnate*, he promotes a shift away from the original literal understanding of Incarnation toward a metaphorical reading. A literal understanding, he argues, must be rejected on the basis that it is impossible to assert this without contradiction; in other words, it is impossible to say that Jesus was genuinely and unambiguously God at the same time as to say that Jesus was genuinely and unambiguously human. As soon as we admit one clause, the other is necessarily jeopardized. Otherwise, we would have to redefine the nature of human being and divinity. See J. H. Hick, *The Metaphor of God Incarnate* (London: SCM, 1993), 103–4.

3. According to de Beauvoir, gestation is of no benefit to women. It demands heavy sacrifices and places harmful limits on their potential (Beauvoir 62). She, therefore, suggests that equality with men is possible but only when women are free from "maternal servitude," free from the "iron grasp of the species" (63) that prevents them from attaining full personhood. Indeed, she is extremely critical of the female body referring to menstruation as the "monthly curse" (64), a "bloody mass," and as a useless burden that impinges on female subjectivity (60); *The Second Sex*, trans. and ed. H. M. Parshley (London: Vintage, 1997).

4. Thus, Irigaray notes: "Woman, in this sexual imaginary, is only a more or less obliging prop for the enactment of man's fantasies. That she may find pleasure there in that role, by proxy, is possible, even certain. But such pleasure is above all a masochistic prostitution of her body to a desire that is not her own, and it leaves her in a familiar state of dependency upon man"; Luce Irigaray, *This Sex Which Is Not One*, trans. C. Porter, with C. Burke (Ithaca, NY: Cornell University Press, 1985), 25.

5. Here Daly argues that since Jesus's maleness serves to support rather than negate patriarchy, the image of Jesus can offer no liberating prospects for women. She therefore presents the women's movement as the Antichrist, as the opposing force, which threatens to destroy Christolatry by calling all women into being. As such, the second coming of women, she argues, marks a new arrival of female presence and a new sense of female pride.

6. "The Verb" constitutes Daly's designation of the divine.

7. The cosmic Christ is mediated through bodies, hence revealing bodiliness as godly as opposed to godless.

8. Jane Flax presents a critique of this perspective in "Postmodernism and Gender Relations in Feminist Theory," *Signs* 12, no. 4 (Summer 1987): 621–43.

9. For more on this, see L. Irigaray, "Volume without Contours," in *The Irigaray Reader*, ed. M. Whitford (Oxford: Basil Blackwell, 1991), 65.

10. For more on this, see Luce Irigaray, *An Ethics of Sexual Difference*, trans. Carolyn Burke and Gillian C. Gill (London: Athlone Press, 1993); and H. J. Bacon, "What's Right with the Trinity? Thinking the Trinity in Relation to Irigaray's Notions of Self-love and Wonder," *Feminist Theology* 15 (2007): 220–35.

11. In "Feminist Criticism in the Wilderness," Elaine Showalter discusses the relationship between writing and the female body. Here she echoes a similar point to my own: that although the body has a role to play in writing and speaking as woman, this body must always be viewed within the context of discourse. She writes, "there can be no expression of the body which is unmediated by linguistic, social, and literary structures" (189). Hence, she firmly rejects the charges of essentialism thrown at Irigaray. See Showalter, "Feminist Criticism in the Wilderness," Critical Enquiry 8, no. 2 (Winter 1981): 179–205.

BIBLIOGRAPHY

Bacon, Hannah J. "What's Right with the Trinity? Thinking the Trinity in Relation to Irigaray's Notions of Self-love and Wonder." *Feminist Theology* 15 (2007): 220–35.

Beauvoir, Simone de. *The Second Sex*. Translated and edited by H. M. Parshley. London: Vintage, 1997.

Bettenson, Henry, ed. *Documents of the Christian Church*. 2nd ed. Oxford: Oxford University Press, 1963.

Boff, Leonardo. *Sacraments of Life: Life of the Sacraments*. Translated by J. Drury. Portland, OR: Pastoral, 1987.

Bowden, John. *Edward Schillebeeckx: Portrait of a Theologian*. London: SCM, 1983.

Butler, Judith. *Gender Trouble: Feminism and the Subversion of Identity*. New York: Routledge, 1990.

Daly, Mary. *Beyond God the Father: Towards a Philosophy of Women's Liberation*. London: Women's Press, 1991.

David, Kenith A. *Sacrament and Struggle: Signs and Instruments of Grace from the Downtrodden*. Geneva: WCC Publications, 1994.

D'Costa, Gavin. *Sexing the Trinity: Gender, Culture and the Divine*. London: SCM, 2000.

Flax, Jane. "Postmodernism and Gender Relations in Feminist Theory." *Signs* 12, no. 4 (Summer 1987): 621–43.

Graham, Elaine. "'Words Made Flesh': Women, Embodiment, and Practical Theology." *Feminist Theology* 21 (1999): 109–21.

Grant, Jacquelyn. "The Challenge of the Darker Sister" In *Oxford Readings in Feminism: Feminism and Theology*, edited by J. M. Soskice and D. Lipton, 302–11. Oxford: Oxford University Press, 2003.

Grosz, Elizabeth. *Sexual Subversions: Three French Feminists*. Sydney: Allen & Unwin, 1989.

Hampson, Daphne. *Theology and Feminism*. Oxford: Blackwell, 1990.

Irigaray, Luce. *An Ethics of Sexual Difference*. Translated by Carolyn Burke and Gillian C. Gill. London: Athlone Press, 1993.

———. *Luce Irigaray: Key Writings*. London: Continuum, 2004.

———. *Speculum of the Other Woman*. Translated by G. C. Gill. Ithaca, NY: Cornell University Press, 1985.

———. *This Sex Which Is Not One*. Translated by C. Porter with C. Burke. Ithaca, NY: Cornell University Press, 1985.

———. "Volume without Contours." In *The Irigaray Reader*, edited by M. Whitford, 53–67. Oxford: Basil Blackwell, 1991.

Isherwood, Lisa, ed. *The Good News of the Body: Sexual Theology and Feminism*. New York: New York University Press, 2000.

Isherwood, Lisa, and Elizabeth Stuart, eds. *Introducing Body Theology*. Cleveland, OH: Pilgrim Press, 1998.

Johnson, Elizabeth. A. *Consider Jesus: Waves of Renewal in Christology*. London: Geoffrey Chapman, 1990.

Joy, Morny. "Equality or Divinity: A Falso Dichotomy?" *Journal of Feminist Studies in Religion* 6, no. 1 (1990): 9–24.

McFague, Sallie. *The Body of God: An Ecological Theology*. London: SCM, 1993.

———. *Models of God: Theology for an Ecological Nuclear Age*. Philadelphia: Fortress Press, 1987.

Ross, Susan A. *Extravagant Affections: A Feminist Sacramental Theology*. New York: Continuum, 1998.

Ruether, Rosemary Radford. S*exism and God-talk: Towards a Feminist Theology*. London: SCM, 1983.

Schreiter, Robert. J. *The Schillebeeckx Reader*. Edinburgh: T&T Clark, 1984.

Ward, Graham. "Bodies: The Displaced Body of Jesus." In *Radical Orthodoxy: A New Theology*, edited by J. Milbank, C. Pickstock, and G. Ward, 163–81. London: Routledge, 1999.

Zizioulas, John. D. *Being as Communion*. New York: St. Vladimir's Seminary Press, 1993.

INDEX